Enjo
Daily Le
Understanding
One Day at a Time!

Author: Ray Carman

MW01293920

    The purpose of this devotional is simply this: to help the reader to Enjoy the Shepherd, Jesus Christ. What I have learned in my short tenure as a shepherd is how much love a shepherd has for his sheep. This love is displayed in many ways, but all for one purpose, to let His sheep know how much he is enjoying them.

    As you read through this devotional, please take the time to read the passages each day and study them for yourself! It is not my desire to take you away from Scripture, but rather encourage you to go to it more often. Allow the passages to sink deeper into your soul and refresh you on your journey. There are video devotionals that coordinate with each day as well (Enjoy the Shepherd on Youtube) if you want a more visual understanding of the words. But most importantly, my heart is that you begin to grab ahold of this simple truth: **You can enjoy the Good Shepherd because He truly loves you and is enjoying you as a member of his body.**

Thanks for reading. Now "Go Enjoy The Shepherd."

About the Author:

Ray and his family live on a small farm in Middle Tennessee. Ray has been in real estate and auctions for over 20 years and enjoys his work. He is married to his best friend, Katie, and together they have 4 children (Hailey, Raygan, Truett, and Knox) and 5 cows, 20 chickens, a horse and 18 sheep!

This whole journey of sharing lessons from sheep started in 2011 when our family took a trip to Colorado to visit some friends. During that time, I fell in love with sheep and immediately upon returning home bought some of our own. I have been blessed to learn much from other shepherds along the way, but the still small voice I began to hear in the fields is what struck me the most. I pray as you read these devotionals, you too will hear the voice of the Good Shepherd and begin to enjoy him forever!

Enjoy The Shepherd
Daily Lessons From Sheep
Copyright © 2016 by Ray Carman

Scripture quotations are taken from THE HOLY BIBLE, NEW INTERNATIONAL VERSION®, NIV® Copyright © 1973, 1978, 1984, 2011 by Biblica, Inc.™ Used by permission. All rights reserved worldwide.

ISBN 978-0-9984858-0-5

Dedication and Acknowledgements:

I would like to take a minute and thank a few people who were vital to this project:

Katie, my dear wife, for your patience and kindness, allowing me the countless hours necessary to complete this project, Thank You! You truly are a gift from God and I thank him daily for allowing me to live life with you.

To my kids: Hailey, Raygan, Truett, and Knox, I pray you will all come to a full knowledge of the Good Shepherd's great love for you. Thanks for sharing me with the sheep of his flock.

To my parents, who poured out hours of their time to teach me the Scriptures and imprint in me the love of a Savior. May God bless you both as you continue to serve him.

To Bill and Connie Kuecker, without your many hours and devotion in training me with sheep and how to care for them, none of these lessons would have taken place. Thank you so much.

To Lenda Selph, your tireless hours of reading through my words to make me sound more eloquent, I just don't know how you did it. Thanks so much!

Thanks to Amanda Runge for her work on the cover art. Photo by Ray Carman, all rights reserved.

To all who prayed for me along the way and encouraged us through this process, many thanks to you.

To God be the glory, great things he has done and is doing. Now, Go Enjoy the Good Shepherd.

In the Beginning
Genesis 1:1-2, 31

I stood idly by, my official title of the day was a "grip." My friend Craig was shooting a video for the NSA (National Sheep Association) at a slaughterhouse in Colorado. The "star" of the day was a lady named Temple Grandin, one of the foremost authorities in livestock of our day. The large truck full of sheep backed up to the ramp and lowered its gate. It was time to unload the sheep. I watched and listened to all that was being done and said. As the sheep came off the truck and entered the large shed where they would be held, I noticed they all leapt in the air when they came to the shadow cast by the building. One after the other, they jumped as if something were blocking their way.

As I watched this unfold, I found myself drawn into the world of these sheep. I looked at them and gazed in wonder at these creatures. It did not take long for this to be the beginning of my love for sheep. I had seen sheep before, but never so up close. I instantly was enamored and captured by these creatures. My heart was taken away from the very beginning.

The Good Shepherd himself tells us of how in the beginning, he fell in love with his sheep. His story from the first day has been about how these "sheep" captured his heart and he looked upon them and decreed "It is good!" He looked around at all these creatures he had made, and his heart was set on the ones he had formed in his image. From the very beginning, he has been in love with you!

Go Enjoy The Shepherd.

Getting Down Low
John 6:38

I stood there in awe and amazement at what I was seeing. Kneeling down in the alleyway where the sheep had been unloaded was the star of the instructional video being shot. Temple Grandin is famous around the world, yet here she was kneeling down in the dirt and filth left behind by the sheep. Her head was mere inches from the ground as she explained what we had just witnessed.

As they unloaded from the truck, the sheep had each jumped over a barrier that was not there. It was as if in unison they had created an invisible gate to leap over. Temple however made it seem so simple. As she was down near the ground, she explained how the shadow cast across the earth caused the sheep to leap. They did not like crossing from light into darkness, or the other way around. She ended her instructions by saying this, "If you want to know how sheep think, you must get down on their level."

The Good Shepherd watched as his sheep constantly leapt back and forth between darkness and light. He watched us struggle and wrestle with the things in our way. He offered his help, but we refused to embrace it completely until, he came down to our level. He lowered himself into the dirt and filth of our lives and placed himself where no other shepherd had placed himself before. He lowered himself down and looked at life through our eyes, all because he wanted you to know how much he cares!

Go Enjoy The Shepherd.

January 3

Being a Shepherd
Isaiah 64:4

I was so excited! I was daily making plans to have sheep in my life. I had been around cows and goats before on our family farm, but sheep were something I knew little about. I researched what I could, but there is nothing like hands-on knowledge. I had heard stories from my dad and grandfather from when they had raised sheep many years before, but I was wanting to speak to someone who was currently raising sheep. That is when I found Bill and Connie living just down the road.

Bill and Connie had been raising sheep for years and Bill was the NSA ambassador for the state of Tennessee. In other words, he knew a lot about sheep. Thankfully, this dear couple loved sharing their knowledge about sheep with a young man eager to learn. They shared with me tons of information on sheep and their needs, but I soon realized the only way to learn how to be a shepherd was to become one! In other words, knowledge about sheep could only take you so far. To really know them, you had to be a shepherd and learn as you go.

What I love about our Good Shepherd is that he is not just full of knowledge about his sheep, but rather, he gives himself to the work and labor of being the shepherd. Bill gave me lots of insights, but the knowledge was only useful once I put my hands to the work. God is not just a God of knowledge about his sheep, he is not simply watching as his sheep wander about, NO, he is a Shepherd who acts on behalf of his sheep every day, doing only what a Good Shepherd can do!

Go Enjoy The Shepherd.

January 4

Preparing for Sheep
John 14:1-3

It was hot and I was not happy. The fences on the old family farm were in pretty rough shape. For years, cattle had grazed the place and so the cross fencing went unnoticed. I had been gone for 6 years but was now returning to the farm with a desire to raise some sheep. I had gathered my info and made an agreement to partner up with Bill. Sheep would be arriving any day, and suddenly I realized the plight I was in. There was no way these fences were going to contain the sheep.

As I twisted the wires, doing my best to make some sense of why the cows had been so rough on the fences and why no one else had cared to repair them, I became frustrated and flustered. When the high tensile wire I was holding suddenly untwisted and popped my already bleeding hands, I finally had had enough. I hollered out, "Why am I out here working fences! This is ridiculous!"

It was in that moment I heard the first of the many still, small whispers in the field. It simply said, "What do you think I am doing for you every day?"

You see, the Good Shepherd knows the needs of his sheep, and he knows one of the greatest needs is protection. He also knows that everything—other animals, the predators, time and weather, and even sheep themselves—over time press hard on these fences of protection, causing them to become torn, twisted, and broken. That is why he is working every day, mending the fences so his sheep can be safe! The work is not easy and often it causes the Shepherd pain, but he does it with a joyful heart knowing his sheep will be safe!

Go Enjoy The Shepherd.

Becoming a Shepherd
2 Peter 3:9

I was so excited! The day had finally arrived! Sheep would be arriving on the farm. Bill had called and he had bought 3 sheep at one of the local sales. All my hours and labor on the fence would be put to use. The water I had provided would be enjoyed. The food we had bought would be eaten! Truly an exciting day for me and my family!

Bill pulled up and we backed the trailer up to the gate. With eager anticipation I watched as the gate was opened and the sheep emerged. I was so excited our first sheep had arrived. I figured I would offer them some grain out of my bucket, but to my amazement, they bolted away from me and ran to the far corner of the field. They appeared nervous and afraid. Bill just smiled and said, "Give them time and be patient, they will get used to you."

God is so patient and understanding of us and our fears. As we enter into his pastures for the first time, it is not uncommon for us to bolt to the far ends of his protected fields, away from his loving hands. We, like sheep, are nervous and afraid of what this new place and shepherd will offer us. Thankfully, he is a Good Shepherd who has great patience and long suffering toward us, knowing our fears will eventually subside as we come to know and understand his great love!

Be thankful today that He is patient with you, and:

Go Enjoy The Shepherd.

January 6

Drawing Near
James 4:8

A week had passed by and I was becoming a little frustrated. Why were these three sheep still being so shy. I came to see them several times a day and even brought them a "treat" in the form of grain. I was doing everything to cause these sheep to understand I was there to care for them. I spoke softly and gently, but I could never could get them to come close. They would always wait for me to leave before coming to get the "peace offering" I had brought.

Finally, I made a decision to pour out the grain and move about 10 feet away. Cautiously they came up and ate, always keeping a wary eye on me. Each day for the next week I put the feed out and stepped a little bit away, each day closing the gap between us. Finally, I poured out the feed and they came and ate at my feet with no concern or worry. They had come to realize I was not there to harm them, but rather to enjoy them and for them to enjoy me.

I am so grateful that our Good Shepherd is slow and patient in his approach to his sheep. He tenderly and carefully places his truth and love in front of us. He does not force himself upon us, but rather slowly earns our trust over time until finally we are able to eat at his feet with no worries or concerns. When we finally realize why he is there we are able to simply enjoy him as he enjoys us!

Go Enjoy The Shepherd.

January 7

The Sick
Mark 2:17

It was another monumental day for me as a beginning shepherd. Bill had made a deal with a rancher in Texas to purchase 1000 sheep and bring them to Tennessee. We did not want too many, maybe a 100 or so, but the best deal was to purchase 500 or more at a time. With the market in Tennessee doing so well, it made sense to go ahead and bring in all these sheep. Bill had great contacts and made a few calls, and before long he had several other shepherds lined up for the additional sheep.

The day came and the sheep arrived. Bill and I planned to look over the sheep first, choosing the ones we wanted. An unfortunate delay on the trip put the sheep coming in a few hours behind schedule, and when they arrived so had the other shepherds. Before I could blink an eye, these other shepherds picked through the sheep, taking the best of course. When it was all said and done, I looked at a group of tired, skinny sheep.

Surprisingly, Bill was not discouraged at all. He knew a few days on good grass, water, salt, and minerals that these sheep would be just fine. As a new shepherd I was somewhat skeptical. However, his words held true and over the next few days on our farm, these sheep quickly put on weight and looked great.

Jesus told us that, as the Good Shepherd, he did not come for the healthy and good-looking sheep of the field, but rather his eyes were on those that are sick and needy. Why? Because his heart is for those who have been cast aside, left behind, and declared unwanted. His heart is for these sheep, because he knows a few days eating in his fields and drinking the still waters he has prepared are just what these sheep need to truly live!

Taste and See, for he is Good and . . . Go Enjoy The Shepherd.

January 8

The Payoff
Luke 8:39

I remember distinctly thinking that after having those first three sheep for a week that I had thoroughly lost my mind. I had made little progress with those three sheep and I just knew I had made a huge mistake. It wasn't till the day that they finally drew near to me and ate near my feet that I started enjoying my decision to become a shepherd.

Amazingly, all that hard work paid off again. As Bill and I unloaded all the sheep from the new purchase, they did the same thing as these three initial sheep, they ran away from me. There were 120 sheep huddled in the far corner of the field and three standing by my side. I anticipated that I would have another long ordeal in front of me in getting these new sheep comfortable with me as their shepherd. But the time it took for these new sheep to settle down around me was much shorter than with the first three. In fact, in the matter of only a few days, these sheep from Texas were gathering around me as I walked in the field to check on them and feed them. Why? Because they had watched the reaction of the first three and followed suite.

In our lives, God patiently awaits for us to settle in to the understanding that He is our Good Shepherd. He gives us time and allows us to draw near to him. He does this because he knows how important it is for the new sheep he gathers into his flock to see the response of those who have been there awhile. He knows that as we draw near to him, the others will quickly follow suit and he will stand there and smile, as I did, as he watches his flock gather around his feet.

Today, draw near to him and then tell others to come with you!

Go Enjoy The Shepherd.

Rotating Pastures
Numbers 9:22

One of the basic principles I was taught early on with sheep was the need to have multiple pastures for them to graze. In the world of livestock it is called rotational grazing. The principle behind the theory is that if sheep are left too long on any one given pasture that they will destroy the grass by over-consuming it. It also can lead to other issues like parasite issues and death of the sheep.

So in my fence preparations, I worked diligently to make sure the sheep had multiple pastures to graze. The idea was that I would move them once a week in order to given them new grass and allow the other pasture to be refreshed by rain and new growth, so when they returned there would be plenty for them to enjoy.

On one of my walks through the field, I again heard that still, small whisper of the Good Shepherd. He explained to me how he also diligently works in the lives of his sheep to prepare new fields for them so they can continue to grow. He knows too well the tendency of sheep to want to stay where they feel safe and comfortable. However, this can easily lead to stunted growth and potential disease and death.

You, like me, may not like change in your life. You feel a comfort in the place you currently are and when the Shepherd calls, you may find yourself reluctant to follow. However, he knows if you stay where you are, you will miss the blessing he has worked so hard to prepare for you.

Today, join me in letting go of what he is calling you away from, and run to follow him into the pasture he has prepared, remembering, it is not only for your benefit and blessing, but also for the "field" you are leaving, so it may grow up and have new growth and life for those who are coming behind you! Go Enjoy The Shepherd.

January 10

Despite the Filth
Romans 5: 6-11

It was not long before these once skinny, bony-looking sheep started plumping up and little lambs began to appear. Watching the birth of a sheep is something to behold. Like most other animals in the mammal world, sheep give birth and then immediately start cleaning up their young. They first have to tear away the placenta and then lick away the thick fluid in order for the lamb to take its first breath. If this is not done, death will quickly overcome the newborn lamb. This process is vital for sheep; however, it is an extremely nasty process that takes place.

The mother has to lick the nastiness away in order for her and her lamb to know each other. There is not only the blood and fluids, dirt gets on the lamb and she has to lick that away too. But I have never seen a loving and mature mother shy away from this process. It is a process that must take place in order for the lamb to live.

The Good Shepherd knows all too well the process of a new birth into the life of his flock. He has endured the process of giving life to new "lambs" over and over. He knows from the very beginning that in order for that new lamb to breathe its first breath of life, he must reach down, get in the filth with this lamb, and clean it up. If he was unwilling to accept us in our filth and clean us up in such a personal way, then we would have no way to breathe.

But praise be to his name, that he made a way where he, our Good Shepherd, can, and does, love us despite our filth!

Go Enjoy The Shepherd.

January 11

The Bonding Process
Colossians 1:19-22

Yesterday we talked a little about the birthing process of a lamb and how a mother helps bring breath into the new lamb by cleaning off the filth. While all this is going on, the mother also makes a very unique sound while she is cleaning off the lamb. It is a low and distinct grunt. Each grunt is very unique to that particular mother. As she cleans her newborn lamb, she makes this noise over and over in order to establish the intimate bond with her child.

This grunt is a very important part of the life of this new lamb for the first few months of its life. As a flock of ewes give birth and many lambs are running through the fields, or taking shelter in the shade, the mother will lift her head and call out to her baby(s) with this unique sound. If they did not listen to their mother's voice at birth, then confusion would quickly set in on the lamb as it heard all the other mothers call for their offspring. However, this bonding call for each mother and her children does take hold and each lamb knows its mother's call intimately.

The Good Shepherd does the same for each of his sheep. He meets them at the place of new birth. He willingly sinks down and wipes away their sin and shame so they can have life. While doing this he speaks softly and tenderly to them with his own unique call for them. He knows that they will hear many voices, all striving for the attention of his offspring, so he takes his time to form an intimate bond with them, using the uniqueness of his voice to form an everlasting Bond! Praise be to his holy name, he cared enough for me to call me his, and let me know he is mine!

Go Enjoy The Shepherd.

January 12

Not the Same
Romans 15:1

One day, I walked upon a mother ewe who had just given birth to twins. The mother was a red-coated Katahdin sheep and the ram who was the father had a red coat as well. Therefore, she had given birth to two fantastic little red lambs. Better yet, one was a boy and the other a girl.

As I sat and watched these twins, something became very apparent. The little girl was weak and wobbly, while her brother was bouncing around. I stepped in to check on the lamb and attempted to help her to her feet. She would wobble for a moment and then fall back down. I worked with her for over an hour, and eventually, she was up on her feet and joining her brother in a hearty meal!

Watching this, I again heard that little whisper in my ear. So many times, we see a new "lamb" born into the family of God and they are up and running in mere moments. A lifetime of teaching has finally taken hold and they are running with gusto into this new life. While other times, a new lamb wobbles and struggles to get their feet under them, continuing to struggle to stand.

Unfortunately, we tend to think that all new believers should be like the little ram lamb, up and running and seeking milk instantly. But we are not all the same and many of us look more like the little ewe lamb, struggling to stand. Thankfully, the Good Shepherd knows our weaknesses and he gently and carefully works with us to get us up and going so we can enjoy the new life he has given to us!

Today, seek someone you know who is struggling and allow yourself to be used by the Good Shepherd to gently help them get on their feet!

Go Enjoy The Shepherd.

January 13

Covered
Isaiah 61:9-10

There are times when a good mothering ewe will have a lamb die and shortly thereafter, another lamb is born to a different ewe who is rejected or abandoned. If the first will ewe will not adopt the lamb, as a last resort, a shepherd can take the dead lamb and carefully remove its skin and wrap it around the living lamb. Hopefully, the scent from the skin will trigger the first ewe to accept this lamb as her own, wrapped in the skin of her dead child. It is a difficult and messy task the shepherd undertakes, going to such great lengths to have this living lamb to be adopted by the mothering ewe, but it is what is necessary in order to redeem the life of the lamb so it will not be lost as well.

I know no greater picture to help us understand the enormous love of the Good Shepherd when we are told he has clothed us in the righteousness of his son. God himself had to give up the prized lamb of his flock, Jesus, and allow him to suffer death. Then he took his son and stripped him of his garments of righteousness so he could drape it over me and you in order to have us properly clothed for our adoption into his family. He had to take away the garments his son rightfully deserved and place it over those who struggled against this new layer of skin. Yet, in his perseverance, the Good Shepherd sewed on this new covering so when he saw us, he no longer saw our filth and wretchedness, but rather, the righteousness of his glorious Son, thus sealing our adoption into the family of God!

Today, sit still and rest in this covering he has placed over you so that you too could be sealed into the adoption process of entering permanently into the flock of God!

Go Enjoy The Shepherd.

Worth It
1 Peter 1:18-19

Oh, those long, long nights. Rising every 3-4 hours for the first two weeks of a bottle-fed lamb's life to be sure it received the milk it needed to live. Honestly, these were not my most treasured times. I can remember having to not only get up, but also walk through the cold, down to the sheep shed to deliver the milk bottles. On each walk I would remind myself that it was all worth it.

I would picture ahead to the days when that little lamb would follow me around the field as a full grown sheep. I thought of how it being willing to be close to me would encourage some of my other sheep to follow suit. I thought of how there would be days I would be frustrated or down and how a simple walk in the field with this lamb at my side would encourage me. These thoughts of how things would be gave me the strength to press on through the difficult times.

The Good Shepherd knows all too well the frustration of raising new lambs. Lambs who require so much attention and who many times do not reflect a gratitude for what he is doing. Even Jesus showed these signs of frustrations with his disciples, yet he pressed on. Why? Because he knew what was to come from all his efforts. He knew that one day these little lambs would walk closely with him and draw others close as well. He knew his patience would be greatly rewarded by his Father in Heaven.

Today, do not be troubled by your struggles as a lamb. Do not fear his constant working on your heart. Be encouraged to know, that he is fully aware of the beauty of your relationship ahead and what the results of all his hard work and time will produce.

Go Enjoy The Shepherd.

January 15

When Sheep Speak, Part 1
Psalm 98:1-4

What most people find very unusual when they visit a sheep farm for the first time, is how quiet it is. Sheep are not a very noisy animal. For the most part they tend to keep quiet, except on a few occasions.

The most prominent time that sheep speak is when they hear the voice of the shepherd. The flock can be out in the field, spread over the countryside, but when the shepherd calls, they will suddenly reply with a chorus of bleating. One after the other, the sheep will call out and run toward the voice, each one seemingly notifying those behind them, "Hey, the shepherd is here!"

What a beautiful picture for us to follow in our lives. To remain quiet and content in our "fields" the Good Shepherd has placed us in until we hear his voice. When he calls out for his sheep to come, we can lift up our voices one after the other, letting all those around us know, "Hey, the Good Shepherd is here!"

Go Enjoy The Shepherd.

January 16

When Sheep Speak, Part 2
John 6:34-35, John 7:38

It really is amazing if you sit in a field with sheep for an extended period of time. I mean, they really do not make much noise. If their shepherd calls them they respond, but other than that, there are only a few times you will ever hear them.

One of those few times is when a mother is looking for her lamb so she can give it the milk it needs. It is amazing, almost like clock work, a mother ewe will bleat out and her lamb(s) will come running to enjoy the milk she has supplied. Her call to her lambs is extremely unique so only her lambs will respond; however, her call will often prompt more mothers to do the same and the other lambs to run to their supply of milk to be nourished and refreshed.

The Good Shepherd, Jesus, does much of the same with his sheep. He comes to us daily, sometimes several times a day, and calls to us, saying, "Come and eat and drink the meal I have prepared for you. Come get from me what you need for life, REAL life!" Just like those lambs who run to their mothers for the nutrients they need, he calls to us to come and enjoy the feast of himself he has set before us.

Go Enjoy The Shepherd.

January 17

When Sheep Speak, Part 3
John 10:14, 1 Corinthians 12:12-27

One of the first things I learned about sheep is that when they have lambs there is a unique grunt the mother ewe makes to call her child. It is not the sound we are used to when a sheep speaks, but rather a low, rumbling grunt. What is interesting is that they start this immediately upon the birth of the lamb while they are cleaning it off. To the untrained ear, each grunt sounds the same, however, every mother's grunt is unique and one of a kind.

I wondered why, until I realized the purpose of this grunt. It was to help the lamb identify the mother's call from all the rest. Sheep tend to lamb "in season," meaning, all the lambs are born fairly close together. So this call is extremely important for when the mother wants to have the lamb near. It was personal, unique, and intimate.

The Good Shepherd is the same with his sheep. Each one he calls to himself in his own unique way and that call he uses sets the tone for that relationship for the rest of that child's life. Some are drawn through preaching, others are moved by music, some through the kindness of a stranger, others are knocked off their horse on their way to persecute the body of Christ. All come to the same Shepherd, but through His own personal, unique, and intimate calling.

What a wonderful Shepherd we serve. Today, listen as He calls out to you in that unique way he called you from the very beginning!

Go Enjoy The Shepherd.

January 18

When Sheep Speak, Part 4
Jeremiah 33:3, Matthew 28:20

The longer you sit and listen, the more you realize how quiet sheep really are. You could almost say, "the silence is deafening." There are times I would prefer them to speak just so I know they are breathing and alive. However, I know it is the nature of a sheep to only speak when necessary!

One of the other times I have heard the "voice" of the sheep is when a lamb is searching for its mother. Lambs take naps on a very regular basis when they are young. They need a lot of rest to grow into the sheep they will eventually be. As they are resting, the mother can often wander a little ways off with the flock, grazing to regain the nutrients she needs to raise her lamb(s). When the little one wakes up, it will instantly call out for its mother, suddenly feeling the urge to eat once again.

We too, like lambs, can find ourselves resting in the comfortable places we have been led. We will rest in preparation for our growth that is to come. In doing so, at times we will find ourselves to have "overslept" in our comfort zone and we suddenly see a distance between us and our Good Shepherd, our very life supplier. He is our supply! He is what we need! He holds our everything in his hands!

What I love so much about Jesus, our Good Shepherd, is that no matter where I am when I call, He is ALWAYS faithful to answer!

Today, if you feel you are far away, call out to him! He promises He will hear and draw near to you!

Go Enjoy The Shepherd.

January 19
When Sheep Speak, Part 5
Psalm 91:14-16, Psalm 80:17-19, Psalm 30:11

The saddest sound a shepherd can hear is that of a lost, trapped, or hurting sheep or lamb. It is such a pitiful noise they make, but amazingly, they only cry out if they are absolutely desperate in their need. They can be trapped, caught, or lost, but they are afraid to speak up because the ears of the predators are always listening for the sounds of distress. They are afraid if they cry out too early, that the enemy will swoop in and snatch them away. But when all hope is gone, and they can sense death coming in upon them, they will cry out in their desperation, hoping the shepherd will hear their cry.

However, that same sheep or lamb changes their tune instantly when the shepherd arrives to rescue them. The cry of despair turns to a simple sound of gratefulness. Once the sheep or lamb is returned to the flock, their cry of desperation turns quickly into a prancing around for joy! As the shepherd wipes his sweat and the dirt away he gathered during the rescue, he simply smiles at the joy he sees before him!

How amazing is our Good Shepherd that he knows the sounds of our individual cries. He hears our cries in our most desperate and crucial moments of despair. When He hears our cry, he comes running to our rescue! His heart leaps for joy as he reaches down to pull us out of the snare that has trapped us, and then he holds us close, whispering in our ears, "Everything is alright my child, I am here!" He restores us to His flock and watches over us with a smile as we leap and run for joy, frolicking in the green pasture he has provided!

May we, like sheep, dance with joy before him and lift up sounds of praise for his everlasting love!

Go Enjoy The Shepherd.

January 20

Come Boldly
Hebrews 4:14-16

I still have a good chuckle when I think of this moment with my sheep. It was a gorgeous morning, the air crisp with the freshness of a new day. I was walking out in the field and headed toward the sheep shed when I heard an unusually fast-paced running behind me. I turned and saw Mauro, my older ram, racing toward me. He was well on up in sheep years, yet here he was charging toward me. I had never had any need to be concerned for my safety around him before, but on this day I faced him directly head on to be certain I was not going to get rammed.

He followed me al the way into the little shed where I kept corn, and here is the funny part! As I was getting the corn out of the barrel, I received a little "nudge" on my backside from him. Evidently, I was not moving fast enough for him. He did not aim to hurt me or to evoke me to anger, but he wanted me to hurry up.

That was a beautiful lesson for me that day as it relates to me and my Good Shepherd. So many times, I see him at work and I run to join him, but my path is reckless and impatient. He confronts me head on and slows me down before continuing on the path he is leading me in. As he reaches out to bless me, many times I impatiently give him a nudge because I long to have what he is offering NOW. Thankfully, he knows the hearts of his sheep, and he smiles at our sense of urgency, knowing full well the blessing he is going to pour out in front of us will come in it's perfectly planned time!

Today, do not be afraid to "nudge" the heart of the Shepherd. He told us to come boldly before his throne with our concerns and fears. He invites us to cry out in our impatience and hurry, knowing full well that he will give us what we need exactly when we need it!

Go Enjoy The Shepherd.

The Exchange
John 10:11

There is a story of a really good shepherd who truly loved his flock. He spent his days and nights making sure they had everything they needed. His sheep were healthy and very beautiful to look at. Among his sheep was a glorious ram who was the favorite sheep of his flock. The ram and the shepherd had a very close friendship and spent many hours simply enjoying one another's company.

Across the fence lived a very cruel and mean shepherd. His sheep were a very poor sight to behold. The cruel shepherd would beat his sheep and deprive them of their basic needs. If they did not produce like he wanted, he would starve them and shave them even in the middle of winter. On many days, you could see these poor sheep staring across the fence, wishing they could have belonged to the good shepherd.

One day, the good shepherd asked the cruel shepherd if he might purchase his sheep. The cruel shepherd hated the good shepherd and despised his kindness toward his sheep of his flock. He decided to offer a trade to the good shepherd, the favorite ram for all of his sheep, with this understanding, "When I get your ram, I am going to beat him, starve him, mistreat him, and eventually kill him!"

The good shepherd momentarily wrestled with this decision, but how could he keep one and leave behind so many. In a move that shocked the cruel shepherd, the good shepherd agreed to the trade. As months passed, the poor, skinny sheep flourished in the care of the good shepherd and across the way a lone, skinny, beaten, and despised ram stood looking across the fence toward what was once his home. If one looked closely, he could see a smile on the ram's face, for he knew that one day the Good Shepherd would redeem him from the hands of the cruel shepherd too!

Remember today, a very HIGH price was paid for your freedom! He loved you so much, the Good Shepherd gave up what was most precious to him because he considered you worth the price!

Go Enjoy The Shepherd.

January 22

Carry Them to His Feet
Mark 2: 1-12

The day was nice and sunny and in the midmorning hours my guard dog was taking a nap up on the hillside while the sheep grazed contentedly in the fields. It was the time of year that new little lambs were scattered throughout the flock and they loved to take naps in the fields. As I was working, I suddenly heard a piercing cry of a lamb who had arisen from her nap only to find her mother was nowhere to be found. The mom had walked over a hill and did not hear the bleating of her lamb. However, my dog did.

As I started in the direction to help this poor little lamb find its mother, I watched one of the most amazing sights I have ever seen. My slumbering dog arose from her nap, walked over to the lamb, gently picked it up in her mouth and tenderly carried it over the knoll and dropped it at the feet of its mother. When she was done, she went back to her spot in the sun and resumed her time of rest.

Many times in our lives, we are faced with a lamb of God who has been separated from the source of their life, the Good Shepherd. Our ears hear their cries and pleadings to be restored to the fount of living water. Many times, we are tempted to try and fix the situation in order to relieve the pain, but the only way we can truly help is if we are willing to pick them up in prayer and carry them to the feet of the Good Shepherd, Jesus Christ.

Today, think of who is in your life who needs to be close once again to our Good Shepherd, then gently pick them up in prayer and carry them to his feet!

Go Enjoy The Shepherd.

The Surprise Lamb
Romans 14:12-13

It was lambing season again and I was watching with much anticipation as the bellies of each ewe grew. I loved walking through the field making my guess as to how many lambs each ewe was going to produce.

This particular year I had one ewe, Ruth, who I was certain had somehow missed being bred. She was not very large and I could not discern any milk developing in her udders. As all the others drew near to giving birth, I was very close to marking her off as a "non producer" and was planning on taking her to market in a few short weeks.

As I walked up early in the morning, I was shocked at what I found. There stood Ruth with a precious little lamb. She proudly groomed her newborn and encouraged it to suckle her fresh new milk. I placed her in a stall and checked to see if she actually had any milk. I was amazed to see that not only did she have milk, she had an abundant supply. Oh, how I smiled as I enjoyed watching her with her lamb.

Many times, we too make the mistake of assuming that one of the members of God's flock is not reproducing and making disciples. We watch them and judge their actions thinking they will soon be cast aside by the Good Shepherd for not bearing fruit. However, the Good Shepherd himself knows what is going on inside this same member of his flock. He knows the beauty of what is being created in each and every one. And when the time is right, He knows great fruit can and will be produced by even the ones we may assume have "missed" the opportunity to make disciples.

Let us not judge by what we see, but rather, let us trust the Good Shepherd to do what only he can do in the lives of each one of his sheep!

Go Enjoy The Shepherd.

January 24

The Shepherd Works Daily
Psalm 66:4-5

Being a shepherd is not just a pastime or something you can "do on the side." Being a good shepherd requires work every day. Sheep are fragile and easily lost if you do not keep a close eye on them. Left to themselves they will quickly become wild in nature, sick from parasites, and easy prey for the predators.

Each day, I have to go out and make sure there is plenty for the sheep to eat, especially during the winter months when they rely on hay, as the grass has quit growing due to the cold and snow. I have to be sure they have adequate and clean water from which they can quench their thirst. At times this means making sure the pond is accessible and not frozen over, at other times that means hauling water in pails out to a trough for them to drink from. I have to watch their health, checking for parasites, illnesses, and potential foot problems. Needless to say, it requires my daily attention.

Jesus told us clearly that he is our Good Shepherd. That means he is daily at work on our behalf. He did not just come and live, die, arise and return home to await our homecoming. No, he said he was going to prepare a place for us. He said he would be working daily to prepare the way before us. His work is never ending as he leads us to green pastures, beside still waters, and even through the dark valleys of shadows. He is at work every single day, tending to the needs of his flock.

Today, simply lift up your hands in worship and praise and thank him for the work he is doing on your behalf today!

Go Enjoy The Shepherd.

January 25

Choosing the Shepherd
Matthew 16:14

It is such a joy to walk out in the field and take a seat on the old white bucket and be joined by one of your sheep. I cannot express to you how relaxing that time is for me as a shepherd. So much of a shepherd's time is taken up with tending fences, checking water supplies, making sure the grass is plentiful, and that no one is sick. When you can just sit and relax in the field with the sheep it is simply amazing.

Even better is when one of your sheep loves you and trusts you enough to come and let you run your fingers through their wool/hair. But for that to happen, the sheep has to ignore every built-in instinct he or she has, because by nature they are skittish and prefer to stay away from people.

The Good Shepherd is much like the shepherds here on earth. He is constantly fighting battles and tending fences on our behalf. He is preparing green pastures and still waters for his sheep. He is plotting the course through the Valley of darkness and preparing a feast for us in the midst of our enemies. However, his joy is made full when his sheep come to him and simply let him love on them. His smile is unmeasurable in those peaceful and still moments when he simply sits with his sheep and we allow him to pour out his love on us!

Today, take a moment and just be still! Let his smile pour down on you and allow him to lift your spirits, and "wag your tail" as a way of showing him your gratitude for taking time just to be with you. Today you have choices, right now, choose to simply be with Him!

Go Enjoy The Shepherd.

January 26

They Are All Valuable
Luke 15:8-10

When I first got into raising sheep, I listened intently to those who had been doing it for years. I was honestly looking for another way to provide for my family, and I figured those who had been doing it would know how to best turn sheep raising into a profitable venture. One of the most important lessons I picked up on was that a "good ewe" would produce twins, as that is considered normal amongst sheep. If you wanted to make a living at it, your ewes needed to be producers of twins. Therefore, a ewe who consistently produced a single lamb was considered a disappointment.

As lambs began to be born in our fields, I honestly was keeping track of who was having twins and which ones were only producing single lambs. I figured I would follow the wise counsel of those wise shepherds and build my flock with the best of the best producers. However, I found myself struggling with this process of decision making. As lambs were being born, I began to see the value in each and every lamb. It wasn't the number that seemed important, but rather the health of each and every lamb. I found myself unable to look at it like a business, but rather found myself seeing it as a reflection of God's love toward each of his sheep.

As I stared at these single lambs with their mothers, I heard again that soft whisper in the the fields. It simply said, "Every sheep and lamb in my flock is extremely valuable in my eyes!" There is not a single one who is despised in his eyes! He places a high value on each and every lamb which was evidenced by the price he paid to have them as his own!

Go Enjoy The Shepherd.

Shedding the Old Man
Colossians 3:9-10, Ephesians 4:22-24

I raise hair sheep. Most people associate sheep with ones that grow big wool coats you have to sheer off. I was surprised to learn there were breeds of sheep that you did not have to help cut their heavy winter coats. Hair sheep shed their thick winter coats every year on their own. During this time, our fields are typically full of chunks of this wooly hair that they rub off.

What is interesting is how they go about this. In order to get rid of this thicker hair, they have to rub up against very rough and coarse surface. If you ever get a chance to see this, I would highly recommend it. They will find a tree, a gate, a piece of fence, the side of a building, or even thick bushes. Once their outer layer is off, a gorgeous, new, and shiny coat is unveiled. It is a spectacular sight to see.

In Scripture, we are told to "shed" the old man and put on the new. The Good Shepherd knows our nature is to become burdened with "heavy coats" of troubles and the concerns of this world. He knows how we are dragged down by the lust and desires of the old man. He created us in such a way though, that through rubbing up against our cross on a daily basis, the old outside layer can be shed. This process will then reveal the gorgeous and shiny new man he has redeemed us to be. It is not an easy process, but when he is finished, it is a beautiful sight to see!

Today, what part of your "old" self do you need to rub against the splintery surface of the cross? Give yourself today to allow the old man to die and be removed so that Jesus can shine through you!

Go Enjoy The Shepherd.

January 28

No Matter the Weather
Mark 4:35-41

It's January and the weather in Tennessee is rather unpredictable. One day we can have a cool day with sunshine, the next it could be raining in sheets of cold rain, or possibly even snow falling on the ground.

For a season in my time as a shepherd, our sheep lived on a farm about 20 minutes from our house. So several times a day I had to make a trip over to the farm to check on the sheep. For the most part, this was not a huge issue, until the snow and ice began to fall.

It was one of those rare years in Tennessee when we were having several days of snowfall and mixed in was sleet and ice. The roads became treacherous and difficult to travel. However, I had to make the trip regardless of the weather, because lambing season had come upon us and new lambs were being born daily. If one was born out in this messy weather, it could mean instant death upon arrival. So, I would make the drive, walk through the fields, looking for any newborn lambs.

It was during one of these days when I realized how great our Good Shepherd is. I realized that if I, a man who preferred not to be frozen and cold or to be out on the roads when they were dangerous to travel, if I would set aside my personal feelings and desires to do what was best for my sheep, how much more would our Good Shepherd do whatever it takes to care for his sheep!

Today, rejoice and give thanks that he will care for you no matter how treacherous the path may be! He gave his all to have you, therefore he will surely give his all in taking care of you!

Go Enjoy The Shepherd.

Bring Him Joy
Psalm 149:4

There are days which require that I leave the farm before the sun rises. Whether it is an appointment for work or to spend time with another brother in Christ for fellowship and discipleship, these days are simply part of my life. I truly enjoy them, but there seems to be something missing from my morning.

I am grateful I am blessed with a wife and children whom I can trust to handle the day to day chores on the farm. However, when I do have to miss out on the chores, I also miss out on simply spending time with the sheep. Now to some, that may sound absurd, but for me, there is a lot of happiness and peace when I am with my sheep. Simply sitting with them and spending time with them fills my heart with great joy, even if it is only for a moment.

As a shepherd, I have come to realize some of my most peaceful and enjoyable moments are when I simply get to be with my sheep. It is great for me and for them. It is no different in the heart of our Good Shepherd. He takes delight in simply being with his sheep. His greatest pleasure is found in enjoying his flock and them enjoying him.

Today, take a moment to bring him joy in your life by simply being still with him. Allow him to enjoy you as you take a moment to simply enjoy him.

Go Enjoy The Shepherd.

January 30

The First Milk
1 Peter 2:2

When a newborn lamb comes into the world, it has a great need for its mother's first milk—colostrum. This milk is vital to their growth and development. There are so many rich nutrients in this milk which will allow the baby to develop its necessary immune systems to fight off diseases. If for some reason the lamb misses this milk, it will be susceptible to many illnesses or even possibly die. That is why it's considered a vital part to its new birth process.

Peter knew this " first milk of the word" was vital to the life of a "newborn lamb" in the family of God. Jesus had told Peter prior to leaving earth that his desire for Peter was to "feed his sheep." Peter, having a basic knowledge of the life of a lamb, knew the major importance of this "pure spiritual milk" which would be vital to our lives as sheep in God's flock.

The Good Shepherd, he knows that our enemy wants to creep in and steal, kill, and destroy. He is fully aware of our enemy's knowledge on the necessary elements of growth in new sheep. The enemy knows if we somehow miss out on this "first milk" that our defense systems will be open to his lifelong attacks on us. Thankfully, our Good Shepherd has promised to supply all our needs, including this "first milk." All he asks of us is that we "crave it" like a newborn lamb.

Today, ask God to supply you His rich "first milk" so that your growth in him this year will be rich and deep!

Go Enjoy The Shepherd.

January 31

Come As You Are
Isaiah 1:18

I have been tending sheep now for a little over 5 years. I can honestly say, it has been an opportunity for real growth for me both in life and in my spiritual walk. There are so many things we can daily learn from that God has placed all around us. For me, he used sheep in order to open up Scripture so I could know him even more fully.

One of those things I learned came from a simple observation of what my sheep do when I call them to come to me. I can walk out in the field, let them hear my voice, and they will simply come running in my direction. Something that struck me is how they never once ran to the pond or stream to take a "bath" or clean themselves up before they came. They simply always come to me just as they are, and I did not mind at all. I did not require they clean up before they came. I wanted to be with them enough that I was willing to accept them just like they were.

It was a truly blessed day when I realized that this was also the heart of the Good Shepherd as well. Each day, when he called my name and asked me to come to him, he did not require that I first run and take a "bath" before running to his side. Because of the great offering of the Perfect Lamb, Jesus Christ, I now could come into the presence of the Most Holy Shepherd with no fear or condemnation. I began to realize that he wanted to be with me so badly that he made sure there was a way I could come, just as I am!

Today, do not hesitate to run to him when he calls. Do not try and be fully clean before answering the sound of his voice. Know today, he loves you and ask you to come just as you are!

Go Enjoy The Shepherd.

February 1

The Rejected Lamb
Psalm 118: 20-24

I will never forget the day that I walked out into the field and found the little lamb all alone. She was crying and searching for her mother. She was nasty and filthy, covered in birth fluid and dirt. I looked around and found her mother with another lamb not far away. I carried her to her mother's side and hoped that everything would be okay.

I took the lamb and mother into a stall, but instead of accepting it, the mother grew more intense with her rejection of the lamb. Her head butts were harsh and severe. Whenever the lamb would try and nurse, the mother would kick it away, then thrust her head into the lamb's side.

In order for this lamb to live, I would have to take this poor little lamb home and raise her myself. This would require feeding her bottled milk every 2 hours, cleaning her up, and loving on her. In essence, I would have to become the one who would give this lamb the milk it needed to live. Although it would require much work, I did not mind, because I knew when the journey was over, this lamb and I would have an intimate relationship as shepherd and sheep!

Many times in life, this is our experience as well. The very one who we think can give us life turns on us, abandons us, and rejects us. Like the butting of the lamb, this pain is almost unbearable as we desperately seek the life-giving milk we think they have to offer. Fortunately, the Good Shepherd sees our pain and he reaches down to lift us up, takes us into his house and raises us as his own. It is not an easy process for the Shepherd, but he knows in the end that all his labors will lead to a deep and intimate relationship with these Rejected Lambs!

Go Enjoy The Shepherd.

In memory of Precious born on 2/1/2016

(Watch this Video on our YouTube channel: *Enjoy The Shepherd*)

February 2

Where He Leads
Matthew 19: 2

One of the joys of raising a bottle-fed lamb is the relationship that is formed. I have had the privilege of raising more than just a few of these lambs in my time. The effort and attention they require is enormous. Having even one bottle-fed lamb limits your ability to go any type of distance from home for several weeks. If you do have to go somewhere for an extended period of time, you must either take the lamb with you, or find a trustworthy undershepherd to fill in during your absence.

However, this time as a privilege because of the close relationship formed during this bonding period with the lamb. In the hours between feedings, the lamb can be taken out to run and play in the yard. Wherever I would go, the lamb would follow, staying as close to me as possible. Yes, the labor was long and at times tiresome, but the joy of seeing the lamb follow my lead was worth it all.

Our relationship with the Good Shepherd is not any different than that little lamb. When he takes us in from the darkest hours of our lives, he is well aware of the long and toilsome hours that will be involved in raising us up in his care. He knows our every need and our every concern. But his joy is made complete when he turns and sees us following him every step of the way. He is willing to put in all the work necessary because he already knows the joy that will come when he looks and finds us standing at his feet!

Today, your life may be screaming that you are alone and rejected by those who love you. Know this, he has you in his care and he does not mind the work because he can already see the joy you both will experience as you follow closely in his footsteps!

Go Enjoy The Shepherd.

February 3

Despite the Smell
2 Corinthians 2:15

"What is that smell?" I ask this same question every time we raise a bottle-fed lamb. Our lambs are typically born during the colder months of the year, and without a mother to snuggle up to, a rejected or abandoned lamb needs a place where they can stay warm. Unfortunately, we did not have electricity run to our sheep sheds, so this meant these cute little creatures were invited into our home.

Many long and hard hours went into not only feeding these lambs, but constantly changing out towels, blankets, or puppy pads in the indoor pen we used for these lambs. No matter what we did though, there was a unique and real stench to the area in which these lambs lived. I remember all too well walking in the backdoor from clean, crisp, cold fresh air and being overwhelmed by the smell in our house.

You might ask, "Why would you put up with this in your home?" The answer is simple, because I looked forward to the days that lay ahead. You see, I knew a time was coming where that lamb would return to my farm and it would become a sheep who would run to me every time I called. I chose to look beyond the smell in the moment and focus on the bigger picture of what was ahead.

The Good Shepherd, he also takes us into his home in all our filth and stench. He invites us to come into his house knowing full well we will be a "Smelly Mess" just like those little lambs. He is able and willing to do this for us because he sees the sheep we will one day become who will run to his feet when he calls, and in the process, lead others to his feet as well.

Remember today, God loves you despite the "smell." He sees beyond your faults to the glory of who he has created you to be!

Go Enjoy The Shepherd.

February 4th

What Is My Name?
Isaiah 43:1-7

I was driving home from the farm with this little white bundle sitting in my lap. She was tired, worn out, and definitely confused. On top of that, she was wet, cold, and extremely thirsty. Her mother had rejected her and left her alone. Without intervention, she surely would have died.

I called ahead to my wife to inform her I was bringing home another lamb for us to raise. At first thought, this idea was not overly exciting, especially for my wife who knew the long hours of feeding, cleaning, and massive amounts of laundry that would have to be done. For a second, we both took a deep breath, then we buckled down for the task ahead. One look at this little lamb, and all concerns of the long hours, days, and weeks ahead disappeared into the wonder of this life in our hands. Like a newborn child, she instantly grabbed the strings of your heart and we were hooked.

I hung up the phone and reassured the lamb everything was going to be okay by softly rubbing her back. She was nervous and afraid, and at times tried to escape from my grasp. I firmly held her in my arms, constantly reassuring her with the sound of my voice. Everything was truly going to be okay.

I decided before I arrived home that this little lamb needed a name. Knowing my young children would probably come up with something a little far fetched, I decided to name her before she met the family. *What should I call you, little one?* I wondered to myself. Several girl names ran through my mind, but only one seemed to make sense! "Precious!" I said it out loud a few times and knew that it was the perfect name for this little girl. When I arrived home, everyone agreed we had found the name that was perfect for her!

When I named this lamb, who became the catalyst for the book you now hold, I did not purposefully choose a name that would lead to the words you are reading. In essence, I assumed she would be like all my other lambs we had raised, known only to us. However, God had a much bigger plan. The story of her rejection spread like wildfire over the internet and she became the lamb a world fell in love with. Her name may have been given to her by me, but it was chosen for her long beforehand by the Good Shepherd himself.

You too, may feel like that lamb! The world has left you beaten, tired, worn out and confused. Riddled with the pain of rejection and being abandoned, you find yourself desperately in need of love, warmth, and something to eat and drink. You feel loving arms you cannot see embrace you and lift you up. However, anxiety and nervousness cause you to want to run away. But the Good Shepherd, he holds you firmly in his arms and comforts you with the tenderness of his voice. He takes you into his own home and proudly introduces you to the rest of his family!

You see, the world may hate you, despise you, and even reject you. But what the world throws away as worthless, the Good Shepherd loves and he calls you "Precious!"

Go Enjoy The Shepherd.

February 5

Grey Days
John 16:33, Matthew 28:20

"Something is wrong," I said. "This lamb is not feeling good!"

As I walked around the yard one day with Precious, the Rejected Lamb, she was clearly not feeling good. She refused her milk and did not want to play. I am not sure exactly what was going on with Precious, but I was staying very close to her that day, watching over her with a keen and loving eye.

It was in that moment that I again heard that little whisper in my ear. It said, "There are days in your life when you do not feel so good either. The grey clouds of life seem to cover up the light inside your heart. The feelings of life overwhelm you as you focus on the hurts, pains, sorrows, and difficulties you face. Your head hangs down low and your desire to eat of the Bread of Life fades away. You begin to feel like you are all alone."

"Little child, know this! Just as today you are staying so very close to this little lamb of yours, on days you FEEL you are alone, the truth is I am closer than I have ever been!"

Today, you may feel like life is dark and grey. Circumstances and emotions are crashing over you like a raging hurricane. The pressure on your chest seems to suck the very breath of life out of you, and like so many others, you cry out, "God where are you?" Remember today, no matter the troubles the world is trying to crush you with, the Good Shepherd is closer to you than he has ever been because he promised to always be with you, especially in the furious storms of life!

Hold on to Truth today and rest in the comfort of his care!

Go Enjoy The Shepherd.

The Evidence
Ephesians 4:17-32

When hair sheep start shedding, there is no denying it. They leave hair on the fence, on the gates, on the bushes, and all over the fields. As the old layer loses its grip, the hair falls out everywhere. While the process is being carried out, it is not necessarily a pretty sight. The old clumps of hair hanging on make the sheep look rough. However, when the coat is finally off, they are truly a beauty to behold.

The same is true for us as we are learning to put off the old and put on the new. It is a process that takes time. It is rarely a simple or quick process as we wrestle against our old man and his desire to cling to what we have always known. As we struggle, we may look gaudy and rough in the world's eyes, but the Good Shepherd sees as we will be, not as we are. He is patient with us, and the evidence of our transformation starts to be seen as the old is pulled away and the new begins to shine through.

Go Enjoy The Shepherd.

February 7

It Takes a Rough Surface
Luke 9:23-24, Matthew 11:27-30

When my hair sheep are shedding their winter coat during the spring/summer, it is amazing the effort they put into it. They literally find the roughest and hardest surfaces on the farm to rub against. Fences, thickets, the barn, panel gates, fence posts, trees—you name it; if it is rough, they will rub against it.

The reason for this is so the outer layer will let go. This old hair is stubborn and really does not want to let go of its roots. They are buried deep in the skin of the sheep, so in order for them to rid themselves of the old, they have to rub it against something extremely rough.

That is why the Good Shepherd offers his sheep a cross to bear. He knows very well how rough that surface is and knows it is the perfect place for us to rub off the stubborn old man and allow the new man to be revealed. He carried the cross himself and invites us to allow the old man to die there while we vigorously rub against its abrasive surface.

But do not be discouraged though, he does not ask us to do it alone. No! If we choose daily to pick up that cross, he carries our cross with us, knowing it is too much for us to bear alone. As we feel the rough surface rub against our stubborn old man, the glory of his redeemed one starts to shine through!

Go Enjoy The Shepherd.

February 8

To Shed or Be Sheared
1 John 1:9, James 5:16, Joshua 7:19-26

I never will forget the first time I witnessed the shearing of a sheep. There was an evident look of embarrassment in the eyes of the sheep. They had been carrying a thick covering of wool, which can hide many imperfections. But once the shearing was completed, everything was on display. They appeared to be naked and ashamed.

This brings up a very clear difference between the two breeds of sheep, hair vs. wool, and the way they shed their outer layer. A wool sheep must be sheared in order to be relieved of the heavy coat while the hair sheep willingly rubs and scrapes against hard surfaces to loosen the old layer so it will come off.

This is something we must consider in our own walks as well. Jesus has called his sheep to come to the foot of the cross and willingly rub their old layers off with the help of his tender touch. However, there are times we are much more like the wool sheep and prefer our thick layers to cover up our imperfections. We refuse to come and "rub" our old man away. When we act like this, our Good Shepherd is forced, out of his love for us, to bring us in and put us under the power of his shearing force to remove the thickness of our heavy burdens.

This process is not pleasant and often leaves us embarrassed with our sins laid bare for all to see. When we are "caught" and our outer layers stripped away, we are often left ashamed of our actions and what is uncovered underneath.

The point is, we need to surrender and die daily to our desire to stay hidden in our sins. We need to confess our sins and allow the family of God and the Good Shepherd to carry us through the process of ridding ourselves of the old man. If we do not, he fully intends to perfect his flock and he will do whatever is necessary to bring this new man to the surface.

However, he wants us to remember, whichever path we choose, whether shedding or shearing, his hands will do it with perfection and tenderness. Thus showing in each process, the amazing love of a Shepherd who cares for his flock!

Go Enjoy The Shepherd.

February 9

The Beauty Underneath
1 Corinthians 13:11-13

When you walk into a field of hair sheep who are shedding, it is not a pretty site. Sheep with old hair hanging off them and partially shed coats make them look awkward. Some have used the word pitiful and pathetic. I will admit, it is not something nice to behold.

However, when the old coat is fully shed, there is a glistening and beauty in the new coat. It shimmers in the sunlight and is radiant. The rams look kingly and the ewes look stunning. As a shepherd, it is lovely to the eyes.

The same is true in our shedding process. As the old man is coming off, clinging as tightly as he can, it is not pretty. As we wrestle and struggle to lose ourselves from what was, to embrace what is and will be, we can often look awkward, pitiful, and pathetic.

However, our Good Shepherd already knows the beauty that is coming. He knows how we will shine once the process is complete. In fact, he knows it because he sees what we will look like when he looks in the mirror. He knows his "rams" will resemble kings and his ladies will be like stunning queens.

It is because he knows this: that he is patient and long suffering throughout our transformation process. How loving our Good Shepherd is as he awaits the beauty that is on its way!

Go Enjoy The Shepherd.

February 10

Fighting in the Flock
James 4:1-17

When you put two rams together in a field for the first time, they instantly fight. It is in their nature to attempt to set dominance in the flock. Sometimes, when a young ram challenges an older ram, it can lead to being paralyzed or in some cases even death.

The ewes fight as well. They fight to set a "butting" order and also to set up territorial rights. They back up and collide their heads together and a loud popping noise follows.

The shepherd of course sits back and chuckles to himself. All this fighting is to see who will be the leader or big shot in the flock; all the while, the shepherd knows he is in control. He knows that if they will stop fighting, they will see there is more than enough for them all to be satisfied.

The same is true in our walk with the Good Shepherd. He sees all of our fighting and attempts to have dominance over a territory or people. He laughs at our feeble attempts to be the "king of the flock" because he knows he is the King and we are all to follow him.

So he tells us to "quit fighting" and enjoy all he has put before us. He has prepared such great pastures in abundance for us all, yet we fight over our own little spot in hopes of controlling it. He implores us to simply enjoy him and enjoy all he has given us in harmony and unity. He knows he has prepared more than enough to satisfy our every need.

Today, instead of fighting to control a territory that belongs to the Good Shepherd, be content to simply be a member of his flock and allow him to satisfy your every longing.

Go Enjoy The Shepherd.

February 11

Meant To Be Together
1 Corinthians 12:12-31

While raising Tessa, a bottle-fed lamb, we ran into something quite interesting. We had raised several lambs before, but none quite as vocal as this one. She would sit and cry in her pen or even while out in the yard running around. She would not become calm, still, and quiet until someone showed up to be with her. As long as I or one of my children sat by her side, she was content. She hated being alone!

Sheep by nature were created to be a part of a family. The flock serves a greater purpose than just having other sheep around; it provides a peace and a comfort in the fellowship. Sheep may spread out over a field while grazing, but when it comes time to settle in the shade or gather for the night, sheep are drawn into a close huddle. This is simply evidence of their need to be a part of something bigger than themselves.

When the Good Shepherd formed us from the dust of the earth, he rightly referred to us as sheep. From the very beginning he said, "It is not good for a man to be alone." He refers to us as "members of one body," each playing its role for the good of the whole. We, like sheep, were not meant to be alone. Yet our old man strives to separate us from the flock in order to beat us down and steal our joy and even our life. I know, I tried this being alone in my life and it simply does not work.

Thankfully, when we were designed, the Good Shepherd made us to be like sheep. When we wander off and graze alone, our spirit always leads us to be back with the true family of God.

Today, if you find yourself off by yourself and your heart is craving the comfort of the Good Shepherd and his flock, ask him to draw you near, and according to his Word, he will answer your prayer!

Go Enjoy The Shepherd.

February 12

Purpose of the Trial
James 1:2-4

Suzie Q is one of my most interesting sheep. She is the one I refer to as my resident knucklehead. No matter how good or kind I am to her, she consistently chooses to keep her distance from me. She does not want to come when I call or draw near even when I bring her favorite treat—corn. She stands back and waits until I walk away to come in and see what it is all the other sheep are enjoying.

Therefore, when the time comes I need to get close, I have to set up an alley way which will force her into the sheep shed. When dealing with sheep of this nature, shepherds will create a funnel through which they can lead the gentle sheep in and then they will put either a herding dog or farmhands behind the flock, thus forcing the others to follow into the shed. What the sheep do not realize is that they have been forced there so the shepherd can care for them and show his love toward them.

Unfortunately, I know the heart and nature of this type of sheep all too well when it comes to my Good Shepherd. There are more times than not when I am afraid of what drawing near will bring about. What my anxiousness displays is a lack of trust in the Good Shepherd.

Thankfully, he is wise and knows exactly how to bring me to a place where I will be close to him. I may not like the journey, I may fight against the circumstances that are pushing me that way. But when he has me in that place, that is when he can finally calm my fears and heal my scars.

Today, if you have been afraid of his touch and you have kept yourself at a safe distance, know that he loves you enough to do whatever it takes to draw you near into his loving arms.

Go Enjoy The Shepherd.

February 13

The Hidden Enemy
James 5:16

When most people think about the dangers facing sheep, we instantly think of predators. Coyotes, wolves, bears, or mountain lions. Amazingly though, one of the top causes of death in sheep is not from these outside predators. Yes, many sheep are lost to them each year, but many more are lost to an enemy we cannot see with our eyes: worms.

Parasite worms love to make themselves at home in the fields of sheep. If pastures are overgrazed or the sheep are not able to rotate pastures on a regular basis, these parasites will infest the flock and can cause complete devastation. By nature, sheep do their best to not show any signs of weakness until death has gripped them and they simply fall over dead. That is why it is very important for the shepherd to regularly check his flock for the signs that these parasites have come into their bodies and then take the proper measures to rid his flock of these devious little creatures.

The Good Shepherd knows that it is not typically the "big predators" that will come in and destroy his flock. A flock of sheep can spot a wolf or lion a good ways off, but those worms can easily sneak into his family and cause destruction or death from within. Our enemy knows our tendencies as well and instead of roaring in like a lion, more often than not he looks for ways to sneak in like a parasite and kill us from within.

Today, if there are worms eating you from the inside out, don't try to hide and let death come upon you. Instead, let the Good Shepherd heal you by taking the gift he has given, Confession. Let your worms be revealed by crying out for help and he has promised to give you what you need to have them removed from your life.

Go Enjoy The Shepherd.

February 14

The Muck and the Mire
Psalm 40:2

It was time again to rotate the sheep to a new pasture. Up on a knoll were two new mothers with their lambs. Reluctant to move their fairly new lambs, these mothers ignored my call to the fresh pasture. I climbed the hill and urged them down the hill with the lambs in my arms.

At the bottom of the hill was our spring-fed pond. To my amazement, one mother, thick with a heavy coat of hair, jumped in the pond. I watched in shock from the bank as this sheep desperately tried to find her way through her current situation. I was certain she was going to drown. Eventually, she did find her way to the edge, but then she sank in the muck and mire at the water's edge. She literally could not move. Once she quit struggling, I joined her in the muck and pulled her out and walked her to the new field.

How often do we, as the sheep of God, ignore the clear path leading us to his provision and we rush ahead, desperate for a shortcut. We dive in and suddenly find ourselves weighed down by the circumstances of our impatience. Desperate and near to death, we become stuck in the muck and mire of life.

Thankfully, the Good Shepherd is there, ever present and always watching. Once we give up our struggling and striving, he comes down into our muck and mire with us and pulls us out! He then gently walks alongside of us, leading us to the blessings he intended for us to enjoy!

Today, if you have rushed ahead of the Good Shepherd and you find yourself "stuck" in the miry clay of life, call out his name and he will be faithful to rescue you and set your feet on solid ground.

Go Enjoy The Shepherd.

February 15

Supplication and Prayer
Philippians 4:5-7

Those 2 a.m. calls from a lamb can really startle you in your sleep. Imagine having just entered into a real rest after having been up for 30 minutes at midnight, only to have that same little bleating reach your ears. Hungry and alone, the lamb calls out to her caregiver to rise again and meet her needs.

This happened every morning for two weeks when we were raising Precious. Although it would have been nice to continue enjoying the rest I was having, I did not mind her calling out to me with her pleading and begging for me to come with her warm bottle of milk. My heart was to see her thrive and live, to grow older and join my flock in the fields. I looked forward to the day she would help lead other sheep back to me because her love for her shepherd would be great. Therefore, none of her bleating was ever a burden, for it brought me pleasure to meet her needs.

The Good Shepherd told us long ago that he looks at each of his sheep just the same. He even encouraged us to bring our prayers and supplications (begging) to him in prayer. He told us he was always near (v. 5) and that it brings him joy to impart to us the peace of being close to him. He is more than thrilled to give us the "milk" we need to grow in grace with him. Why? Because he is already looking forward to the day when we too will help lead others to his feet!

Go Enjoy The Shepherd.

February 16

First in Line
Matthew 10:31

When I walk in my fields and call my sheep, I have no doubt whom I will be greeted by first. There is never a question who will be in the front of the line. He is always leading the flock as they run to greet their shepherd. His name is Caesar.

There is a reason I know Caesar will always be the first to me. He was a bottle-fed lamb that I raised along with my daughter Hailey. Caesar grew up in our home and played in our backyard. In other words, we formed a bond of trust with each other. He knows when I call, I always have something special for him. I may have corn, shrub leaves, fresh hay, or maybe just a good back rub (which he really enjoys). It always brings a smile to my face to see him sprinting to be by my side. In truth, there is nothing special or amazing about Caesar. To all the world he is just another sheep. But to me, he is a sheep who brings me great joy!

Sometimes I wonder why the God of the Universe, the Good Shepherd, would care to spend his thoughts and energy on me, a sheep. In the eyes of the world I am just another man who wakes up and goes to work, struggles through life, wrestles with self- confidence and the old man who is constantly leading me to do things I do not want to do. In other words, in the world's eye there is nothing special about me, but in the eyes of my Good Shepherd, when he calls and sees me running to his feet, I am the sheep who brings him great joy.

Today, allow his voice to drown out the screaming of the world that you are "just like everyone else" and listen to his voice when he calls. You are his, and like Caesar causes me to smile, you bring a smile to the face of God!

Go Enjoy The Shepherd.

February 17

My Border Collie
John 6:44

Having dove into the world of sheep,,I went and bought a partially trained border collie named Ben. While I was training Ben, I was also learning some valuable lessons about sheep. Sheep move by peripheral sight. If I sent Ben left, they would go right. If he went right, they would go left. As Ben worked to bring the entire flock to me, he would constantly move back and forth, left to right, right to left. The sheep wanted desperately to get away from this dog, but Ben's goal was to press them toward to their shepherd.

The Good Shepherd knows our tendency to both be afraid of our shepherd when we do not trust that he has our best in mind. We also tend to be afraid of whatever it is that seems to be pushing us forward. Like sheep, we would prefer to be left alone to graze our pastures and relax in the sun. But he knows that what we need most is to follow him.

So the Good Shepherd employs many "border collies" who have been trained to do one thing. They have been through his school and they know exactly what to do to keep us walking a straight path back to his feet. When we swerve to either the left or to the right, his helpers, knowing our nature, move back and forth, forcing our eyes to remain forward, steady on the Good Shepherd himself.

Today, whichever of the "border collies" he has enlisted to use in your life, give thanks to him. Although they make you uncomfortable, remember they have been trained to drive you closer to his feet.

Go Enjoy The Shepherd.

Sweetheart
Job 1

When Sweetheart arrived on our farm, she was different than all our other sheep. A member of the hair sheep family, it was evident that Sweetheart had some close heritage to a wool breed in her genes. She carried a much thicker coat and was not able to shed much at all. When I looked out over the hillside, she was easy to spot because of her thicker and heavier coat.

Another thing that made her stand out was her evident dislike for me. I could not get her to come close to me no matter what I tried. Eventually all the other sheep had grown accustomed to me, but Sweetheart maintained her distance. If I put out corn, she waited until I was gone to join the others for a nibble. She seemed to be aware of what might happen to her if she entered the pen.

As I was training my border collie, I used a particular method to pick sheep for him to practice in the pen with. I put corn out and the last three to four sheep who had their heads down eating would be the "chosen ones." One day, Sweetheart got herself trapped in the pen and I put Ben to work. Instantly Sweetheart's dilemma became apparent. Behind her was a dog she feared and in front of her was a shepherd she despised.

As Ben forced the three sheep to me, they would get next to me and he would lie down to hold them steady. I would release the sheep and he would repeat the process. After four times of working the sheep to me, I congratulated him and gave him a break. As he was lying five feet away, I suddenly felt a heavy leaning on my leg. I looked down and there was Sweetheart, panting heavily from her running from the dog to me. I reached down and petted her back and that was the day she received her name. I turned them loose and again worked Ben. This time, Sweetheart wasted no time running to my leg and leaning into me.

She had learned, as long as she was close to me, the dog was not going to bother her. On the final run, I had no more given Ben the order to bring the sheep that Sweetheart was by my side.

That day, I heard that voice again. The Good Shepherd taught me that those situations in life that seem to constantly cause me to struggle, and even fear, have a very valuable purpose. When they come and surround me, pushing me and aggravating me, they are simply training me that there is safety at his side. At first, I am slow to come to him. Over time, as he trains me through the circumstances, hopefully I learn to run immediately to his side and rest in his protection just like Sweetheart did.

Go Enjoy The Shepherd.

February 19

No Longer Last
Luke 8:35

Something very interesting happened after that ONE day that Sweetheart spent in the pen with me, being chased to my leg by Ben. From that day forward, I could walk out in the field and call my sheep and Sweetheart would be the first to me. She had gone from being the last sheep to come in, the one who stayed as far away from me as she could, to being the first to be by my side. Something in her that day in the pen had changed and she became the sheep who was closest to me at that time.

Many times in our lives we can be frustrated by circumstances or other people. They constantly are pushing us and forcing us to rely and rest on our Good Shepherd just to get through. We have been forced to draw near to the Shepherd despite our fears of even him. We hate the process of this training we go through, but the glorious purpose shows up when he is finished. We will go from being the last to come to him and choosing him as a last resort, to being his sheep who are the first to his feet when he calls.

Today, if you find yourself being forced toward the Shepherd and you wonder why he could possibly be allowing this circumstance in your life, just know he has a greater purpose! On the other hand, if you hear his voice calling you to him, don't be afraid, run to him and enjoy his love today!

Go Enjoy The Shepherd.

February 20

Be The One
Luke 17:11-19

As time went on, I came to enjoy a great relationship with Sweetheart. As sheep came and went in our operation, I was determined to hold on to Sweetheart. She was not the prettiest of the sheep or even the healthiest, but she was close to me because she trusted me to come close.

Eventually, we sold off most of our flock and kept only 20 sheep. Of the ones we kept, Sweetheart was a part. We also kept another one whom we simply named Crazy! The only reason she remained is because we could not catch her to sell her, thus by default she became a member of our flock. Any time I came close to the sheep, she would bolt for the hills. She reminded me of how Sweetheart used to be.

On a hot summer day I went out to the field where the sheep were resting in the shade of the maple tree. I really wanted to go sit with them, but I knew if I tried to get close, Crazy would jump and run and all the other by nature would follow her. Therefore, I stood 100 feet away and spoke to them. I said out loud, "I would love to come sit with you all, but I know if I try you will all run from me!"

I kept my distance until my guard dog, Yado, came out of the shed and went to the maple tree. The sheep were very comfortable with her as she was "just one of the flock" as far as they were concerned. Yado went straight to the tree and begin to paw in a little crack in the tree. I quickly realized what was going on. My daughters, Hailey and Raygan, had held a "picnic" at that tree the day before and a ziplock bag got shoved in that crack. I knew if Yado got it she would attempt to eat it and that would lead to an expensive surgery. So I made my way to the tree and just as I expected, all the sheep jumped and ran because Crazy had taken off.

As I put the bag in my pocket, I turned and was face to face with Sweetheart. She too had jumped up, but she fought her natural instinct to run with the other sheep and stayed close to me. I sat down under the tree and Sweetheart lay back down. Within five minutes after we sat down, the rest of the sheep, including Crazy, had joined us back under the tree.

That is when I heard the still, small voice whisper to me, "See, Son, if one will sit at my feet, the rest of my sheep will follow. Now go and Be The One!

Go Enjoy The Shepherd.

February 21

Rest in His Arms
Matthew 11:28

Lambs are extremely energetic. As soon as they get their feet under them they are off and running. Within days they are frolicking around with other lambs, bouncing and prancing through the fields. I really enjoy watching them at times seemingly frustrate the older sheep with their bubbly joy as they run around. Once they have expended their energy, they find their mother and sibling (if they are a twin) and they snuggle up and rest with the ones whom they trust.

For a bottle-fed lamb, their energy is the same. They have within them the same desire to run and play, frolic around and bounce with joy. When we had Precious at home, one of her favorite games was to chase my younger boys, Truett and Knox, as they ran through the back yard. Thankfully, the boys were young enough that they could run as long as she could. Then when she was tired, she would come to me ready for a rest. One day, I lay down in the grass and she literally snuggled into my arms and quickly drifted off to sleep. Her place of comfort was with her shepherd!

All who have believed have been covered in the righteousness of Christ and adopted into the "flock" of God. We have become his very own and he has given himself totally to us as our Good Shepherd. He loves to watch us as we run, jump, bounce, and frolic in the fields he has prepared for us. Then, when we are tired, worn out, and maybe even beaten up by this world we are in, he lies down in his fields and invites us to snuggle up into his arms and rest.

Today, take some time to simply rest in the arms of the Good Shepherd.

Go Enjoy The Shepherd.

February 22

Dragged to the Barn
Proverbs 22:15

Bam-Bam was by far the biggest ram I had ever owned. He seemed rather docile and content for such a big ram. Until...one morning when I went to bring in his ewes to the barn. About halfway to the barn, Bam-Bam turned and faced me from about 50 foot away. Suddenly, he lowered his head and proceeded in my direction. With nothing more than a few sticks to defend myself, he quickly had me at a disadvantage. The look in his eyes showed that his intent was to remove the shepherd.

After a few minutes, I was left with two broken sticks in my hands and I knew he would not quit until someone was victorious. In a last ditch effort, I timed his next attack and caught him by his horns and twisted his head to the side. Pausing to catch my breath I now wondered what I was going to do. If I let go we would be at war again. If I held on, it meant dragging this massive ram about 400 feet to the barn, with him trying to escape the entire way. I opted for option two and about 30 minutes later I had him locked in a stall in the barn.

So many times in my life, I find myself angry that Good Shepherd is driving me in a direction I do not want to go. In my pride and arrogance, I attack the Shepherd who is pressing me to the place he knows I need to be. In his patience, he offers me opportunities to end my struggling, using staffs to correct me in the fight. At times, I have pushed it to the point that he has had to drag me by the horns and "lock me in a stall!" until I remember he only has my best in mind.

Today, if you are fighting the Good Shepherd, I encourage you to STOP. You may not like where the path is leading, but he only has what is best for you as his plan.

Go Enjoy The Shepherd.

February 23

Meeting the Rod
Genesis 32:22-32

Bam-Bam was not happy being locked into that stall. In fact, he was enraged. As soon as I got him in there and locked the door, he tried to knock the door down in order to get to me. There is only one way I knew of to put this squabble to an end. We were going to have to fight!

I grabbed my rod and entered the stall. This time I had grabbed something much more substantial than a flimsy stick. What I held was thick and sturdy, enough to make a point. Bam-Bam backed up into his corner and lunged in my direction. I stepped to the side and quickly struck him across his forehead, striking him as if I were another ram. When he gained his footing again, he looked at me and lowered his head in recognition of his shepherd.

You may think this is a harsh story two days in a row, but what took place in that barn was absolutely necessary. If I had not made the decision to fight Bam-Bam head on (no pun intended), he would have continued his attempts at dominance and put both me, and anyone else who entered my field, in danger. So out of love for him I fought him until he realized that I was in charge.

Praise be to God that he loves the strong-headed rams of his flock and that he was, and is, willing to allow them to fight with him head-on in prayer until they bow their heads in surrender to his lordship as the Good Shepherd.

Go Enjoy The Shepherd.

February 24

The Rod of Love
Proverbs 13:24, James 1:1-4

As a shepherd I get asked many times about the story of a shepherd using the rod to break the leg of a lamb who is constantly wandering off. The question usually goes like this, "Did shepherds really do that to their lambs? That seems a bit cruel!" Research has shown that in fact this method was used in order to train a sheep who was consistently leaving the comfort of the flock and the protection of the shepherd, going its own way. However, there is much more to the story.

Whenever a shepherd was forced to use this method of correction, it also meant the shepherd would then have to carry this lamb or sheep on his shoulders every time they moved to a new pasture. Because the sheep was lame, the lamb would live within feet of the shepherd, be fed by the shepherd, given its daily water from the shepherd's hands, and carried to each new destination. In this process, the lamb and shepherd form an intimate bond, and when the lamb's leg has healed, it would live the rest of its life at the feet of the shepherd, no longer prone to wander.

Much like sheep, we are prone to stray away from the comfort of the flock and protection of Jesus' hands. If we consistently live in this pattern, in his great love, he pulls back the rod of love and "breaks a leg" so to speak. We scream in pain, looking in anger at this one who has caused us great pain. However, if we listen and watch, we will realize what a great gift this suffering has become as we learn to rely on the Good Shepherd to supply our every need which he is faithful to do.

Today, if you feel as if the Shepherd has broken you and you are wondering why, realize he has reached out in love to you, and though the pain be great, his purpose is only this: to show you his great love!

Go Enjoy The Shepherd. (even if right now it seems to hurt!)

February 25

Running Toward the Danger
1 Samuel 17:33-36

The evening air was crisp as the howl of the coyotes rang out. I was sitting on my front porch when their eerie cries pierced through the evening air. Having lost several sheep to these critters, I jumped up to grab a gun to fire at the first one I would see. That is when I saw something that would bring me joy for years to follow.

I had just purchased some guardian dogs from another local goat herder in Middle Tennessee. That evening, I realized the enormous value of these animals as I watched our new members of the flock round up our sheep and then one of them took off like a bolt of lightning in the direction of the pesky predators. Roaring with her bark each step along the way, she fiercely took the fight to the enemy. Literally within seconds, I heard the sounds of retreating coyotes and my new best friend reappeared, walking with the confidence of a victorious warrior.

The Good Shepherd defends his flock just like this guardian who was now with my flock. When the cry of the enemy fills the air, he does not simply wait for the fight to come to him, but rather, staff and rod in hand, he runs head first into battle with our enemy, roaring every step of the way. Yes, the enemy is strong and mighty, but he is no match for our Good Shepherd. When the battle is over, the enemy will run in defeat and our Shepherd will return to his flock as the Victor!

Today, you may be hearing the sounds of the enemy all around you, but fear not, nor be dismayed, for your Mighty, Good Shepherd is already running to the front-lines of the battle to bring secure the victory on your behalf!

Go Enjoy The Shepherd.

February 26

The Rod of Protection
John 10:11

In Old Testament days, a shepherd was often alone in the fields with his sheep. He had his staff and rod in his hands as he watched the sheep peacefully graze. As he sat overlooking the fields, he would notice a stir in the high grass as a lion or bear was about to attack. Swiftly he would grab his staff and rod and run toward the enemy, placing himself between his flock and the danger. What we know through stories told in history, many a good shepherd lost their life while defending their flocks. As he fought the mighty beast, the sheep would have time to flee to safety. His last breath of life would be given to make sure the sheep would be able to live.

The Good Shepherd, his rod in his hand, sat and watched as his sheep grazed peacefully in the green grass he had provided. He smiled as he remembered the still waters they drank from earlier in the day. In the distance he noticed a stirring in the high grass. Swiftly he ran, rod in hand, toward the roaring lion who was roaming around. A battle raged as he defended his flock. His blood poured out as the lion pierced, his mighty claws slashing through his frail skin. He looked up and saw his sheep swiftly running to safety, and then with his final breath, he sacrificed his own life, allowing the lion to devour his torn body, so that his sheep could live!

Jesus said, I am the Good Shepherd. I lay down my life in order to save my sheep! Today, take a moment and remember what he has done for you, and then...

Go Enjoy The Risen Shepherd!

February 27
Bolt for the Shepherd
Proverbs 18:10

Tessa was a few weeks old when we started letting her spend some time in outside in a pen. Raygan, our daughter, had raised her mainly by herself, getting some help from her mom and me through the nights. Many days, as Tessa basked in the warmth of the sun, Raygan would sit by her pen as she read or worked on school. In other words, they spent a lot of time together.

One day, the neighbor kids were over playing and Raygan decided to join them in the front yard. Alone in the backyard, Tessa paced back and forth, crying at the gate of her pen. I decided to go outside and sit with her for a bit myself. When I reached her pen and opened her gate, Tessa made a mad dash to the front yard. I called her name, but she was not interested in me at all. She could hear the voice of "the one" who she knew loved her most. As I rounded the corner into the front yard, I saw Tessa standing at the feet of my daughter. She had bolted to the feet of her shepherd. This would be the first of many times that she would rush to be with my daughter if ever given the chance. She found comfort being close to her shepherd!

The Good Shepherd loves to love his sheep. His heart is to be with them and for them to bask in the warmth of his care. So many times in life, we are caught in the pen of circumstances and sin. We find ourselves captives to our own desires in life. Thankfully, the Good Shepherd never leaves us or forsakes us, and in times of trouble, he tells us at the first chance to bolt to his side, for in him we will find rest, comfort, and protection!

Today, drop all your worries and cares and BOLT to the Good Shepherd's feet. I promise, you will not regret it!

Go Enjoy The Shepherd.

February 28

One on One
Matthew 18:15-17, Matthew 5:21-26, John 14:23-24

As a shepherd, you are bound to see a fight or two in the field. No matter how gentle or easy-going your flock is, some kind of strife is going to arise. However, there is something I have never seen my sheep do. I have never seen two sheep who are fighting go "bad mouth" one another to the other sheep. I have never seen sheep try to get other sheep on their side of an issue and join them in a fight against their brothers or sisters. No, they simply deal with their issue one on one, and when it is over, they are done and go back to being as gentle as they were before.

The Good Shepherd knew beforehand that issues would arise inside of his flock. He knew that there was going to be differences of opinions and arguments. He knew feelings would get hurt and frustrations would mount as offenses grew. However, he left a very clear message that we are to go to anyone who has offended us, One on One, and deal with the issue. He warned against going and gathering up troops for our side of the issue because that causes discord and gives the world reason to laugh and mock our Good Shepherd. So he commanded us to deal with it, one person to another, and hopefully in the process win our brother/sister back.

Love One Another, thus showing your love for Jesus by obeying his commands!

Go Enjoy The Shepherd.

February 29

Change Is Necessary
Joshua 1:9

Sheep hate change. They are creatures of habit, and if left to themselves would never leave the field in which they were born. They find comfort in the normalcy of consistent surroundings. Any type of disruption to their life can throw them into a state of anxiety. This is evidenced by upset bellies, a tendency to be sick, lowered heads displaying a depressed look, and lots of bleating in the fields. Change is simply something they do not like!

However, change is necessary for sheep to properly grow. Each year I have to sell my lambs to other shepherds. The simple fact is they must go to new farms. If the ewe lambs remained with their father and the ram lambs stayed with their mothers, some negative consequences can occur, causing lots of suffering. The fields would suffer from overgrazing and the sheep would suffer from inbreeding. Neither of which a shepherd wants to see happen on his place. In order for the sheep to properly grow into who they were born to be, they are going to have to move to a new farm and deal with change.

The Good Shepherd also knows his sheep do not like to deal with change. Our natural instincts tend to lead us to stay where we are comfortable. However, God did not redeem us so we could remain the same—he has a plan for us to grow. That growth often comes through major changes in our lives. It is his way to help us become who he created us to be. This will also allow us to in turn, to become reproducing sheep (disciples) and draw others closer to him.

Today, if your life is in the middle of a whirlwind of change, rest easy knowing he is preparing you for a time of growth which he can use to help others grow as well.

Go Enjoy The Shepherd.

March 1

Resting in the Shade
Psalm 91:1-2, Psalm 121

When I look at fields that my sheep will be in, there are several factors that are extremely important. First, it must have a good supply of food and water. There also must be a sense of safety for my sheep, so I make sure there is a good fence to keep the enemy out and protect my sheep. Then, I check to make sure there is a place of rest for them from the heat of the day.

Sheep require shade, especially during the heat of summer. If left out in the sun all day, sheep can easily overheat and die. Therefore, I check to make sure there is either sufficient trees or bushes to provide them relief from the sun, and if not, I build a shed for them to escape from the heat. Without these places of rest, sheep simply cannot survive.

The Good Shepherd knows our need for rest as well. That is why a place of refuge is mentioned in Scripture many times. It tells us his wings are a place for us to gather under, and that there is shade provided by his right hand. He speaks of a place to rest when you are weary from the battle and heat of life. Amazingly, it is not just that he has prepared a place for respite, our Good Shepherd IS the place for us to find rest for our souls. He is our shade, our place of refuge when we weary in our walk through life.

Today, take a moment and lie down in the shade he has provided and…

Go Enjoy The Shepherd.

March 2

The Shepherd Gives Thanks
Psalm 136

One of my greatest joys is when I sit in the field with my sheep. I really enjoy just hanging out with them in the shade, or watching them graze in the pastures of green grass. I simply enjoy spending time with them.

When I do, Caesar, a ram whom we bottle-fed, likes to stand next to me and let me pet him. I enjoy watching his tail wag back and forth as I scratch his back. I experience a feeling of great joy seeing him enjoying time with me. I speak to him and tell him thanks for allowing me to love him and I reward him with what I know brings him great joy.

The Good Shepherd enjoys being near his sheep and having them rest in the shade he has provided. He smiles as his sheep draw near to him, allowing him to touch them with his tender loving hands. He smiles as they wag their tails in praise and worship for the kindness he has shown to them. It brings him great joy and satisfaction when his sheep allow him to love on them and experience his joy of being close by his side. When we remain still, and allow him to shower his love over us, he says thanks by rewarding us with things that bring us great joy!

Today, be still and allow him to shower you with his love!

Go Enjoy The Shepherd.

My Head is Stuck
Psalm 46:10

"Dad, please hurry! Her head is stuck and I cannot get it out."

That is what I heard one day as Raygan was feeding her bottle-fed lamb. I was standing off a bit and watching as my daughter was growing into quite the caretaker. When she finished and came out of the field, I turned my head for only a moment, then suddenly I heard my daughter cry out for help. As I turned around, I noticed her struggling with her lamb who had managed to get her head stuck in the fence in her efforts to get to her "momma."

I encouraged my daughter to try again, to which she responded, "I can't because she won't quit pushing forward!" I took only a few steps in her direction to lend a hand, when suddenly the lamb quit fighting and she was quickly freed by my daughter's efforts.

As I watched all that unfold, I saw a lot of myself in that lamb. How often in my desire to get through an obstacle in my path do I end up in a mess with my head "stuck in the fence." Thankfully, the Good Shepherd comes to my rescue, but instead of allowing him to do his work, I usually press even harder against the circumstances and wrestle against his helping hands. That is when he whispers to me, "Cease Striving" and invites me to simply trust him in his work!

Remember today, God has whatever you are struggling against under control and he is working to set you free. All he asks of you is to be still and allow him to do what only he can accomplish!

Go Enjoy The Shepherd.

March 4

Black Sheep
Genesis 30:34-36

The term "black sheep" is typically used to describe someone who stands out from the crowd or does not "fit in." I have heard it said quite often that "they are the black sheep in the family." I always connected that term with a negative thought, or something you did not want to be.

Now here I was with my very first sheep and all three of them were black sheep. If you read the statistics, having a black lamb requires a lot of genetic coding in both parents for it to happen. I personally have never had a "pure black lamb" born on my farm. I have had spotted sheep born, but not just a pure black one.

So thinking this through, I had what one might consider "the outcast," or black sheep as my very first sheep. However, these so-called outcasts played a very important role in my first lessons as a shepherd, and they became extremely important to what was about to happen on our farm.

Though we may think of black sheep as a negative thing, the Good Shepherd has shown throughout Scripture his love for the outcast and those who were considered "different" or unwanted. Just look at the family tree of Jesus himself, it is filled with misfits and outcasts, those we would have called "black sheep." In fact, God chose to love them dearly and used them in many mighty ways. "Black sheep" in the family of God should never be despised, as God takes great joy in doing big things through his "black sheep!"

Today, if you look in the mirror and you think the world considers you a black sheep, be of good cheer, for God loves to use people just like you to do his glorious works.

Go Enjoy The Shepherd.

March 5

Enjoying the Shepherd
Luke 10:38-42

When I enter my fields with my sheep, many times it is just to find a quiet place to think and rest. Having four children at home can sometimes lend itself to noise and distractions. There is nothing wrong with either of those things in the course of life, but there are times that stillness and quiet bring calmness to the soul. It is during these times God will often speak something of importance into your life.

On one of these occasions in my life, I grabbed an old five-gallon bucket and took to the fields. I drew in close to the sheep, being careful not to disturb them in their time of grazing. I took a seat and began to simply watch my sheep. That is when Caesar chose to leave the rest of the flock and come be with me. He had acres of grass to choose from, and plenty of companionship with the other sheep in which he could have found joy. However, he chose to come stand next to me over all of that. As you can imagine, this brought a smile to my face.

You see, Caesar chose to ignore all the good things in front of him in order to come and simply stand next to me. He chose to leave behind the things that might possibly bring him joy in order to simply enjoy the shepherd.

Today, turn your eyes away from the things around you that might be good, and take time to enjoy the great. The Good Shepherd has come to be with you. He is simply waiting for you to come and Enjoy Him.

Go Enjoy The Shepherd.

March 6

Purpose of a Good Fence
Genesis 3:1-7

Good fences are a vital part of a livestock farm operation. Countless hours and dollars have gone into putting up fences for sheep all around the world. I know I have spent a fair share of my time and money investing in a good fence.

During those long, hard, hot hours working on fences, I will have to admit there were moments of frustration and pain. I remember more than once just wanting to quit, give up, or go back to something easier. Putting up fences is just not an easy or quick chore.

Like many people, when I saw a fence I assumed it was for the sole purpose of keeping the sheep in. However, during one of my days of putting up fences, the still, small voice whispered to me, "Ray, the fence is not to keep you in, it is to keep the enemy out!" What a simple, yet profound, revelation that was. For in the hills of Tennessee, coyotes run wild and free. If I did not have a good fence, then the first line of defense for my sheep would be worthless and my losses would be great.

The Good Shepherd, in one of his very first acts of kindness for his sheep, he set up a fence—one simple rule—"Don't eat of that tree!" His goal was never to keep his loved ones from something good, it was his way of keeping the enemy out.

Today, as you struggle with the purpose of the seemingly rigid and difficult fences you feel God has placed around you, know this: his purpose is simply to keep the enemy out of the fields of blessing he has prepared for you!

Go Enjoy The Shepherd.

March 7

Greener on the Other Side
Philippians 4:19

At our current farm, Namrac Farms, we have a large pasture for a rather small flock of sheep. They can never keep the grass eaten down, as it grows faster than they are able to eat. However, I have on occasion found my sheep staring at the" greener grass" on other side.

One summer I had decided to add another two acres to their field as another rotation paddock for them. While I was doing this, often the sheep would stand at the fence, seemingly waiting on me to finish the fence. They had plenty to eat and drink where they were, but evidently what was available on the other side is what they wanted more.

I know many times in my life, I am like those sheep. The Good Shepherd has provided me all my needs, but I stand at the fence and stare, looking at the pasture he is preparing for my tomorrow, but I am wanting it today. He knows what is best for me, and he longs to give me the desires of my heart. But he must first do the work to prepare that pasture with the proper protective measures, so when I do enter it I will be safe in his care.

Today, instead of staring at what is on the other side, give thanks for his provisions of today. Knowing this, our Good Shepherd is diligent at work, never stopping to rest, preparing for us bountiful fields of green. However, in his wisdom, he knows not to let us enter these new green pastures until he has first prepared them properly for the highest value for his sheep!

Go Enjoy The Shepherd.

Overwhelmed by His Love
Isaiah 53:10, John 13:34

As a child, many times I would hear my dad tell stories of when he was a young boy and raising sheep with my grandfather. My dad, being a pastor, would many times relate illustrations and true stories, using lambs as the main character. One of his true stories was of a butcher's encounter with a lamb.

The old butcher had been at his job for years. Killing a lamb did not even phase this man, for his heart had grown hard and cold from the many years at his job. One day, a shepherd brought in a lamb who seemed more of a pet than a scared sheep. The shepherd was clearly upset, but he needed the meat from this lamb in order to feed his family. He asked the butcher to please wait until he was gone to slaughter this dear lamb of his.

The butcher thought of the shepherd as weak and too tender, but he agreed to his request. Once the shepherd was gone, the butcher grabbed the lamb up without even a chase. The lamb had been hand raised by the shepherd and was comfortable around people. The butcher grabbed his knife and slit the animal's throat. As the blood poured out and got onto his hands, something happened that would shatter this butcher's cold heart. The lamb, as it lay bleeding to death, suddenly licked its own blood from the butcher's hands. On that day, the butcher laid down his knife and he never returned to his former job. He could not bear the thought of living a life like that anymore.

The Good Shepherd took his favorite Lamb and laid him on the butcher's block. He turned his head as his Precious Lamb was slain. The blood from this Lamb poured forth on those who had taken his life. Then, in a shock to them all, this Lamb began to clean his own blood off the hands of those who had caused his death!

Why would a Lamb do such a thing? Because of his great love for those whom he had laid down his life! May our response be like that of the butcher! May we lay down the instruments in our lives that caused the death of God's Perfect Lamb, and may we never return to the life we lived before the day that he washed his blood off our murderous hands!

He Loves You So Much!

Go Enjoy The Shepherd.

March 9

Even the Little Things
Luke 12:7

After a long hard day working on the farm, I sent one of my daughters into the field to feed our guard dog for the evening. As I was cleaning up the tools from our day of putting up a new fence, my daughter came running up to inform me that Vasella (our Karakachan dog) was nowhere to be found.

I took off walking the field to see for myself, and it was true, she had somehow escaped the field. I called her name and scanned the horizon, but there was no sign of her anywhere. I had to get my girl to an appointment of hers, so we left the farm and said a simple prayer that Vasella would return.

I also put out a call for prayer to our friends and family on Facebook. I was instantly overwhelmed by the sheer volume of people who said they were praying and asking for Vasella to return. I sat through my daughter's meeting for an hour and a half and I prayed one simple prayer. "Father, please bring her home if for no other reason but to prove to me and all these people that you have heard our prayers."

Darkness had set in, but I chose to drive out to the farm before going home. We kept our eyes open along the road for a possible glimpse of our missing dog. Without her in the field, it was possible the coyotes might find a way to disturb our sheep. We pulled up the gravel drive to the sheep gate and I got out of the truck. For a moment, I wavered in my faith, but made the decision to call out her name. Once, nothing. Twice, still nothing. I turned to my daughter and said, "I will try one more time." As I did, I noticed a dark figure running through the fields. "A sheep" I thought to myself. As it drew closer though, I realized our dog had returned home. (Even until this day, I do not know how she got out or back in!)

What a great reminder to us that our Good Shepherd cares even about the little things. The dog, though just a dog to the world, is an invaluable part of our sheep farm's safety. Without her, many sheep would possibly be lost to the predators all around. But this story was not merely about the dog. It was more of a statement from our Good Shepherd that he hears our prayers and wants us to bring to him ALL our requests.

Go Enjoy The Shepherd.

March 10

It's a Family Affair
1 Corinthians 12:12

Putting up new fence on our farm was no easy chore. In my younger days, I attempted to put up some fences by myself. I got them up, however, they were typically not great fences even after all my hard labor. Woven wire fences really requires a hard working group of people all functioning as a unit.

That is why our fence work has always been a family affair. This particular year, it was my wife and I and our four kids. Our daughters were 13 and 11, and our boys were 6 and 4. Each member of the family was responsible for a specific part of our job, and when we worked together we got the fence up in a short span of time. Meaning, our sheep would get to enjoy the fresh green grass they had been longingly waiting for.

The same is true in the body of Christ. The Good Shepherd has called us to work together as the body of Christ, each member functioning in its proper role. The work is not easy, but when the body functions properly, we can accomplish much, including, preparing the fields for both God's sheep and the new lambs that will be born.

Our loving Good Shepherd has graciously allowed us to join him in his work. So today, give *yourself* to do the part he has created you for, and let's work in unity to accomplish the work he has put before us.

Go Enjoy The Shepherd.

March 11

The Shepherd's Pleasure
Jeremiah 29:10-14

What a joy it was to fling open that gate and let the sheep come through. Once my family and I had finished the fence work and checked the fields for any possible dangers to the sheep, we let them come over and enjoy the grass they had been waiting for. As I watched them graze and enjoy this new pasture, my heart was filled with joy and excitement. It brought me pleasure to see them simply enjoy what had been prepared for them.

The Good Shepherd smiles as he watches us walk through those new open doors he has opened in our lives. He has seen our longing stares and heard our prayers and petitions for the next step in life. He has been hard at work preparing those places for us to enjoy, and when the time arrives for us to enter in, he smiles as we simply enjoy what he has prepared for us.

Today, prepare yourself to bring joy to your Good Shepherd by simply enjoying what he has prepared for you today!

Go Enjoy The Shepherd.

March 12

Lift Each Other Up
Galatians 6:2

If a sheep is left to itself for long, something interesting happens. Because they are by nature animals who tend to live in a flock, a lone sheep will quickly show signs of depressions and despair. After crying out for a while and receiving no response, the sheep will lower its head and you can literally see the sadness set in.

Being alone is not how sheep were created to live. Their nature says they should stay close to one another, be a part of a family in which they can thrive. If they do this, they can lift each other up simply by being close to each other.

The Good Shepherd was clear when he referred to us as his sheep. Part of this was because he created us and he knows our nature is to be a part of something larger than ourselves. He knows if we get off to ourselves, we can quickly be overcome by despair and depression. Therefore, he tells us to stay close to one another, so we can lift each other up.

Today, look around you for someone who is carrying a heavy load, and trying to do it on their own. Go join that person, and carry their load with them, and in this way we can help Lift Each Other Up.

Go Enjoy The Shepherd.

March 13

Pawing For Attention
Isaiah 55:6-7

Hanging out in the backyard with Precious was truly some of my most relaxing moments. It was a cold time of year and frost would be on the ground in the early morning. However, I took great joy in simply spending time with her.

As I would lie on the ground, she would bounce around me, and at times climb on my back. She treated me like I was her "mothering ewe" and she apparently enjoyed being with me. If at times I turned my attention to something else, like my phone, she would literally paw at my feet, begging for my attention. This is a natural reaction every sheep has when trying to get attention or to be noticed. What she was saying through her actions was, "Please notice me!" In response to this, I always gave her my full attention.

The Good Shepherd truly enjoys spending time with his sheep. His joy is found in being with them and seeing them thrive in the life he has provided for them. At times, as his sheep, we may think his attention has been diverted away, so we come and "paw" for his attention. When we do this, he simply smiles and turns his face directly upon us.

Today, "paw" at his feet. Cry out for him to notice you, because it is his joy to give you his full attention.

Go Enjoy The Shepherd.

March 14

Tell Your Story
Mark 16:15

Learning about sheep is not something you really want to do on your own. If you just get a flock of sheep and put them on your farm without any training or knowledge of sheep, you are headed for heartache and grief. You can research sheep on the internet and gain some mental knowledge, but there is no better way to learn than from another shepherd.

I was privileged to be able to spend time with a long-time shepherd when I first started up with sheep. Before I even had my first one, I spent several hours on different occasions listening to stories and watching this shepherd work. He gave me some hands-on experience in how to be a shepherd. Without his help, I am certain I would not have continued long in the work of being a shepherd.

The Good Shepherd knows the excitement that can fill our hearts when we think about being his undershepherd. He knows how we love to speak of his great love. However, he also has told us that in order to tell others of the Good Shepherd, we first need to know him. Not just facts and figures that we can obtain from research and study, but first-hand knowledge only gained by spending time with the Good Shepherd.

Today, be still and listen to the voice of the Good Shepherd. He loves to train you and teach you in all of his ways through the Holy Spirit. Allow him to pour out himself into you so that when you, like Peter, start tending the flock he has given you, you will be properly prepared to teach them about his glorious love.

Go Enjoy The Shepherd.

March 15

Giving Thanks
Psalm 107:1

Nothing quite compared to the first time I had to take a bottle down to the building and give it to Babe. Babe was our very first bottle-fed lamb we had to raise. I was nervous and unsure I was fit for this chore. I had helped my father as a child bottle-raise some calves, but this lamb was so small and fragile. She was born sickly and was therefore rejected by her mother. I called my shepherd friend for advice and tips, but when it was time to do the work, it was up to me.

At first, the lamb turned away from the bottle. It was not a natural feel to her, nothing like what her mother's would have been. With patience and perseverance, I was able to get Babe to take the bottle. As she began to suckle the milk, her little tail began to wag. What a joy it was to watch her express her thanks every time she drank from our hands.

The Good Shepherd, he is patient and kind. He knows our every need! He also knows our natural tendency to turn our heads away from the supply of his hands. He presses on, undeterred by our reactions, persevering until we learn to drink the milk necessary for our growth. His smile bursts forth as he watches our tails wag as we give thanks for all he has done for us.

Today, lift your voice in praise and thank God for all he has done for you! Think of the air you breathe and "wag your tail" in response to his great love!

Go Enjoy The Shepherd.

Preparing to Go Out
Matthew 10:1-16

The day came up so fast. All the long hard hours of raising Precious at home had paid off and it was time for her to go back to the farm. She was twice her original size at birth and full of life and joy. All she had known was being a part of our family, but in order for her to reach her full potential, it was necessary for her to return to the fields of green grass and to be with the other sheep.

However, I could not just take her back and drop her off. I had to first take her to the fields and spend time with her among the sheep. She had no clue how to be with the sheep, so it was crucial that I slowly graft her back into the flock. This meant hours at a time sitting in the field with her near the rest of the sheep.

The Good Shepherd, Jesus Christ, spent time with his disciples, training them and teaching them how to live and love as God intended for them to. He walked with them and displayed how to live with the other sheep of his flock. Before he sent them out into the world, he trained them, walked with them, and instructed them how to live.

That same instruction has been passed down through the ages, but his methods have not changed. He calls us to make disciples as he did. This means giving them milk for early growth, teaching them to simply Enjoy the Shepherd, and spending time with them among the lost sheep of the world, training them how to raise up other sheep to know the Good Shepherd.

Today, spend time with your Good Shepherd and the one(s) he has given to train you. Then, go out with the ones he has called you to disciple, spend time with them among the flock and lost sheep, preparing them to go into the fields of harvest.

Go Enjoy The Shepherd.

March 17

Being Sent Out
Matthew 28:19, John 16:7

I cried a few tears when the time had finally come. I had spent the time with Precious feeding her and raising her. I had sat in the field with her among the other sheep, watching to make sure she understood how to graze and find the watering hole. I watched her interactions with the other sheep, making sure she would not be pushed away too much or hurt by one of the larger sheep. But this was the day I had to leave her there and walk away. As I walked away from the gate, she paced back and forth, crying out for me. My heart ached to hold her and comfort her, but I knew this is what was best for her.

This was another time I heard his still whisper and he reminded of the time he walked away from his precious lambs. Jesus had spent years walking with these men, loving them, training them, teaching them. After his death and burial, these men were dazed and confused, losing the Shepherd they loved so much, only to have him return. What joy must have run through their spirits, seeing their beloved alive again. However, he kept saying he had to leave. Why would he leave?

Just like Precious pacing at the gate, the disciples stood staring up in the sky where they had last seen their Good Shepherd disappear. They cried out for him, called to him, begged him to return. How his heart must have longed to go back to them and be with them, but he wanted only what was best for them. If he would have stayed, they would have not received the even greater gift, his Holy Spirit living inside of them. In order for them to have the best, he left them, but he never forsook them, his spirit always there with them.

Rejoice today, for he is leading you into the perfect pasture where you can become who he has created you to be.

Go Enjoy The Shepherd.

March 18

The Fruit
Psalm 128:2

My heart burst with joy the first time I saw the fruit of my labor come to pass. I was out in the field, walking along; of course, Precious was following my every step. I turned and smiled at her and that is when I saw it! As she was following me, my other sheep were following her back to me! Oh, the Joy that filled my soul! All the hard work had paid off and I was reaping the fruit of my labor.

The Good Shepherd, oh, the hours of labor he has put in with each one of his sheep. Each one, at times, pressing hard against even his patience. (Remember Jesus showing frustration with the slow growth of the disciples; Matthew 17:17 is one example.) But he presses forward, knowing one day his labor would produce great fruit. I can see his beaming smile now as he watched Peter, James, John, and the others begin to lead the other lost sheep of the world to him from the heavenly pastures he was working to prepare for our future. What joy must have flooded his soul.

Today, remember, as you press onward in the sometimes frustrating work of training others to follow him, know that you will one day see the fruit of your labor. Like Jesus, you may watch it from "those distant shores," but he who labors does not labor in vain. Do the work he has put before you and trust him to produce the fruit. Above all, remember this, he is smiling from ear to ear as he watches you lead others to him.

Go Enjoy The Shepherd.

March 19

Helping the Weak
Romans 15:1

Nothing is quite as fun as calling for your sheep and seeing them run to you. I would stand at the sheep shed and call out for my flock, and they would each appear from their grazing place or place of rest to come running to me.

One day I noticed a ewe struggling to make her way to me. She had developed an issue with one of her legs, causing her to walk with a limp. She desperately wanted to run with the rest, but her ailment kept her from making it to me like she wanted to. But it was not her that really caught my eye. It was the other two ewes who were perfectly healthy who chose to walk alongside of her and behind her. They could have easily run to me, but instead, they chose to stay with this hurting sheep, apparently as an encouragement along her way. Eventually, they all made it to the shed and I responded by giving them each a special portion of corn that day.

How exciting it must be for the Good Shepherd when he sees some of his prime and healthy sheep willing to choose to help others who are struggling along the path. In a flock of sheep, they tend to respect what is known as the "butting" order, showing respect to those who are ahead of them. In our lives, we have brothers and sisters who along the walk of life become sick or ail with a struggle in their life. Our natural tendency can be to run ahead to gather quickly up to the Good Shepherd; however, he smiles when he sees us encourage the weaker ones along the way, choosing willingly to give up our own abilities in order to help those who are struggling.

Today, who can you willingly choose to lay down your rights for today in order to encourage them on their way to the Good Shepherd?

Go Enjoy The Shepherd.

March 20

Meet Him at the Gate
Psalm 5:3, Psalm 16:5-11

After we took Precious back to the farm to stay with the other sheep for good, she would repeat the same process every morning. As I pulled up to the farm, she would run to the gate. I would gather my supplies, including her bottle for the day, all while she waited for me to enter the gate. Upon my entering the gate, she would immediately lunge for the bottle in my hand and give herself completely to eating from my hand. I had what she needed and she would always meet me at the gate to receive what I had.

The Good Shepherd has ALL we need in his hands. Each day, he invites us to meet him at the gate and receive the life-giving food from the palm of his hands. For those who greet him at the gate each day, he offers life-giving food from which our souls can be satisfied. His eyes light up as he looks up and sees his sheep waiting each day for him at the gate!

Today, greet him at the gate and enjoy the life abundant he has for you in the palm of his hand.

Go Enjoy The Shepherd.

The Shepherd's Patience
2 Peter 3:9

In my original flock of sheep, I had a few Hawaiian Black Sheep. This breed of hair sheep is much leaner than others, resembling at times more features of a goat than a sheep. I was happy to have a diverse flock of sheep to enjoy, and one of these Hawaiian Blacks stood out because of her horns.

Unfortunately, she stood out for another reason, her persistence in finding a way out of the fence. She constantly was trying to get to the "greener grass" on the other side. It really did not matter if the field she was going to was better or not, she just wanted to get out. Each time she left, I would go get her and bring her home. She was so frustrating to me, and yet, I was doing all I could to remain patient with her, hoping she would eventually stay with the flock.

The Good Shepherd is so patient and kind. His love goes far beyond any boundaries we can imagine. He knows we are prone to go astray, yet he comes each time to bring us home. At times we are certain to press hard against his patience, but his well of patience runs deep for the sheep of his flock.

Today, if you find yourself outside the protection of the Good Shepherd's watch, look back for he is certainly on his way to bring you back home.

Go Enjoy The Shepherd.

March 22

The Agonizing Decision
2 Peter 2:1

I was in great pain from a gall bladder attack when the call came in that there was about 40 of our sheep on the neighbor's farm. At the head of this pack of sheep was that horned Hawaiian Black ewe. This time, not only had she gotten out, she was increasing her following to almost a third of the flock. After several hours, and calling in a master herdsman with his highly trained border collie, we had the sheep back home.

I sat in my house with more than just a gall bladder pain in my gut. I knew what had to be done, yet I wrestled with the decision. I loved each of my sheep and desperately wanted to have each of them as members of our flock, but I could not overlook the fact that this one sheep was now leading so many astray. With deep sorrow I had to make the decision to remove her from the flock. If I did not, in time she would eventually lead them all away from my protective care and into the jaws of the waiting coyotes.

How agonizing it must be for the Good Shepherd when he sees one of his own leading others away from him. How his heart must break knowing the countless hours he has spent working with this one to teach him/her to stay close. Yet, He has made a promise to always do what is best for the flock as a whole, and at times that has meant removing the one who is leading others astray.

I know this is a hard lesson to swallow, but the Scriptures are filled with God's promise to protect his flock, even from enemies that come from within. Today, lift your hands in praise to a Shepherd who will make even the agonizing decision to remove one of his own so that others will not be led astray.

Go Enjoy The Shepherd.

Chewing the Cud
Philippians 4:8

Sheep are ruminant animals, meaning they have more than one stomach. They will graze on grass, filling their belly, then go lie in the shade. As they lie there, they will be chewing over and over the food they have eaten earlier. Bringing it up from one stomach, they grind it more in order to extract nutrients further. As I watch this take place, it is a joy knowing they are receiving the full benefit from the grass they have eaten.

The Good Shepherd loves to watch his flock "chew the cud" as they ponder the things of his word. As we take time to graze the green pastures of his Word, we are given time to enter into the shade of his wing in order to ponder the full depths of his love.

Today, take a moment and simply go "chew the cud!"

Go Enjoy The Shepherd.

March 24

Building the Shed
Hebrews 2:10

I grimaced yet again as I grabbed my thumb one more time. "How many times am I going to hit myself?" I wondered. I was out doing my best to build a shed for my sheep. My hope was to provide them a place of rest from the elements of the weather. Not really knowing much about construction or building, I was literally learning as I went, and my thumb was paying the price.

Many times in the process of building this first shed I was tempted to simply quit. My arms ached from the swinging of a hammer and lifting boards into place. I was not able at this time to secure much help because my children were still all very young and Katie was pregnant with our fourth child. Every muscle and joint seemed to be screaming for me to give up, but I knew I had to finish what I started so my sheep could enjoy the comforts this shed would provide.

I can barely imagine how many times our Good Shepherd wanted to give in to his pain and suffering. Daily surrounded by the sin of the world, his soul must have suffered greatly each day. His very muscles and joints must have ached from the mocking and scorn thrown his way as he claimed to be the Son of God. Then, as he hung on the cross, how his body must have begged for him to give up and give in to simply calling ten thousand angels to rescue him from his suffering.

But for the joy that was set before him, he endured! He had to finish the work he had started because the sheep of his flock desperately needed the provision only he could supply.

Today, rejoice that our Good Shepherd did not give in to the cries of his flesh, but rather, he held steady to the work at hand because he counted you more valuable than his own life.

Go Enjoy The Shepherd.

March 25
Training the Lambs
Proverbs 22:6

Mother ewes are fascinating to watch. As they walk around with their lambs each day, that fact that they are training them is evident. Sheep do not raise their lambs haphazardly. They teach them along the way. Each movement and sound the mother ewe makes has a purpose and a reason.

When the lambs are young, only days old, they use a special call to bring the lambs in for feeding. When the lambs need to rest, the mother will lie down and call her babies to herself. As they grow older, she intentionally forces them to learn how to graze, shortening their time of sucking milk from her. She leads them to the water's edge, teaching them how to drink from the fresh water to quench their thirst. In other words, she is training them to become grown sheep able to eat on their own.

The Good Shepherd has supplied the lambs of his flock with "mothering ewes" to train them in the way they should go. Parents for children. Teachers for students. Shepherds for disciples. Like a mother ewe, they have been given a charge to train up these young ones so that they may one day function as fully mature sheep. Giving them milk, yet teaching them to eat the food they will need. Showing them how to rest in the shadow of His wings in order to gain strength for the journey ahead. Leading them to the infinite well of his loving water supply that never goes dry so that their thirst can be quenched.

Today, give thanks to the Lord for his "mothering ewe" in your life and then tell them thanks for teaching you how to follow the Good Shepherd!

Go Enjoy The Shepherd.

Bad Advice
1 Kings 12:1-15, Isaiah 11:2

"Hey, Son, when you have to give those sheep some medicine, just take your thumb and run it down their jaw and that will force their mouth open so you can put the medicine in with no problems." This was the sage advice I received from my grandfather as I was explaining my shock to find out sheep had no top teeth. I quickly learned that my grandfather was having a little fun at my expense.

The first time I followed his advice, I quickly learned that sheep do in fact have both top and bottom grinding teeth in their jaws. My thumb hurt for weeks and at one point was so infected I had to give it special attention. To this day, my grandfather just smiles at the thought he was able to "pull one over on me" when it came to sheep. (I have a feeling his father did this to him when he was young.)

Sometimes in life we seek advice on situations we are facing. If there is one thing most people have, it is an opinion on how we should handle a particular situation. Rarely is everyone's advice the same, so we are still left with a choice.

However, the Good Shepherd himself has offered unto us his very own Spirit of wisdom. We have the blessed opportunity to enter into his presence and seek his guidance for all situations we face. All we have to do is enter in!

Today, as you listen to the advice of those around you, take a moment and ask the Good Shepherd to lead you in his path, because only he has promised to NEVER lead you astray.

Go Enjoy The Shepherd.

That One!
Luke 15:3-7, Isaiah 53:11

It was raining and the last thing I wanted to do was to go searching for sheep. Wintertime was starting to set in and that meant the rain drops would each be like a chilled bullet hitting my skin. The call of the easy chair was loud and clear after a long day at work, but I knew if I did not go and look, I would be up all night wondering if the coyotes had found my wandering sheep first.

As I walked along those hillsides, cutting through the rain, I thought about what was compelling me to do what I was doing. Was it money? No, that was not really my motivation. Was it my reputation? No, I do not think anyone would have thought less of me, really. So what was it? What would drive me to ignore myself and do what was best for the sheep? It must have been my love for the sheep that had grown in me from my time watching over them.

Can you imagine how deep the Father's love for us must be that he would even dare to ask his very own Son to leave the comforts of glory in Paradise to come find and rescue you? How much value the Good Shepherd must have placed on you to ask his Son to become one of us, to live in the midst of our filth, in order to redeem his sheep and return them to the comforts of his care.

Wow, the Good Shepherd must think very highly of each one of his sheep to have paid such a high price!

Go Enjoy The Shepherd.

March 28
Life of a Sheep
Psalm 69:7-12

Where I live in Tennessee, the most profitable means of farming is in cattle and crops. Depending on what type of farm you have, level or hilly, this typically determines how you will most profit from the land. Everywhere you turn, you can see cows roaming large farms and being hauled to the market for sale.

On the other hand, sheep are not looked upon highly by livestock producers. Yes, some people raise large flocks, but in general, having sheep as your sole livestock is not given a lot of thought. Sheep are hard to keep alive. They tend to die quickly and often. They don't carry a high price at the market for the most part, even if the market is high. I once figured out if I wanted to feed my family solely by raising sheep, I would need a flock of over 500 to make it work. In other words, sheep are not highly favored as the livestock of choice.

Ever wondered why Jesus came as the "Lamb of God?" In the Old Testament it is clear that those who brought sacrifices, who wanted people to notice, offered big bulls! Sheep played a major role in the sacrificial process, but even in those days, sheep and shepherds were not regarded highly. In order to avoid be considered a threat to the Egyptians, Joseph told his family to call themselves shepherds because it was a despised occupation in Egypt (Genesis 46:34). So why be known as the Lamb of God?

Again, how great his love for you must have been, to come and live among us, despised and rejected. Considered nothing more than a "sacrificial lamb," he was mocked and scorned. But in the eyes of the Good Shepherd, the value of this Lamb was the payment necessary in order to redeem the lost sheep of his flock, which includes you!

Go Enjoy The Shepherd.

The Willing Walk
John 10:18

Watching those sheep in Colorado as they were being herded up at the slaughterhouse was an interesting day for me. I watched hundreds of sheep being unloaded from trucks and each one gathered together in pens. They were not making much noise at all, just waiting. When the time came for each group to be slain, they walked down a path, then up a ramp, directly through a door where they would meet their end. Not once did I see one sheep try to turn and flee down the ramp. Not once did they fight or squirm; they willingly walked the path that would lead to their death.

What a beautiful picture of the Lamb of God, Jesus Christ. As he was being beaten and tortured, walking the path to his own death, he did not make a sound or open up his mouth in defense. Not once did he turn to flee, trying to escape his fate. When he reached the "ramp" of the hill to Golgotha, he willingly moved forward, knowing what was awaiting on the other side. As they pierced his hands and his feet, raising him up to breathe his last, he counted the cost and said you were worth his pain!

Go Enjoy The Shepherd.

March 30

Death and Burial
John 19:38-42

When death happens, the process of properly disposing of the body falls to the shepherd. A dead carcass is only an attraction to predators to come and inflict even more suffering on the other sheep. Moving a living sheep around is hard enough, but when they are dead it can be even more of a chore. Lifting "dead weight" to take it to a place away from the flock so you can bury it can be a very difficult job. I remember my first time well as I went up on top of a hill and dug the hole to place the body in. I covered it with minerals and lye to cover and mask the smell, hoping the coyotes and dogs would not find it to dig it up. Each shovel of dirt cast over the body was done so with the reality of sorrow over the loss.

Can you fathom how the Good Shepherd felt as the dead body of his precious Lamb was carried away to be buried? As they wrapped the body, torn and twisted from such a cruel death, he must have grimaced at such a sight. The Roman soldiers mocked and laughed as this "King of the Jews" was carted off to be placed in the tomb. Sorrow must have coursed through the veins of the Good Shepherd as they sealed the tomb, covering the body of his precious Lamb.

Today, reflect on how our Good Shepherd's heart must have felt, seeing his Son die and be buried. The immortal becoming mortal flesh, being ripped to shreds, hung naked on a tree for all the world to see, then cast into a pit to rot away. Then remember this. He saw this unfold, then he looked at you and said "You, my child, are worth it all!"

Go Enjoy The Shepherd.

March 31

Once Dead, Now Alive
Revelation 1:17-18

As I was driving up one day, one sheep in particular was missing. *Where in the world could Caesar be?* I wondered. He typically is just among the other sheep, but I couldn't spot him anywhere. So, I put on my walking shoes and took off through the fields. Despair was already setting in on my heart when I saw what I feared most. There was the body of Caesar lying on the ground, appearing to be stiff. I simply could not believe my eyes. What could have gone wrong?

I reached down to grab his leg to prepare for disposing of his body. As I touched his leg I jumped back with a jolt. This lamb that I was certain had died moved frantically back and forth. After recovering from my near heart attack, I reached down, stood him up, and watched him walk again. It was evident something was not exactly right, he was carrying the evidence of a great battle (probably with his father). You cannot imagine the joy I felt as I realized that this lamb I was certain was dead, was in fact alive!

This day allowed me to experience in a very small way what it must have felt like for the disciples of Jesus when they realized he was no longer dead. I can see them stumbling back in shock, as I did, wondering how could this possibly be. His body revealed he had been in a major fight, carrying the scars from the cross. But here he was, the Lamb of God, who once was dead, but forever more is Alive!

What joy must have flooded the heart of the Good Shepherd, God himself, as he watched his precious Lamb breathing again. His perfect sacrifice being accepted as the price, allowing our Good Shepherd to once again abide in the fields with his precious sheep.

He did this all for You, so … Go Enjoy The Shepherd.

April 1

Joy of Spring
Isaiah 55:10

It has been a long winter season and the reality of wanting fresh grass is not only on the minds of the sheep, but also the shepherd. Feeding hay to ensure the sheep do not starve has been a daily chore throughout the winter. But as the weather warms and the sprouts of grass shoot forth, I join the sheep in their longing look for the green grass to appear.

It is such a joy to turn the sheep loose into that pasture which has been barren for most of the winter, but now bursts forth with new life. The sheep wag their tails as they start munching the grass before barely even making it through the gate. At times, I have had to actually urge them on a little further into the field so I could get the gate shut behind them. To fully appreciate the joy of the abundance of the green grass, the sheep first had to live through a period of living without it.

The Good Shepherd's heart is looking forward to the day when his sheep can barely make it through the gate before they begin to enjoy the blessings he has prepared for them. He bursts with excitement as he watches his sheep eat from the fields he has prepared for them. However, he also knows, that in order to fully enjoy the blessings of what is to come, the sheep will have to experience what it is like to be without!

Today, thank him for not only the times of blessings overflowing, lift your hands up also and give thanks for the times of hardship and suffering. Because without the one, you cannot fully appreciate and enjoy the other.

Go Enjoy The Shepherd.

April 2

Walking the Fields
Deuteronomy 31:8

Part of my chores of raising sheep has to do with walking the fields to make sure there is a sufficient supply of food for them. I walk in the field where they are currently grazing, checking to make sure the grass is still plentiful. But that is not all. I also go before them into the next field to which they will be moved to make sure they will also have enough there when it is time for them to move.

I love how Scripture, time and again, gives us the picture of the Good Shepherd going before us. What a comfort it is to know that he is not only making sure we have enough for today, but that he is also in our tomorrow, making certain the fields ahead will have exactly what we need when we reach that next day in life.

Go Enjoy The Shepherd.

April 3

Change of Plan
Matthew 2:19-23

There have been times, as I have walked the fields ahead of my sheep, when I realized the field was not ready. The grass had not yet recovered from the previous time the sheep had grazed it. The reasons could be many, like the lack of rain, or overabundance of rain and lack of sunshine. Whatever the reason, it simply will not support them properly.

As I go back to the field they are in, I also realize the current field will not sustain them much longer. So I have a choice to make. Will I leave them where they are a little longer, or do I move them forward despite the field not having recovered as it should?

The answer is neither. When this would happen, I would go and search a different area of the farm and see if there was another area that would best be suited for their needs. I walked until I found a place that the sheep could find both the food and water that they required.

In Scripture, this truly was a job the Good Shepherd had before him. He was constantly looking ahead to what was before his flock, and he was willing to change their course in order to meet the needs of his sheep. Look at the story of Joseph as God went years ahead in a plan to rescue Jacob and all his sons from certain starvation. The path was not always easy, and the road was at times a way of suffering, but in the end, the Good Shepherd is always preparing the best for us!

Go Enjoy The Shepherd.

April 4

The Shepherd's Reputation
Ezekiel 20:9, Isaiah 48:11

I learned quickly that the reputation you had as a shepherd spread fast. If you were known to over-graze your fields or mistreat your animals, you quickly were considered someone to not do business with. So, part of my motivation to be known as a good shepherd was I did not want a bad reputation with my peers. When they spoke of me in terms of how I cared for my sheep, I longed to have them say kind and good things regarding my labors.

God is not in need of anyone to uphold his reputation as a Good Shepherd. However, he has allowed his reputation to be put on the line before all the world and universe to see. He has claimed the honor of the Good and Great Shepherd, and he dares anyone to defy his claims as such. As the whole of his story unfolds, he asks anyone to step forth and accuse him of mistreating or doing his sheep any wrong. Many may point to the death and martyr of saints and catastrophes throughout the ages, but God again dares you to look at the whole of the story and see how even those hardships and sufferings were not for the greater good of his people.

How comforting is it to know today that God does all that he does for the glory of his namesake, his eternal reputation as a Good Shepherd!

Go Enjoy The Shepherd.

April 5

New Life
2 Corinthians 5:17

Spring in Tennessee is the time for new birth! What a glorious time it is!

My very first year as a shepherd, all our lambs were born between the end of March and first of April. I loved to gaze out in the fields as they were covered with little lambs. Each one unique, yet so much alike. Each one depending totally upon the care of the shepherd and its mother to survive. If left alone, death would surely come quickly.

What a great time to stop and reflect on the glorious truth that our Good Shepherd loves to gaze out over his pastures and see the new lambs covering his fields. He smiles as he watches them run and play in his fields. He knows without his watchful eye and the milk they need to grow, death can easily set in. So, he watches, making sure those who have received new life can grow and prosper in his fields.

Go Enjoy The Shepherd.

April 6

Crushed by the Mother
1 Kings 3: 16-28

She was a great sheep, one of the most unique on my farm. She was a hair sheep, yet her coat was much thicker than the others. Her coat was white, but her face and legs were black as night. When she gave birth to a set of twin lambs, they were each a spitting image of her. It was instant love on my part, seeing these magnificent lambs.

As I arrived at the shed one morning to turn out the sheep, this ewe and one of her lambs were already out of the shed and waiting for me at the gate. Curious, I looked around to see if I could spot the other lamb anywhere. When I realized she was not in the pen area, I entered the building. There, in a corner, up against the post, was the body of this beautiful little lamb. It was clearly evident she had been crushed and smothered by her own mother during the night.

I asked God, what can you possibly teach me through this? This beautiful lamb suffocated at the side of her mom. Lord, please show me how you could possibly use this for your glory.

That is when I hear him say, "The heavy coat on the mother is like sin in your life. It keeps you from being sensitive to the needs of those around you, like this mom was unable to feel the dying lamb at her side. When you continue in sin, you are like this mother, slowly taking the life out of the lambs I have put under your care!"

Today, if you are carrying a thick coat of sin, run to the Good Shepherd and plead with him to shear you, removing the thick and hard coat you're wearing. If you do not, it is not only your life being affected, you are also contributing to the slow and harsh death of those around you.

Go Enjoy The Shepherd.

April 7

Meat # 1
John 10:3

Okay, so today is be honest day, as every day should be. When I first entered the world of being a shepherd, it was not so I could learn about God and his heart for his sheep. I was looking for an opportunity to make money. Sort of like a second source of income.

We brought in over 100 sheep to our farm from Texas in the middle of the summer. These sheep were desperate for food, seeing as Texas was suffering a drought in the summer of 2011. When they arrived, it was easy to see that these sheep had mostly been left to fend for themselves on a wide open plain. And, it was clearly evident many of them were heavy with lambs about to be born.

The first ewe gave birth to a big and good-looking crossbred ram lamb. He was tall with a greyish color coat and long black legs with a black face. Not having names for any of these sheep, I decided to call the ewe "Momma 1" and my daughters wanted to name the lamb. However, I was adamant they not give him a name because I knew where he was going to end up. Therefore, we called him "Meat 1."

Now you might be asking, "How is this a lesson about the Good Shepherd?" Simple, he has never named any of his lambs "meat." Unlike here on earth, where shepherds must sell lambs and sheep in order to not overgraze the earth, and supply food for the needs of people, God never has to "sell" or remove any sheep from his pastures, for his pastures are limitless and beyond imagination.

Today, Praise God that he is the Good Shepherd with no limitations to his ability to provide. Thank him for bringing you into his flock and calling you by name!

Go Enjoy The Shepherd.

April 8

Wedding Day
Revelation 19:6-9

Weddings are glorious events, and throughout history, they have been closely connected to sheep and lambs. In Biblical days, sheep were often used as part of dowry payments, securing the right to marry the beautiful bride. Lambs were also sacrificed to supply the meal for the feast of the wedding.

Today, across the world, this tradition continues on in many areas. Sheep are bartered as a dowry payment and lambs are used to prepare the feast for the wedding celebration.

Now look ahead, through the eyes of the Good Shepherd as he is preparing the wedding of the Lamb of God. He is preparing a great feast and celebration for that great day, when his Son, Jesus Christ, will receive the promised Bride. Yet, in Revelation, we see a turn of events where the sheep of his pasture, purchased by God through the sacrifice of his precious Lamb, will join together in one body to become the Bride of the Lamb. Instead of a lamb being used for the Feast, it is the Lamb who will finally receive the reward for his great sacrifice and a supper Feast will be held to celebrate this unforgettable day.

Today, lift your hands and sing, "Worthy is the Lamb!"

(Happy Anniversary to my dear wife Katie! Thanks for serving the Good Shepherd by my side!)

April 9
The First Step
1 Thessalonians 5:14

I watched with attentive eyes the first time I had seen a lamb born in real time. I had been told that lambs can actually go from birth to walking in less than seven minutes, so I was curious to see if that was correct. I kept my eyes on the lamb, watching as the mother cleaned it off. In just about five minutes, the little lamb was doing its best to stand up. It would get up and wobble a bit, then fall back down. The mother would nudge the lamb, encouraging it to try again. After several attempts, the lamb finally found its strength to stand and go get the first drink of milk from its loving and patient mother.

What a beautiful picture of how the Good Shepherd tenderly watches over each of his newborn lambs. When they first arrive on the scene, they are weak, cold, and in need of cleaning up. Then, with patience and care, he gently urges them to stand on their feet. They attempt in their own strength to stand, only to fall back down again. With a gentle nudge, he prods them to try again until they are finally able to stand and drink the first taste of life he has to offer them.

Today, rejoice in the gentle touch and patience of our Good Shepherd.

Go Enjoy The Shepherd.

April 10

The Hireling
John 10:12-13

I left for lunch that day and smiled as I saw the sheep grazing in the 50-acre field. Beside them stood the miniature donkeys who were there for the purpose of protecting the flock. It had been said that coyotes hated the braying of a donkey and would run when they heard it.

When I returned home an hour later, I saw the carcass of one of my sheep lying in the field. Curious, I walked over to it only to discover it had been eaten from head to toe. This was no doubt the work of a pack of coyotes. I lifted my eyes to see the rest of my sheep continuing to graze, along with the donkeys, about 150 feet away.

On that day, I realized the donkeys are good at defending against coyote attacks, but only if it means defending themselves. They could have cared less about the well-being of my sheep—they were only concerned with their own lives. They were nothing more than hirelings in my field. What I needed was a true undershepherd who would defend my flock.

In Scripture, Jesus talks about those who were no more than hirelings watching over sheep. He tells us that at the first sign of danger, they would protect themselves and leave the sheep to the clutches of the wolves. That is the true difference in someone who actually loves the sheep and one who is only there to earn a living for themselves. One cares for the life of the ones they are watching, the other cares for his own life.

Today, give thanks to the Lord, as he was not an hireling who cared more for his own well-being, but rather, he is the Good Shepherd who willingly laid down his life for his sheep.

Go Enjoy The Shepherd.

April 11

Why Guard Dogs
John 10:11

After losing nine sheep on the donkey's watch, I went out and found me some guard dogs. I was desperate to find a guardian who cared as much for my sheep as I did. I was looking for protectors who were willing to lay down their lives for the sheep, like the Good Shepherd was.

I was blessed to find my now beloved Karakachans. They are a very special and rare breed of dogs, originating from Bulgaria. What is most fascinating about these, and other Livestock Guardian Dogs, is the way they literally become one with the flock. In a short period of close contact, they literally adopt these sheep as their own family and defend them as such. There are many stories of these animals fighting to the death defending their flocks.

I have found these LGDs a beautiful picture of our Good Shepherd who willingly laid down his life for his sheep just as he promised. He came down and became one of us, adopted us as his own family, and then defended us accordingly. He saw the enemy, a roaring lion, ripping through the fields toward his family, then he went and willingly laid down his life for you and me so that we could live!

Today, we, like Peter have been called to be like Jesus and tend to his flock. Your flock may be a congregation who meets on Sunday and through the week. Your flock may be those you gather with in homes. Your flock may be your co-workers. It could be that your flock are those you go to school with or share a dorm room with. Or maybe your flock is your family and children you are raising. Ask yourself today, "Who is the flock he has asked me to tend?" Then, be willing to lay down your life so that they may live.

Go Enjoy The Shepherd.

April 12

For Eagerness
Hebrews 12:1-2

I often get asked "Why do you want to raise sheep?" It is a valid question, especially since we only raise a small flock. There is no real gain in it from a world's point of view. As I have mentioned before, in order to experience enough financial gain one would literally have to raise a large flock of sheep. So why do I do it?

At first, I admit, it was for personal gain and interest. I figured I could find a way to make it profitable to my family. After being around the sheep, I began to just consider it a joy. I liked walking in the fields, staff in hand, hanging out with the sheep. I loved hearing the lessons I was learning from God as I walked through the fields. Eventually, my heart changed from looking at it for gain and I began to realize it was for the pure joy of being with sheep that I was a shepherd.

So why would the God of the universe declare himself to be a Good Shepherd? If he knew in the beginning there would be no gain or profit for himself, why would he do it? Why would he become a Shepherd?

Hebrews 12:2 tells us to fix our eyes on Jesus who is the perfecter of our faith, **who endured the cross because of the joy set before him,** ignoring its shame. Once he had conquered that, he sat down at the right hand of the throne of God.

He did it simply for the joy of being with his sheep! (That means You!)

Go Enjoy The Shepherd.

April 13

Be Eager
1 Peter 5:1-4, Hebrews 12:3

In real life, working with sheep can be extremely frustrating at times. Sheep just have a way at times to push the shepherd to his limits. I can remember dealing with a whole set of sheep in my flock who simply liked to be stubborn. They would only come half of the times when I called. The other half, they would disappear up the steep hill into the dense cedar thickets. It is simply a fact of life, your sheep at times can get under your skin.

However, the key to dealing with this is patience and perseverance. I got through those walks up a hill, through the thickets, to bring the sheep back by remembering why I did it. For the joy of being a shepherd and for the love of my sheep.

It makes me smile to look in the Old Testament and see God himself at times dealing with these types of sheep. Look at the Israelites in the wilderness, at the foot of Mt. Sinai, worshiping a golden calf and claiming this statue had brought them out of Egypt. How frustrating that must have been for God as the Good Shepherd to those sheep. Yet, Moses, a shepherd himself, reminded God of why he took these sheep as his own. For the joy of being a shepherd.

Today, your flock may be causing you great frustration. It may be a stubborn congregation, teenager, husband, wife, kids, students, or disciple you are teaching. When those moments of frustration arise, remember the love and patience the Good Shepherd has shown to you and be eager to press on!

Go Enjoy The Shepherd.

April 14

Grazing Stripped Croplands
I Corinthians 3:6-7

I was absolutely fascinated by the video I was watching of shepherds leading their flocks into corn and wheat fields that had been harvested. From the look of the naked eye, there was nothing there for them to eat. The wheat had been all taken up and the corn fields were seemingly nothing but stalks. However, there was something you could not see with just a first glance.

Anytime fields are harvested, there is always some of the corn or wheat left on the ground. The stubbles of the wheat are like candy to sheep, and the left-behind corn is pure satisfaction to their bellies. So they graze these fields with joy, evidenced by a wag of a tail every so often.

However, there is a greater benefit in this for the farmer of those fields. As sheep walk through and graze, they also are fertilizing his ground. As the sheep enjoy what is left behind, they are preparing the ground for the next abundant harvest.

Sometimes, to our untrained eye, we think the Good Shepherd has led his flock into a barren place where there is no food. We watch in wonder as to why He might leave them/us in such a place. However, as the Shepherd, he knows what all is there for his sheep and that their needs will be met. But even more, he sees how the sheep will make this seemingly barren land into a future abundant harvest.

Today, if you believe you are living in a deserted wasteland and you are not doing your Shepherd any good, remain faithful and obedient. You may not be there to see what will come from your labor, but he does and he is pleased with what he sees.

Go Enjoy The Shepherd.

April 15

Paying Taxes
Mark 12:17

Tax day in the United States. Not really a day I personally look forward to. Giving away my hard-earned money just does not feel good. I don't like it.

You know, sheep have those days each year as well. Wool sheep especially go through this. They spend so much time growing their nice coats of wool, only to be marched into the shearer to have it removed. The shepherd calls them into the shed and asks them to give back to him for all he has done for them. Their wool is needed to make clothes for the shepherd and his family or to be sold at the market so the shepherd's family can buy food. If you watch sheep get sheared, you will notice how seemingly embarrassed they are when it is done. Yet, the shepherd, year in and year out, calls them in so he can take their wool.

Our Good Shepherd, Jesus, told us to give to Caesar what was his. To pay the taxes that were due. More importantly, he told us to be like sheep, and render unto God what belongs to him. The coin had the image of Caesar. We are created in the image of God. When he calls for us to give to him what is rightfully his, sometimes it does not feel good. However, we must trust that he has a purpose for our good and know what we give will be used to bring glory to him.

Today, do not be afraid to render unto God what belongs to him.

Go Enjoy The Shepherd.

April 16

The Heavy Coat
John 15:2

Yesterday we looked at the shearing of the sheep and how that sometimes feels like "tax day." However, the shepherd has more on his mind than just taking away the wool.

You see, if sheep are allowed to go untrimmed for extended periods of times, there can be many disasters for that sheep from this. The wool can become so heavy that it brings pain to the joints and feet of the sheep. This burden could eventually lead to disease and death.

If these heavy coats become too moist, the sun cannot reach the inner layers and the moisture could invite skin diseases and sores. Also, a thick heavy coat that is soaked by rain has also caused a sheep to become "cast," basically causing it to fall on its side and unable to get up. If this happens, then the sheep will soon have gases built up in its belly and will die a painful death. Therefore, a good shepherd makes sure his flocks are sheared in their proper times.

The Good Shepherd is not slow to care for his sheep. He knows all too well the dangers of built-up coats of sin or self-righteousness. He is timely in his work to prune away these burdensome coats before they can cause immense damage and decay to his sheep, sometimes even leading to death. The only question remains. Are you willing to trust his hands to do what is best for you, removing the burdens of the coats you now bear?

Rejoice today, for he cares enough for you, loves you enough, to prune away your heavy coat!

Go Enjoy The Shepherd.

April 17

Stubbornness
Hosea 4:16

Part of our farm operation is raising not only sheep, but some cows. Ever since I was a boy, I have been privileged to be around cattle. My brother and his sons tended cows for many years on the old family farm on behalf of my grandfather.

One year, they brought home this magnificent-looking cow. Her coat was a light red and she had almost perfectly symmetrical horns. From a distance, she was a fine cow to see. However, there was a reason another farmer sold her at the cattle sale. She was a stubborn and ornery as they come. She would leap fences and gates to go where she pleased. On several occasions, in our attempts to return her to the correct field, she would lower her head and charge right at us. She became a danger to everyone around.

When she became sick during a pregnancy, we had to get her in the barn. What a chore that was. When the vet arrived to check her, she literally attempted to go through us and the panels to get out. She did not even want the necessary care that could keep her alive!

In Hosea, the Good Shepherd referred to his people acting more like this stubborn cow than lambs in the field. What a drastically different picture this paints for us to realize who he has redeemed us to be. I know at times, I find myself fighting against the very hands that are attempting to make me whole instead of calmly living in the pastures of my Good Shepherd.

Today, ask him to search your heart and make you like the lambs of his pasture.

Go Enjoy The Shepherd.

April 18

Leading the Flock
Psalm 77:19-20

When those first sheep came to our farm, they had no idea what it was like to be led. For their entire existence, they had only been pushed from one place to another. The fear of either a dog or person on their heels drove them around, rooting a deep sense of fear of people in these sheep.

However, once we had been with each other long enough and I had given them enough corn from my bucket, they soon learned to follow me when I called. I had earned their trust and they were willing to follow me, knowing if I was in front, they would never face anything that I had not first confronted.

How great is our Good Shepherd, who gently leads his flocks of sheep. He calls you to follow him, sometimes through the very valleys of trouble. But we can take heart, for he is in the lead, and we can follow knowing we will never face anything that he has not first confronted.

Rejoice today, that just as he led the Israelites through the Red Sea, going before them, he too is ahead of you in every step you take!

Go Enjoy The Shepherd.

April 19

All My Life
Genesis 48:15

When Caesar was born, from his very first day, he has only known one shepherd—me. He has been loved on by my family and cared for by friends when I have had to leave town, but he has never known another shepherd in his life. Because of this, Caesar has no issues trusting me. He will follow me wherever I go.

Look at Jacob's declaration in the verses above. He says that the Good Shepherd has led him all his life and it is clear that Jacob loves and trusts his shepherd. I have asked how could this be because I know the story of Jacob very well. He endured much pain, rejection, heartache, suffering, and lived in foreign lands for fear of his brother Esau. He suffered at the hands of his own children, who sold his beloved son into slavery, and then told him Joseph was dead. Yet, he still claimed the Good Shepherd had led him each step of the way. How could he say this? Because he knew the heart of a shepherd.

Jacob tended to sheep when he was young, and he knew what it was like to love his sheep. He knew at times, he would have to lead them through extremely difficult situations; however, as the shepherd up front, he knew the blessing he had for them at the end of the journey. Therefore, he trusted that his Good Shepherd had a bigger plan despite his current pain and suffering.

You may not feel like God has been watching over you all your life, but he never lies and he has told us he knew you before you were in the womb. (Jeremiah 1:5, Psalm 139:13). So today, give thanks that he has been your Good Shepherd all your life, and rejoice knowing he already knows the blessing he has prepared on the other side of your difficult journey.

Go Enjoy The Shepherd.

April 20

Gently Leading
Isaiah 40:11

Moving a flock of sheep for a great distance can be difficult on them. It can be especially difficult on ewes heavy in their pregnancy and mothers with new lambs. So, as a shepherd, I do my best not to move them much during these times if at all possible. Taking care not to cause early births or miscarriages or for lambs to be accidentally left behind is the job of the shepherd.

However, if it is necessary for me to move them, I do it slowly, being careful not to cause a major disturbance to the pregnant ewes and making certain no little lamb is left behind. If the lambs are too young to understand, and the mother is being good, refusing to leave their young behind, I simply scoop them up in my arms and carry them to the next place and the dutiful mom follows me with her babies in my care.

I love this picture of the Good Shepherd here in Isaiah. He knows exactly where we are in our walks with him. He knows our every need, and he knows where we are in our walk with him. When a time comes that we must be moved in order to best enjoy his provisions. He is gentle with those who are like a ewe heavy with child, and he carries in the folds of his garments those little lambs who do not quite yet understand.

Give thanks today, for we have such a Good and Kind Shepherd!

Go Enjoy The Shepherd.

April 21

Sheep Follow Sheep
1 Corinthians 11:1

There is one fact that will forever remain. Sheep follow Sheep. I have watched this time and time again. If a sheep comes to me, the other sheep will follow. That is why a trusting sheep in your flock is of great importance. He or she teaches the others to trust. However, if a sheep runs from me, guess what, the others will follow. By nature, sheep follow sheep.

How wonderful of the Good Shepherd to send to us the perfect sheep to follow. Showing us what it is like to have complete trust in the care of the Good Shepherd, even to his death on the cross. God knows how our hearts are prone to follow others around us; therefore, he places in our lives those sheep in his flock who have learned to trust him and therefore show us how to follow.

Today, go thank the "sheep" whom he has placed in your life who lead you back to the Good Shepherd's feet!

Go Enjoy The Shepherd.

April 22

Judas Sheep
Matthew 7:15-20, 1 John 4:1-3

The place I was standing the day I fell in love with sheep might be considered an awkward place for that to happen. I was standing in a slaughter facility assisting a friend on a video shoot. I had never really considered sheep much before that day, but by now, you know the rest of the story.

One particular sheep really stood out that day. They called him the "Judas Sheep." The name is given to that particular sheep because he is trained to lead the other sheep straight into the slaughter pens. Sheep naturally follow other sheep, therefore this natural instinct is used against them in order to get them through the slaughter process quickly and precisely.

We are warned by the Good Shepherd to beware of the wolves who come dressed as sheep. I have said before, sheep will not follow a predator, but they will follow other sheep. Unfortunately, there are some dressed up like sheep who have been trained to lead others astray.

Thankfully, the Good Shepherd has given his sheep the ability to know his voice and has sent an ever watchful eye over his flock in the Holy Spirit. He knows the tactics of the enemy and how he loves to try and lead us astray by masquerading as one of the flock. Be alert and listen, my friends, for the Good Shepherd has given us warning to this tactic of the enemy and if we are not careful, we may find ourselves following "Judas" to the slaughtering grounds of sin and destruction.

Go Enjoy The Shepherd.

April 23

Replacing the Ram
Hebrews 12:1-3

There are many difficult days in the life of a shepherd. You find yourself torn between doing what is necessary and doing what your heart wants to do.

Sheep do not live forever. That is just a simple fact. They have a finite amount of days and whether we like it or not, they grow older just like we do. Rams are probably the ones I notice the most because when you get used to having a good ram around it is hard imagining your flock without them. However, the day eventually comes when father time says their work is finished and it is time for a new ram to lead the flock.

I do not like these days because I tend to get connected to my rams. I enjoy them, especially ones who have been so good to me, producing great lambs and leading the flock. However, I also know it is the best for my flock to bring in a younger ram to eventually take his place.

The Good Shepherd watches carefully over his flock as well. He loves his sheep who are going out and leading more lambs (disciples) back to his feet. However, his ultimate joy comes when he calls those who have gone before us to pass the mission of making disciples on to those who will carry it on into the future. When this happens, he rejoices as he welcomes his great sheep into that cloud of witnesses who will cheer on those who are left behind to carry on his work.

A personal word of thanks to those who have paved the way for ones like me to carry on the mission of telling others about the Good Shepherd!

Go Enjoy The Shepherd.

April 24

The Sound of His Voice
John 10:27

Once sheep come to know the voice of the shepherd, he can literally call them and they will follow him wherever he goes. I learned this lesson after having sheep for a few weeks and needing to lead them from one pasture to the other. It brought me great joy when we finally made the connection and they began to respond to my voice. To be able to simply open a gate and call my sheep and hear them come running my way brought a huge smile to my face.

The well-known verses of John 10 referencing the relationship between the Good Shepherd and the sheep speak of hearing his voice and following. He says, "My sheep hear my voice, and I know them, and they follow me!" What a beautiful picture of the relationship between the Good Shepherd and his sheep.

How big his smile must be when he calls his sheep and they recognize his voice and follow him. It must bring him great joy to call his sheep from where they are today and lead them into the next phase of life he has prepared for them.

Today, listen for his voice and simply Follow him!

Go Enjoy The Shepherd.

Never Give Up
2 Timothy 2:1-13

I truly love it when you see a fighting spirit in someone. I mentioned before, a time the shepherd faces when he must replace his ram. This comes about when a ram has reached the end of his life and a new ram is required for the flock. I recently bought a new ram because our current one is nearing the end of his journey. However, immediately upon turning the new ram in, the old ram quickly put the young ram in his place as if to say, "I am not finished yet."

This made me very excited because this young ram will now have the opportunity to watch an older ram and learn how to be a leader in the flock. He also knows that the older ram is not going to give up until his time is fully completed.

The Good Shepherd loves to see his sheep continue to stand firm and run the race set before them all the way to the end. Giving up is not an option in our pursuit of following him, and his heart leaps with joy when his sheep continue strong all the way to the end!

Never Give Up!

Go Enjoy The Shepherd.

Stay Close to the Shepherd
Psalm 44:11

When watching sheep for the first few months, we had a huge problem with coyote attacks. They are a common predator here in our area of Tennessee and my flock suffered great losses due to coyotes. What was interesting was the craftiness of the pack of coyotes in how they chose their prey.

Sheep, as we know, have a natural tendency to wander off from the flock. A sheep can get so captivated with the green grass it is enjoying, or something they think looks good, that they simply stray away from the shepherd and the flock. The crafty coyote is smart enough to wait and watch for one sheep to be off to itself and that is where they would attack. When the sheep gets far enough away from the shepherd, it becomes an easy target.

That is true with the Good Shepherd and his sheep as well. We have a tendency to stray and wander off, enjoying the pleasures of this life. Sometimes, that includes becoming too engrossed in the very blessings he has provided. When we do this, we can become so distracted by the beauty and wonders all around us that we simply get too far from the Good Shepherd, and therefore we make ourselves an easy target for our enemy.

To avoid being a target for the enemy, you must stay close to the Shepherd!

Go Enjoy The Shepherd.

April 27

The Guardian
Psalm 91:11, John 6:39

When I first became a shepherd, I had a few frustrating weeks of losing some of my flock to coyotes. Coyotes are crafty hunters and usually attack at night and in a pack. I kept a head count daily and every so often one would go missing and I would find what was left of the carcass.

That is when I went and found myself some guard dogs. I purchased three dogs and brought them home. It took a few days for them to bond with my sheep, but once they did, I ceased worrying about coyote attacks on my flock. I would watch with joy as the coyotes would yelp and my dogs would send a vicious warning back their way with a deep and loud bark. I never lost another sheep to coyotes once the guardians became a part of my farm.

The Good Shepherd has his guardians on alert for his sheep as well. The enemy is always lurking, seeking whom he may devour. Often, he attacks the flock if he senses even the slightest opening. However, the Good Shepherd never leaves his flock unprotected, as he sends his guardians to oversee and protect his sheep! He smiles knowing he will never lose any of his flock as He watches over them!

Today, think of who God has put in your life as a guardian, and give thanks to the Good Shepherd for watching over you!

Go Enjoy The Shepherd.

Notifying the Shepherd
Matthew 18:10, Isaiah 19:1

Having guard dogs on the farm was such a huge help when it came to predator control. Once they bonded with the sheep, it was clear nothing was going to come and bother my sheep without a huge fight.

One of the first things I noticed about the dogs was their natural tendency to respond to the voices of the enemy. When the coyotes howled, the dogs responded with a very heavy and thick howl of their own. One of the purposes of this howl was to let the enemy know they were ready for his attack, but most importantly, it was to notify me, the shepherd, that danger was near so I could be prepared to defend against the enemy.

The Good Shepherd's guardians act in much the same manner. When the enemy howls in an attempt to frighten the sheep of God, the guardians respond to let him know they are ready. Most importantly though, they cry out in prayer to alert the Good Shepherd that they sense the attack of the Evil One, and he is always swift to come and defend his flock!

Rejoice today, for you are under the wings of his protection!

Go Enjoy The Shepherd.

April 29

Ferocious in the Fight
Psalm 24

At one point, early in the stage of having guard dogs on the farm, I was suddenly down to one dog. I had sold the youngest, thinking all I needed was two dogs to work together. Unfortunately, my female died shortly thereafter while giving birth to pups. I found myself having only one dog to defend a very large flock (110 sheep) against some aggressive coyotes.

The coyotes, being an intuitive pack, must have figured my situation. Soon after losing my female, I heard the mighty ruckus of a coyote pack at 4:30 in the morning. I jumped out of bed and ran to my front porch to assess the situation. It was still too dark for me to see much, but it was evident the coyotes were attacking from two different directions. I was certain I was about to lose several of my sheep.

Then, through the darkness came a ferocious loud bark followed by the yelping of a coyote! Just as soon as the enemy had come, the entire pack of coyotes fled with their tails tucked. I grabbed my flashlight and a gun and took off toward the fields to check my losses. What I found was my lone dog, Cheta (said cheetah), standing tall and all my sheep safe and sound. Because he had been mighty in the battle, my entire flock had been spared.

You can rest assured there are no weak guardians under the Good Shepherd's command. He would not send a fearful soldier to protect his flock because he cares too much for us. If a guardian has been placed by the Good Shepherd, watching over you, you can be certain they will be ferocious in the fight!

What a Mighty God We Serve!

Go Enjoy The Shepherd.

Peaceful Warrior
Proverbs 25:21-22 & Romans 12:14-21

Buddy is what I called a very laid-back and relaxed Great Pyrenees. He does not stay in the sheep field and his preference is to wander about over multiple farms and eat whatever the neighbors throw out to him. Looking at his face, you would make the assumption he would never hurt anything. In fact, he is even a little bashful around small dogs and cats.

But one must never judge a book by its cover. The reason Buddy has become one of my favorite dogs is because of his protection of my family and my farm. Once, when on a walk with my family, a couple of donkeys became a little rowdy and got too close to my daughters. In the blink of an eye, Buddy leaped into action and ran them off. On another occasion, he brought a coyote and laid it on the driveway like a trophy because the coyote had gotten too close to the house. He walks around and constantly marks his territory, letting all the surrounding animals know "this is my place." Buddy may look like a "man of peace" but when necessary, he becomes a mighty warrior.

The Good Shepherd has many warriors, who for the most part, look like they would never even fight. One look at them and you might assume they are weak and unable to do battle. However, these "men / women of peace" can often be found waging war in prayer. Or you may find them waging war by being kind to those who are attempting to persecute them, as my father would say, "killing them with kindness."

Some of God's greatest warriors are those who may appear to never fight any battles. However, when danger comes near, they rise up and become Mighty Warriors for their Shepherd.

Praise God for these Peaceful Warriors!

Go Enjoy The Shepherd.

May 1

Always on Duty
Psalm 121:1-5

It does not matter if it is a beautiful day, blistering hot day, freezing cold, or miserable with rain, every day I go out and check the sheep. My job does not depend on how I feel or if I am sick; every day the sheep require my attention. If I cannot go personally because my body refuses or I am out of town, I make sure someone is there to check the sheep.

I can remember days when my body ached so badly from illness, but I went to the fields anyway. I remember days that it was just miserably cold, but I was there no matter. The point is, sheep require daily attention and as their shepherd, I am there to take care of their needs.

I am grateful that the Good Shepherd, Jesus Christ, is not in need of a sick day or kept away by weather. He, as a Good Shepherd, is always on duty watching over his flock. His watchful eye is not turned away by sleep or slumber. He did not shy away when his body was beaten and bruised. He kept his eye on the prize before him, his glorious flock, and today he maintains an ever watchful eye over me!

Go Enjoy The Shepherd and thank him that he is always on duty!

Blazing a Trail
Deuteronomy 31:8, Isaiah 45:2

When you visit a sheep farm, one of the things you will notice is a well-worn path leading to the sheep shed and watering holes. As you walk through the fields or look on the hillsides, you will see very distinct trails that have been traveled many times. These are the paths that the sheep follow to get to where the shepherd has made provision for their needs. Paths to food and to water. Paths to their source of life. Many times, these paths are created as I have walked in front of the sheep, leading them to where I want them to go. As time goes by, these sheep continue in these same paths we walked when I call them to come to me, thus forming a very narrow trodden path.

The Good Shepherd, Jesus Christ, has left a path for his sheep to follow. He, being the perfect Lamb of God, blazed the path leading us back to his Father. He went before us so that we would have a Way to follow back to our source of real life. He told us he would show us the Way, and he did so by becoming the Way back to God.

Today, thank him for the narrow and worn path that he blazed for you, leading you back into the arms of the Great Shepherd, God our Father.

Go Enjoy The Shepherd.

Narrow Path
Matthew 7:13-14

I was blessed to be visited by a dear sister in Christ who had spent 40 years raising sheep in a state just north of us. As we walked through our fields, I was like a little boy soaking in her stories from her years of tending sheep. One that really stood out was why the sheep path was so narrow.

She said if you watch sheep walk, they literally place one foot in front of the other. It almost appears as if they cross their legs as they walk. Because of this, the beaten down paths to the shed and watering holes are extremely narrow. If the sheep walk as they should, in the proper "butting" order, they will each stay on this path and follow it back to where the shepherd is calling from.

In Matthew, Jesus, our Good Shepherd, told us that the way to life was narrow and the way to death was broad. I can see Jesus pointing out little sheep paths to those listening, pointing out how these paths are paths of life for the sheep as they follow their shepherd to the next grazing ground or to still waters. In contrast, the roads they walked, where herders drove the flocks to the place of slaughter, were broad and wide leading the sheep to their destruction! On these roads, the sheep would bustle about, not staying in line, feeling the anxiety of the pace at which they were being driven.

Today, we have a choice, to follow the narrow path as the Good Shepherd leads us to life, or, to join the masses on the wide and broad road as we are being driven to our destruction. Today, I urge you, choose to follow the Good Shepherd and enjoy the life he has set before you.

Go Enjoy The Shepherd.

May 4

One Foot in Front of the Other
Philippians 3:12-16

During the stormy months of the year, when there is a lot of rain, sheep can get sore feet. Many times their feet become tender and sore as their hooves over-grow and bend back into the soft tissue. During these stormy times of year, it is important to keep an eye on the flock to see if anyone needs special attention given to their feet.

One thing I have noticed as sheep struggle with tender feet, despite the pain, they press on along the path leading them back to the place where their food or water is. When I call, they still come to me, putting one foot in front of the other, through the pain, to come to my side. In their desire for the shepherd, sheep are resilient in their efforts to get to where they need to be. As I watch them press on, placing one foot in front of the other, I always reward them with some corn or a treat at the end of their journey.

We also face stormy times in life, when our lives feel beaten, battered, and bruised. We often feel as if we cannot go on any further, but the Good Shepherd, he calls out to us, encouraging us along the path. He tells us to continue to press on, looking ahead at him, our Prize at the end of the path. He smiles at his sheep as they fight through the pain and suffering in their lives and he cheers for them as they press on toward their goal, to be at his side.

Today, if your "feet" are tender from the journey, press on, placing one foot in front of the other. If you do this, at the end, you will receive a great reward from the hand of Jesus himself.

Go Enjoy The Shepherd.

Stay on the Path
Psalm 37:23-26

Sheep can be entertaining creatures at times. I have seen them do some silly things that will make you wonder "What are you sheep thinking?"

The first farm I raised sheep on is what we call here in Tennessee a "hillside farm." Some places on this farm were fairly steep and rough. Over time, the sheep made their well-worn paths on those hillsides, and when they followed these paths they offered the sheep a solid place for them to walk. However, when called to come to another pasture, every now and again, one of the sheep would attempt to break away from the path to get to the new pasture ahead of the others. In the attempt to take a shortcut, many times the sheep would end up in a precarious situation and all too often they would stumble and fall. I would look at them and say, "If you would have stayed on the path, you would have been just fine!"

The Good Shepherd, Jesus, has gone before us and blazed a solid trail for us to follow. It is a path that is now well worn by both him, and the saints who have gone before us. When followed, this path offers us a place of sure footing for each step we take. However, like sheep, we tend to try and jump ahead and take shortcuts on our way to eternity, which will most certainly leave us in a precarious place where we often stumble and fall.

Praise be to God, when we do act like sheep and fall along the way, our Good Shepherd is always there to lift us up, set our feet back on the solid path.

Today, don't look for a shortcut, but rather, stay on the path he has prepared for you to follow. At the end, you will find your joy in him!

Go Enjoy The Shepherd.

May 6

Watching over the Provisions
Psalm 121:8

We are blessed to have multiple types of livestock on our farm. It truly is a joy to watch them when they all get along. However, every so often, a bully shows up in the crowd and tries to hog the blessings of corn or hay when it was given.

One particular situation took place when I decided to treat the sheep to a little corn. We happened to have the cattle, sheep, and horses all in the same field at that time. As the sheep were eating, the larger animals came in to run them off so they could have the food themselves. Of course, as the shepherd, I was not going to allow that to happen, and as long as I stood with my sheep, the others stayed back and allowed them to eat in peace.

On this day I was reminded of how the Good Shepherd stands watch over everything he has blessed us with. Without him to guard it, the Enemy would certainly come in and attempt to steal the blessings away. However, as long as the Good Shepherd is standing watch over us, nothing can touch us or the blessings he has placed in our lives.

Go Enjoy The Shepherd.

The Shepherd's Delight
Psalm 147:11, Psalm 149

It really is the simple things in life that offer us the greatest joy. One of my favorite activities is to go out into the sheep field and just sit with my sheep. That is it. Nothing more or less. I love to sit with them and watch them graze and sit in the shade. I love watching them be simply what they have been created to be, sheep. In this I find not only joy, but a true satisfaction in knowing they can enjoy me as I enjoy them.

How amazing is it to know that the Good Shepherd takes delight in his sheep. Like a shepherd sitting with his flock, he loves to watch as we enjoy the blessings he has provided for us. It brings him great joy to watch us rest under the comfort of his protective hands. He smiles as the sheep of his pasture are simply being who he has created them to be. He finds great satisfaction in his sheep enjoying him as he in turn enjoys being with them!

Today, bring a smile to him as you . . .

Go Enjoy The Shepherd.

Learning His Voice
Psalm 37:23, John 10:27

Recently we added a new ram to our flock. He came to us from another shepherd who lives up in Kentucky. Of course, when he arrived on our farm, he immediately went to be with the other sheep, but it was clear he had no idea who I was. He had never heard my voice before, so when I called he would not answer.

However, what he would do is follow the other sheep. When I would call those who know me, he would by nature follow them. Now, he was very leery of me at first and took up with our resident knucklehead sheep and kept his distance. But, over time, he slowly began to learn my voice and my call and knew to come when he heard me. This process simply takes time and patience on behalf of the shepherd.

What is so sweet about the Good Shepherd is the time he is willing to put in training the sheep who are new to his flock. He knows they will not immediately recognize his voice and his call, but he is patient as he teaches them the sound of his voice. His patience is everlasting, and his love for all his sheep is immeasurable. Because of his kindness and constant calling of his sheep, he knows that one day, the new sheep who have been added to his flock will eventually learn the sound of his voice and they too will come when he calls.

Go Enjoy The Shepherd.

Too Many Sheep
John 6:60-66

I was so excited about the fact we would have sheep on the farm. This was a new adventure in my life, and I could not wait to get started. I remember the joy of having over 100 sheep grazing the fields I had prepared for them. I watched with joy and excitement for the first few months as they covered the hillsides.

I found it very difficult for me to keep up with my sheep individually at this time. So many of them looked just like the other. Differentiating between individuals was not an easy task. There were a few in the crowd, to those I gave names. The rest, I did my best, but it was very difficult for us to really form any bond. There were just too many for me to know them individually.

This eventually led to frustration on my part. Because I could not get to know them well, they in turn did not get to know me very well. We had at best a shallow relationship. This led to many times going and hunting for sheep instead of them coming to me. While this was happening, I was spending less and less time with my own children and this caused even more problems in my home.

Eventually I had to make a decision to cut back on the number of sheep I was going to raise. My joy had turned into complete frustration, but I was determined to still raise sheep. We settled on the twenty I had named and the others we sold to farmers around us.

Amazingly, this led to a complete change in my joy as a shepherd. Once I had it down to a reasonable number of sheep, I could name each one and keep up with it. Most of my frustrations were gone as these sheep became very accustomed to me and my voice. We became like family.

Many times in life, we attempt to "shepherd" too many sheep in the family of God and it can lead to frustrations and even burnout. We lose the ability to have a deep and close connection because we are spread so thin. That is why our Good Shepherd, Jesus, calls us to see his example. He had the opportunity to create a movement by tending to large crowds, but he focused on 12 followers. Through these he created a worldwide movement of disciple-making that continues and will continue until the day he returns for his own.

Today, if you find yourself on the verge of burnout and frustration, ask the Good Shepherd to "trim down" your flock of disciples. Focus in on the few you can know deeply and pour yourself into like family, then watch him multiply your flock as you teach others to shepherd like he did!

Go Enjoy The Shepherd.

Why?
Mark 15:33-37, Isaiah 53:11

Why Lord? Why did you have to take her! She was literally Precious in my eyes. What could you possibly be thinking, God?

These are all questions I asked when our little Precious suddenly died. We had raised her, watched over her, cared for her, and she was perfectly fine when I last saw her only hours before. My mind swirled with questions and confusion. It was very clear that she suffered and struggled for her final breaths. This was the lamb who began my journey of sharing lessons from sheep with so many people. She was the one who inspired me to write what you are holding today. So why would God let her to die?

I am so thankful that I was allowed to ask those questions. They led me to a place where I could draw near to God. Precious passed away on Easter weekend, and the more I learn, there was no greater weekend to share such a story. For it was the same weekend that God turned his head away as his Precious Lamb died on a cross. He watched from his throne as his Lamb suffered and struggled for his last breath of life.

Many will question why God, the Great Shepherd, would allow his Precious Lamb to die such a horrible death, just like I asked why he would let Precious die at such a young age. Many have asked why he would watch as his final breath slipped away, then turn his head. Why, you ask?

Because He saw something he wanted so much that he was willing to give up his most Precious Lamb to have. You!!!

Today, do not be afraid to ask God why he did such a thing, but realize, the answer to your question is You!

Go Enjoy The Shepherd.

Don't Run
Hebrews 13:6

Every so often it is necessary to get all my sheep together for what I call a "wellness check." This involves getting them put up into a small pen or stall so I can look at them up close and personal, one by one. By nature the sheep do not like this experience, not even the ones who trust me the most. They prefer to be out in the open where they can flee if they begin to feel uncomfortable. So, when this time comes, if they spot any opportunity to get out, you can bet they go for it.

However, if they do not allow me to check them for potential life threatening issues, they can quickly become sick and die. So even though they do not like being in the pen, it is a necessary process for their own well-being.

So many times we, like sheep, have been brought into a pen in which we are not comfortable. Inside this pen, we feel closed in, hindered, and everything in us screams to break free. We look up at the Good Shepherd, wondering why he has brought us into a place he knows we dislike. But we should know, whatever he does is so that we can experience life as he meant for it to be.

Today, you may find yourself in the "pen," but do not try and escape. Allow him to do the work that must be done in you, as he checks you over thoroughly for any potential dangers to your life. For through this, you will see, his purpose is to give you real life, a life of truly knowing him!

Go Enjoy The Shepherd.

Quarantined
Leviticus 13:4-6

Whenever I have a sheep who has become sick, I immediately put that sheep in a pen or stall by itself. Just like with a person who is contagious, the last thing a shepherd wants is an illness spreading throughout the entire flock. In order to keep that at bay, I keep that sheep put up until it is healthy again.

When we become sick in our walk with the Good Shepherd, having allowed sin to cause us to become weak. The Good Shepherd will put us in a pen, just like a shepherd does his sheep. He knows that if sin is left unchecked and unattended, it could spread far and wide among his flock.

Today, if you find yourself in a pen, suffering the illness of a sin in your life, thank the Good Shepherd for caring enough for you, and the sheep around you, to put you in a place where he can tend to your needs.

Go Enjoy The Shepherd.

A Place to Heal
Psalm 41:1-4

As I walk into the sheep shed, I can hear the sound of sheep walking the edges of the stall. Clearly, they are not happy to be in there. They look through the cracks and see a wide open field of green grass and wonder why they have to be kept up like this. Some may consider it cruel treatment, but the truth is, I am only doing what I know is best for them. I have brought them in so they can heal.

What has always been of interest to me is that in the pen, the sheep really have even more access to what they need. I keep them furnished with some of the finest hay there is. I bring them their favorite treat on our farm, organic corn. I keep a mineral tub in their stall and clean, fresh water. This is all extra work for me, the shepherd. It adds to my list of things to do that day, but I am happy to do them knowing that the sheep will eventually heal and return to the pastures and the flock it so longs to be with.

Today, if you are in a pen, be still! Do not look for the quickest way out, but rather, call upon the Good Shepherd to heal you of your sicknesses. Cry out like David, and confess your sins, asking him to bring you healing. Then, trust him, simply because he is the Good Shepherd, and he too looks forward to the day you will be restored to the green pastures he has prepared for you!

Go Enjoy The Shepherd.

Feed My Lambs
John 21:15-17

Every year we go through the process of what we call "lambing season." This is the time when sheep are producing new lambs in the flock. After months of carrying these young inside the womb, these moms give birth to beautiful new lambs.

Common sense would tell you that if those lambs were never fed the milk that their mom supplies, they would surely die. Sadly, I have seen this happen more than once, as a lamb is refused the milk its mother has to offer. If I do not step in and make sure the lamb is fed, it will not live long here on earth.

I say all this to point out, that if we do not follow the command given by the Good Shepherd to feed his lambs, they too will surely die. So many times, people are born into the family of God, yet no one takes the time to give them the necessary milk of his Word which will cause them to grow into fully mature disciples of Christ. The Good Shepherd has given each of his sheep the ability to join him in the process of giving birth to new lambs, but that is only the beginning. Just like a real lamb, they must be fed the "first milk" and given a constant supply of the milk of his Word in order that they may live.

Today, join the Good Shepherd and obey his command, Feed His Lambs!

Go Enjoy The Shepherd.

The Conflicted Heart of the Shepherd
Isaiah 6:8

As a shepherd, each time I walk in the field, I end up with mixed emotions. I have such great joy as some of my sheep come and gather around me, longingly looking for something from my hand. I also have such sorrow as I look at the sheep who refuse to draw near to me. My heart longs that all my sheep would come and enjoy time with me, but some are either just too busy or they are simply do not trust me. I look at those around me and I hope one day that by their example these others will one day join them at my side.

The Good Shepherd deals with these same issues every day. He comes each day to spend time with his sheep. His heart is thrilled as some gather in close to see what it is he might offer them from his hand. Yet, he also feels great sorrow as he looks around at all the sheep in the fields who seem to not know he is there! They are either too busy to notice he has come, or they simply do not trust him enough to draw close to his side. His heart longs for them to know the depths of his love, but they refuse to come and sit at his feet.

Today, do not be afraid to draw close to him. Let your heart be not troubled, trust in him so that by your example, hopefully, others will see and draw close to our Good Shepherd.

Go Enjoy The Shepherd.

I Will Gather My Sheep
Ezekiel 34:11-12

It was with sheer determination that I would consistently climb those wooded hills searching for that handful of sheep who always went to the top. It was a long tiresome walk up that wooded hillside covered in cedars, fallen trees, and rocky ledges. However, I was determined those sheep would be down in a place of safety for the evening, whether they liked it or not.

These few sheep were clearly not treated well by their previous shepherds. They were not loved and cared for, but rather, treated simply like a means to gain money. Therefore, they had no desire to be with a man or around a man because of their past experience with them. But I was going to make sure they knew at least I cared enough to climb that hill, day in and day out, to be sure they were not left as easy prey for the coyotes.

The Good Shepherd, with fierce determination, says he himself will go and gather in the scattered sheep whom the other shepherds had mistreated. This passage in Ezekiel tells the story of the shepherds of his flock who raised sheep merely for financial gain. But God was determined that these sheep would know what it was like to be cared for by the Good Shepherd, that he himself went out and gathered them into his fold.

Today, give thanks that our Good Shepherd seeks out his sheep with such fierce determination because that means that he sought you with all his heart!

Go Enjoy The Shepherd.

Lost None
John 6:35-40

I have spent my time as a shepherd priding myself on my hard work to keep my sheep safe. I have done everything in my power to be certain that they all come home each evening when they are called. I have raised fences for their protection. I have placed guardians in their midst. I have taken every precaution I know of to be sure they are safe from the coyotes.

However, despite all my efforts, I have still lost sheep under my watch. How painful it is for me to go out and see that my best efforts have for that one sheep gone in vain. I tried, yet in my humanity, I have not always succeeded in keeping all my sheep safe.

That is why I love this passage about our Good Shepherd. Jesus says that of all the ones the Father has given him, he will not lose a single one. From our human point of view, this seems almost impossible. However, Jesus assures us that he has done everything to save his sheep, and as a reward, his Father is going to make sure he does not lose even a single one.

Rejoice today in the truth that there is nothing that can steal his sheep from his hands.

Go Enjoy The Shepherd.

At His Feet
John 4

There is little doubt that I want my sheep to come to me and follow me when I am leading them. My desire is that they go with me wherever I go in the fields in order for them to receive from me what they need. What I have learned regarding this process is that the simplest way to have my sheep follow me is to have one of my sheep who is willing to go wherever I lead. Because sheep tend to follow sheep, having one who trusts me beyond all doubts allows me to realize my desire of having my sheep follow me. As long as that one sheep will come to my feet, the others by nature will follow.

Look at the passage of John 4 and the story we see. Jesus spends time developing trust with one of his sheep, giving her what her heart is longing for, acceptance. Once she realizes his enormous love and acceptance of her, she runs and brings the other "sheep" of her town back to his feet. What a joy it must have been for the Good Shepherd to see all this unfold before his very eyes! Sheep leading sheep back to the Shepherd.

Today, if you want to be the most effective in leading others to know the Good Shepherd, then be willing to stay at his feet! When they see your example, their nature will cause them to want to follow.

Go Enjoy The Shepherd.

May 19

Let It Go
Leviticus 19:17-19

I have watched many fights take place in my sheep field. It is a normal process in which sheep set what we call the "butting order." This is the order of dominance among the sheep, and you can see the order of this by watching who leads the flock on the path and who is in the rear. Every so often, one of the sheep will attempt to improve its position in the flock by challenging one of the sheep who is ahead of it.

One thing I have noticed in my years as a shepherd is this: sheep do not tend to hold grudges. I have never personally noticed a fight in which the two rams or two sheep seem to leave the fight disliking each other. Once the contest is over, they typically will go to eating grass again right beside each other. In other words, once the fight is over, it is over.

The Good Shepherd has also given his sheep a command to not hold a grudge. He is well aware that we will act like sheep and take up petty fights to set a dominance amongst ourselves. A "butting" order of sorts. However, unlike sheep, we tend to hold to these frustrations long after the argument is over. We separate and divide, leaving the flock of the Good Shepherd scattered and divided.

Today, let go of any petty differences you have, come together in the bond of his love, and let us lay aside our differences, so the world will see our love for each other and give glory to our Good Shepherd!

Go Enjoy The Shepherd.

Grief Among the Flock
Colossians 1:9-10

Every year the time comes that I must sell the lambs to reduce the number of sheep on the farm. I cannot keep all my lambs or pretty soon my place would be unfit to raise anything but weeds. We watch the lambs grow and then find them new homes to go to. These young lambs are sent on their way to be a part of someone else's home.

When this times comes, it is a time of difficulty for both the mother ewe and the lambs. The moms cry out for their young ones hoping to hear the familiar cry back. When we have brought lambs onto our farm, they each cry out for their mother, longing to be back where they consider life to be normal. However, after a period of time has passed, both the moms and the lambs settle into the next phase of their life, pressing forward to the next goal.

The Good Shepherd, by his designs, does not allow us to always remain in the place of our comfort. At times, he will separate us from the ones we have learned so much from, but he has a greater purpose than we can see. Yes, we can cry out for a time in grief over our separation. However, it is important that we, like these sheep, eventually settle into the place he has put us, pressing on forward in the next phase of life.

Today, if you find yourself facing one of your lambs moving forward (high school graduation, off to college or a new career, or maybe even marriage), rejoice in knowing your Good Shepherd has them in his care, and rest yourself in the comfort of his arms.

Go Enjoy The Shepherd.

May 21

Relentless Enemy, Steadfast Shepherd
John 10:7-10

The coyotes were absolutely relentless this particular weekend. They were coming back at all hours of the night. Their first attempts starting at 9 p.m. then again at 11 p.m. As if that was not enough, they tried again at 3 a.m. and 4:30 a.m., desperate to find their way to my sheep. Thankfully, my guard dogs were very steadfast that evening and never let down their guard. They held their ground, returning the coyotes' cries with barks of warning to leave the sheep alone. It was great to hear as the shepherd that my sheep were safe despite the constant attacks of those wily predators.

The Good Shepherd has told us that he is steadfast in his watch over his flock. Our enemy is constantly crying out, attempting to reach his sheep in order to devour us and overcome us. However, our Good Shepherd never lets his guard down as he stands at the gate, protecting his flock!

Go Enjoy The Shepherd.

Praise for the Shepherd
Psalm 79:13

Raising sheep eventually turns into a generational growth in the flock. Retaining some of the lambs to become replacement ewes in the future is a typical part of a shepherd's life. What is fun to see is these lambs grow and become mothers themselves and then watch even the third and fourth generation come. When a flock is being cared for properly, they respond by being healthy and producing great lambs each season. These new lambs, following their trusting mothers, trust the shepherd from an early age and this cycle continues on and on. By doing this, these well-cared-for sheep are praising their shepherd for his great care.

Asaph tells us in this Psalm that we, the well-cared-for sheep of the Good Shepherd's pasture, can praise him from generation to generation. As we grow in our understanding and trust of his care, we will by nature pass this knowledge of his love on to those who come behind us. By doing this, we create a flock of sheep who will praise his name through trust from a very early age, who again will pass it on from generation to generation.

Today, praise his name simply for being your Good Shepherd!

Go Enjoy The Shepherd.

Trust in His Provision
Luke 12:27-34

If there is one thing my sheep do not have to worry about, it is whether or not they will have something to eat or drink. I give my full attention to make sure they are either provided for through the grass growing, or during the winter, with plenty of hay to eat. My sheep do not have to be concerned about looking for food elsewhere or on the other side of the fence. At times, some of them choose to go looking outside anyway, but it is not for lack of provision from my hands.

The Good Shepherd, in his tender kindness, has told his sheep that we do not have to worry or be concerned about our everyday needs. He points us to look at the flowers of the fields and how he cares for their every need. Then he tells us to remember, if he cares so much for things that are here today and gone tomorrow, how much more shall he care for us!

Today, hear the words of your Good Shepherd when he says, "Do not be afraid, little flock, for your Father has been pleased to give you the kingdom," meaning, he will provide for your every need.

Go Enjoy The Shepherd.

Childlike Faith
Matthew 18:2-4

In my tenure as a shepherd, Caesar has by far been my greatest example of a trusting sheep. Raised on the bottle by our hands, he began at an early age to learn to trust me for his care. He ran and played in my presence, and once returned to the farm, continued to come to me with no worries or concerns.

When he reached the age of about five months, he ended up in a fight with his dad. This fight left him near death, but thankfully he survived. However, it was clearly evident this fight had left him broken in some way. His head and neck never appeared to be the same, slightly cocked to the left at all times. He also seemed to have another issue in the sense he did not appear to grasp when he was becoming a full-grown ram. He did not act like a grown ram, but rather seemed to remain in the mindset of a lamb. His fight left him with a "childlike mind."

However, this childlike mind has served him well. He does not fight with the other rams for dominance in the flock, but rather simply enjoys being a member of the flock. He also has never become aware of any reason to distrust me as his shepherd, even when the others run. He comes to me in full confidence that I will care for him no matter the situation.

What a beautiful picture of what Jesus, our Good Shepherd, tells us in the passage above. Telling us that we should come to him with a simple childlike faith, trusting that he will supply our every need. Trusting that he will take care of us no matter the situation.

Today, come to the Good Shepherd with a simple childlike faith. It is the only way to truly approach him in full and complete confidence.

Go Enjoy The Shepherd.

May 25

Replacing the Bad Shepherds
Jeremiah 23:1-6

The news is filled today with stories of sheep who are treated cruelly by those who are in charge of them. No type of livestock animals have escaped being in the news for being mistreated at some time or the other. This is unfortunately not a new thing to our planet, but has been going on since the beginning of the fall into sin. Shepherds mistreating their flock and leaving them battered, skinny, and sick. These sheep are an unsightly thing to behold.

Thankfully, we have seen rescues made and these animals delivered from the hands of their cruel or inattentive shepherds. These same animals who appear to be near death are given to someone who will give them proper care, and in a short time seem to thrive again at the hands of a good shepherd.

Through the prophet Jeremiah, the Good Shepherd has declared he will also rescue his sick and dying flock. He cries out against those whom he put in charge of his flocks, warning them of the destruction that will fall upon them by his hands. Then, in a beautiful picture, he declares that he himself will rescue his sheep and place them under the care of undershepherds who will tend to their needs under his watchful eye.

How wonderful is his love that he would not leave his sheep to be "terrified and afraid," but will bring them into a place where they are tended to and cared for properly!

Go Enjoy The Shepherd.

May 26

Hanging from a Tree
1 Peter 2:21-25

On our farm we have a row of huge shrubs that were planted years ago by a previous owner. They were put in a fence line evidently to block the view of the fields from the original farmhouse. You can look in my fields today and see sheep doing their best to eat the leaves from this shrub as they seem to love the taste of them. However, after reaching as high as they can, they are left to only look up at the leaves they can no longer reach.

One day, while walking through the field with Caesar, I decided to grab a part of the shrub and bring it down to his height. As he ate with great joy, the rest of my flock all ran over to join in. Seeing their reaction, I reached up and grabbed more branches and hung my weight on them so they could enjoy the life-giving food that was on that tree.

This is when I again heard that still, small voice while in the field. It said, "Ray, as you hang on the tree so that your sheep may enjoy their life, I too hung on a tree, placing the weight of their sin upon my shoulders, so that my sheep could enjoy the abundance of true and eternal life!"

Today, take a moment and remember that the Good Shepherd allowed himself to hang on a tree so that you could enjoy life eternal as a sheep in his pasture!

Go Enjoy The Shepherd.

When You Are Exhausted
Matthew 11:26-30, John 16:33, Hebrews 4:15, Psalm 4:8

There is nothing like scorching heat to literally suck the life right out of sheep. When temperatures reach the three-digit range, sheep seek shelter from the heat. They will scratch and paw at the ground to uncover bare dirt to lie in under a thicket of bushes. They desire shade and relief from the exhaustion of the heat, only coming out to get a drink of water or to eat a little grass. They quickly again escape the heat by running to the shade and recover from the exhaustion of being in the scorching sun.

Life for us is much like that, whether we are talking literally, mentally, emotionally, or spiritually. We, the sheep of God, often face the extreme heat this life has to offer. Some of the heat is literal, simply being in the rays of a hot sun. The other heat, maybe the most draining of them all, is the heat from the difficult circumstances of life. Faced with fiery trials and temptations, we can reach the point of collapsing from the intensity of it all.

But the Good Shepherd, Jesus, faced every one of these same trials and temptations that we face today. He knows our burdens, our sorrows, and our physical exhaustion because he lived as a man. He endured the same things we face in every area of life. When we are worn out, and ready to faint from the heat, he simply calls us over to rest in the shade he provides. He offers a cool place to lie down, and he simply says to his sheep, "Rest!"

Today, go and rest in the shadow of his wing!

Go Enjoy The Shepherd.

Too Comfortable in the Dirt
2 Corinthians 6:1-13, Romans 10:11-15

There are always dangers for sheep, even when they are resting in the shade from the heat of the day. If sheep find a favorite shady spot, they rest there every day until it becomes nothing but dirt all around them. However, trouble lurks on every side as flies, ticks, and parasites also like these shady areas and can cause great trouble if a sheep stays there too long.

That is a danger we face as well, as the sheep of God. Living in this world of trials, troubles, and tribulations can be very unappealing. If we are ever invited into the shade of rest, we can become too comfortable there and not want to leave. However, this would be to our own detriment as the comfort of our shade can lead us to not feasting properly on the pasture he has provided. It can also lead to living in the "dirt" of laziness, failing to enjoy the provisions he has given us.

So the Good Shepherd, in his love, sometimes moves us out of the shade and into the "fire of tribulation" we know as life. He never sends us away, only sends us out. This is so we may receive what we need, but also, so we can lead other sheep back to his feet. The Good Shepherd always has a purpose for everything, even when he moves his sheep out of the place of rest they have become too comfortable in.

Go Enjoy The Shepherd.

Adversity
Isaiah 30:18-22

Some of my most trying times with sheep had little to do with the sheep at all. Being a shepherd who also holds down a full-time job and raises a family, sometimes the stresses of life are what bring on my most difficult moments with the sheep. It never fails that when I am having a rough day, something would happen to the sheep. Coyote attack, fences down, lambs lost, sheep separated from the flock, just normal things in the life of sheep, but was added pressure on me as the shepherd. These were simply times of adversity I had to face.

Thankfully, I have been blessed with a wife and children who are always supportive of me. When things are the hardest, they have stepped up the most. They encourage me and help take some of the burdens off my plate. If the need is immediate, they will drop everything to come and help me.

Praise the Lord, he is always with his sheep. His eyes are on us when we go through difficult times. The fact is, it is not "if" we will face trouble, but when! We have been promised trials and struggles in this world, but we can know that even in those storms, he is worthy of our praise! He is the Good Shepherd who does not have to divide his attention with a job or family. His focus and attention is always on his flock, especially in times of adversity!

Go Enjoy The Shepherd.

May 30

Simply Come
Isaiah 55:1, Matthew 11:28, Matthew 19:21

When a shepherd has provided everything a sheep needs, the sheep has only one task remaining, To Come. The shepherd has provided the grass, so the sheep only need come and eat. The shepherd has provided the water, the sheep only need come and drink. The shepherd has provided the protection and shade, and the sheep only need come and rest. The shepherd leads the way to the new fields, water, and place of rest, the sheep need only to follow. That is all they must do, come and enjoy what the shepherd has provided.

The Good Shepherd calls out to all his sheep and says, "I have provided all the food, water, protection, and paths you need to follow. I will not promise this will always be easy, but it is simple, all you must do is Come! Come eat of the meal I have prepared for you. Come drink from the Living Water I have provided. Come Rest in the comfort of my shade. Come follow Me and I will do the rest!"

Go Enjoy The Shepherd.

Lanolin Oil
Psalm 107:29

Sheep have a very unique oil in their wool. It is known as lanolin oil and is used widely around the world for commercial purposes. However, sheep have a very unique use for it themselves.

Lanolin oil is a waterproofing oil in their wool which helps them shed the rainwater when it storms. This oil also helps insulate them when having to cross a stream of water to reach their desired destination. It keeps their skin from becoming too wet under their coat of wool or hair which keeps their skin from rotting. This is why sheep can stand during a storm.

When the Good Shepherd calls his sheep into his fold, he gives them a natural covering of an oil from his hands. This oil, given through his sacrifice, covers his sheep, allowing them to stand in the storms of life. This covering allows them to shed the cares and concerns that come with each storm. This oil he has given keeps the worries of this life from being able to set in and destroy us by rotting away our trust in him. What a wonderful Shepherd we serve!

Go Enjoy The Shepherd.

June 1

The Good Shepherd
Psalm 23

In my time as a shepherd, I have learned there are several different kinds of shepherds. There are good shepherds, indifferent shepherds, and cruel shepherds. Word spreads quickly as to which kind of shepherd you are in the small world of sheep and shepherds.

An indifferent shepherd simply has sheep to have sheep. He does not give them much of his time, just enough to make sure they are bringing him in some profit. He is driven simply by what the sheep can do for him.

The cruel shepherd is careless with his sheep and treats them poorly. He does not care if they have proper water and food or a place to rest. He does not care for the sick, but rather disposes of them quickly if they will not provide him a good profit. He is heartless and the condition of his sheep reflect his attitude.

Then, there is the good shepherd. The shepherd whose heart is that his sheep have the best that is available. He watches over them carefully to tend to any and every need. If he sees an illness, he takes his time to treat each sheep individually. He provides all the food and water his sheep need and watches over them with a keen and protective eye. He provides guardians to defend against the predators and even puts himself out there in the midst of the battles. His work is evidenced by the healthy condition of his sheep!

Today, dwell on these words alone, "The Lord is my shepherd!" The God of the universe, the King of kings, the Lord of lords, is who claims to be your shepherd and he calls himself Good! Rest in the fact you belong to the Great Shepherd's flock, and in that you can find peace!

Go Enjoy The Shepherd.

June 2

The Good Shepherd #2
Psalm 23

Sheep are some of the most needy livestock animals in the world. Sheep cannot provide for themselves in any form or fashion. They require constant attention. The food source must be just right or they could suffer malnutrition. The water source must be still and clean or they will not drink from it. If it is not clean, they could pick up bacteria or parasites that can cause sickness and death. Sheep are extremely needy, and without a good shepherd watching over every detail of their life, they simply will not survive. This is why sheep are not considered a prized livestock to raise because they require so much care.

That is why Jesus is called the Good Shepherd. He knows that his sheep are extremely needy in all areas of life. He knows without his care we will not have the Bread of Life or the Living Water which we need to truly live. He knows without his keen and watchful eye, we will pick up small parasites of sin which can kill us from within. He knew all this BEFORE he took the position, and he accepted it willingly because he loved what most of the world considered unlovable.

Today, give praise that we have a Good Shepherd who took on a task many others despised. He did it with joy, considering you worth the price he had to pay!

Go Enjoy The Shepherd.

I Need Nothing More
Psalm 23:1

My goal with my sheep is to make sure they have everything they need. Grassy fields to enjoy or a supply of hay to satisfy their hunger. We have a pond fed by a spring, but in dry seasons the pond becomes mossy and therefore I need to supply fresh water. During the winter, both supplies freeze over and require my daily attention. I also watch my fences to make sure there are no easy entrance paths for the coyotes or escape routes for the sheep. I provide guard dogs to protect my animals from the outside predator threats. I also keep a keen eye out for signs of worms in my sheep that can quickly kill them from within. As a shepherd, I take very seriously my role to provide for the needs of each individual sheep I own.

By definition, that is what a "good shepherd" does—he provides everything his sheep needs. Therefore, if sheep have a good shepherd, they can literally just live a life under him without any worries or concerns because they know they will have everything they need.

David knew, as a good shepherd, that his sheep were lacking nothing as long as they were in his care. He also knew, that if the Lord was his shepherd, he would lack for nothing he needed at the point of need. That is why he could say, "The Lord is my shepherd, I need nothing more!"

Today, we share the same Good Shepherd as David did. This same Lord is watching over our every need. If he is true to his Word, which he always is, we can take comfort in the fact that we will never lack for what we need if he is our Shepherd!

Go Enjoy The Shepherd.

Green Pastures
Psalm 23:2

In Biblical days, when most of the Scripture we have today was written, sheep were a very important part of the way of life. In fact, in that region of the world, sheep are still a major part of the landscape today.

When I want to lead my sheep to the next field here in Tennessee, I simply open a gate and walk them through. Typically, the journey they make from one lot to the next is not very long or hard. However, when we read of sheep in Scripture, when those shepherds took their sheep to a new pasture, they had to go on a very long, grueling, difficult journey. They led the sheep through rocky hillsides that had very little food or water. The paths they traveled were difficult and hard. After such a long journey, the sight of a green pasture was a welcome site for both food and rest.

The Good Shepherd knows what is best for you as his sheep. He also knows there are seasons in your life where you will have to travel some very difficult and hard times. Many times, you will feel as if you are on the verge of collapsing from the length of the journey and the extreme circumstances you have faced along the way. Sometimes it will be hard to continue to follow the Good Shepherd on these paths because your soul will become weary from the journey.

However, take heart in the fact that he has already planned out the next "green pasture" for you to find rest in. This place is not only so you can have food and supply of your physical needs, it is also a place where he offers you a place to lie down, or even collapse, in the comfort of the meadow. It is a time to rest, to be restored, to be rejuvenated, and to be prepared for the journey that lies ahead of you.

Go Enjoy The Shepherd.

Beside Still Water
Psalm 23:2, Psalm 63:1-5

When we transported sheep from Texas to Tennessee, one of the major concerns with the sheep was water. The trip was made at night to avoid being in the heat of the day, but even at that, the sheep had to be allowed to have something to drink along the way. The trucks would stop and find a way to provide water to the sheep. Otherwise, they would not have survived.

In Biblical days, a good shepherd would go ahead of the sheep and chart out the course to the next pasture. He would make sure there were plenty of places for the sheep to stop and refresh with water. Knowing that sheep are extremely picky about their drinking spots, he would know exactly where the best places were to lead them for a drink. Sheep refuse to drink from a body of water that is moving too swiftly. If the shepherd found water, he also had to make sure there was a place the water was relatively still so the sheep would actually drink. If there was no pool of still water, the shepherd would dig out an area along the bank, creating a place for the water to come in and be still so his sheep could quench their thirst. Once the path was prepared, then he would lead his sheep along the charted course where all their needs could be met along the way.

The Good Shepherd has already gone ahead of his flock, and he knows the journey that you must face. He knows your needs and how dry and parched you will become on this journey through life. So he has gone ahead and prepared the Living Water that you will need, making sure it is a body of still water from which you can quench your thirst. In his amazing love, he will lead you right up to those waters and he will smile as he watches you satisfy your thirst from his pool of Living Water!

Go Enjoy The Shepherd.

June 6

Restore My Soul
Psalm 23:3

Once I had my farm set up for sheep, and things were ready to go, we brought in our first big load of sheep from Texas. It was middle of summer, so the rancher who was going to deliver the sheep made the decision to drive them through the night. He loaded them up and drove straight for 12 hours.

When they arrived, we immediately unloaded into a place where we had provided plenty of fresh hay and water. These same sheep, who seemed to have little life left in them, suddenly had renewed energy once they were given the food and water they needed. This was followed immediately by them finding a place to lie down and rest. Once they had rested for a bit, we moved them into a field of tall green grass which they devoured with great joy. In a matter of just a few days, these sheep who looked tired, skinny, and frail from the long trip from Texas, looked healthy, fat, and content. They were the picture of a sheep who had been restored.

Your journey in life will take you on some very long, difficult, and tiresome roads. On this journey, there is no doubt you will at times be ready to give up and die. You will lose your strength and sometimes even despair of life itself. From your point of view, the journey may seem like it will never end. However, the Good Shepherd knows what he has prepared for you. He has a place ready where your soul can fill up on life-giving food and Living Water. It is a place where you can lie down and rest and enjoy the comfort of his provision. The Good Shepherd knows exactly how much you can take, and when you can go no further, he provides a place for your soul (mind, will, emotions, and strength) to be restored.

Go Enjoy The Shepherd.

June 7

He Leads Me
Psalm 23:3

It is a very interesting fact about livestock, sheep in specific. They can be either led or driven. If driven, sheep show signs of great anxiety and fear. This is evident if you watch sheep moved by a herding dog or herding shepherds. They are uncomfortable being driven along.

I watched this on my own farm using my border collie with the sheep. The sheep would instantly respond to the dog's maneuvering, but it was out of fear and anxiety. This fear was all for good reason, for if they got out of line or tried to fight the dog, he would nip their noses or heels to press them along. Their only comfort was in getting to where the dog was pushing them to go, for that was the only way to find relief from the pushing.

On the other side of this coin are the times I would call my sheep to follow me to the next pasture land. They would come and there was no anxiety or fear in simply following me. We moved at a pace that was proper for the sheep and easily made our way to where we were going. Once there, the sheep were under no duress and could quickly move into the enjoyment of what they had been led to.

How comforting is it to know that your Good Shepherd leads you! He is not behind you, shoving you, poking you, or nipping at your heels. He is in front, blazing the trail that he has mapped out for you. He guides you tenderly along your journey, not rushing you along, but gently guiding you to the next destination. As long as your eyes remain on him, you will certainly be led in the correct path!

Go Enjoy The Shepherd.

June 8

Paths of Righteousness
Psalm 23:3

When moving sheep there is always more than one option. We can take either the quick and easy path, or, we can take the sure, solid, and safe path. Now, temptation often leads me to want to move them in as quick a manner as possible, but this often leads to frustration and something negative happening to my sheep. In order to avoid this frustration and potential harm, I do my best to follow the most certain and sure path that will get them where we are going safely.

When David spoke of these "paths of righteousness," he was referring to the proper path to get his sheep to their next destination. David knew there were shortcuts and quicker ways to get his sheep from point A to point B. However, these paths would be unsafe, filled with potential dangers. Wild animals stalked these "easy paths" and they were filled with potholes that could bring great harm to any sheep who fell in, or areas of sinking sand that would swallow them up. So, David knew what it meant to lead his sheep in a path that was sure, solid, and safe.

Today, the Good Shepherd has also gone before us and checked the roads ahead. He knows there are shortcuts that appear to be easier and that could get us to our destination faster, but these roads are filled with dangers beyond our imagination. All paths, even the righteous ones, have trouble enough, but these shortcuts are roamed by the enemy. They are filled with gaping potholes waiting to cause you to stumble and fall. Areas of miry clay and sinking sand long to cling to your feet and trap you in a pit of despair. That is why the Good Shepherd has gone before you, charting out a course that may not be the easiest, but he knows your footing will be sure and solid, and on this path, you will be safe!

Go Enjoy The Shepherd.

For His Name's Sake
Psalm 23:3

A shepherd's reputation means everything. I know the first thing I learned about shepherds in my area was what type of shepherd they were, based on their reputation. Therefore, I wanted to raise my sheep in such a manner that when my name was spoken in the circle of shepherds, they would speak highly of both my efforts and the quality of my sheep.

Look at this small verse David lays before us. It says the Good Shepherd led his sheep in paths of righteousness "FOR HIS NAME'S SAKE"! Scripture is filled with stories of how God did things to uphold his high reputation. When he was ready to destroy Israel in the desert, Moses dissuaded him by reminding God of his reputation. "What will the Egyptians say, God?" (Exodus 32:11-14).

God is also interested in the quality of his sheep. That is why he is spending so much time perfecting them, making them into a beautiful flock that all will see and brag about. He is at work, removing each imperfection his sheep have, again, for His Name's Sake! (Isaiah 43:25). A shepherd is judged by the quality of his sheep, and that is why the Good Shepherd has spent so much time in grooming, loving, and perfecting his own.

Today, rejoice in the knowledge that God is at work in you and it is not your reputation on the line, but rather, his reputation as the Good Shepherd. Rejoice, because he has never failed to keep his Word, and He has promised to uphold his glory at all cost! (Isaiah 48:11)

Go Enjoy The Shepherd

June 10

Yeah Though I Walk
Psalm 23:4

There is one certainty you can always count on with sheep. If they are frightened, they are going to run! Simple as that. I have watched my sheep literally run in a panic away from my guard dog that they were well accustomed to, simply because the dog came upon them too quickly. The slightest hint of fear or uncertainty will put sheep into a full-out run.

Here, David is talking about walking sheep. These are sheep who are certain and comfortable in their surroundings. They have nothing to fear or be afraid of, therefore, they can simply walk. Why? Because they are with their shepherd!

How sweet of the Good Shepherd to give you this picture for your day! Circumstances may scream at you, friends may hurt you, but through it all you can walk! Why? Because the Good Shepherd is with you, no matter where you are!

Go Enjoy The Shepherd.

June 11

Through
Psalm 23:4

When I move my sheep from one pasture to another, I walk them through a gate. On the family farm, one of the fields required a walk through a narrow area about 300 feet long. As I moved the sheep, we never tarried long in this narrow area as it was usually grown over and the low hanging limbs of trees covered us in shadows. My goal was to move the sheep steadily through this area to reach the next field.

David was well aware of the fact his sheep did not like the valley, therefore, as a shepherd he would keep them on a slow, but steady pace THROUGH the valley so they did not have to tarry there very long. His heart was to move them out of a place of anxiousness and into a place they could be free to enjoy themselves. He never left them in the valley of shadows for long.

You may think you have lived in the valley of shadows your entire life. If you believe this, then you are correct. For life on earth is spent in the valley of the shadow of death. However, your Good Shepherd is guiding you through this valley toward his everlasting place of peace and comfort. As you walk through the valley with the Good Shepherd, remember he is leading you through and this life is but only for a moment. Your troubles will soon be behind you and you will be free to enjoy him forever.

Go Enjoy The Shepherd.

The Valley
Psalm 23:4

Hang around sheep long enough and you start picking up on some of their tendencies. Here in Tennessee, where I first brought sheep, we had a hillside farm. I would watch my sheep and they constantly preferred the high ground over the valley below. They do not like darkness and shadows; they prefer living in the light of the sun. They want their shade, but they also prefer a high spot from which they have a good vantage point.

That is what makes this mention of a valley by David so interesting. He knew the nature of sheep was to avoid places like this, yet he talks about them being led through a valley. He prefaced this by saying they "walked" through the valley, meaning they went against their nature, yet without fear. This again begs the question, how could they walk through this dark place with no panic or fear? Because they were with their shepherd.

The Good Shepherd already knows that you do not like the dark and difficult places in life, yet he knows the best way to get you through to the Promised Land. He has already scouted out this trail himself, and he knows this valley is where you need to travel through to reach the proper destination. Though shadows and darkness surround you, you can walk through these times with confidence that you will be all right because he is with you!

Go Enjoy The Shepherd.

The Shadow of Death
Psalm 23:4

Watching my sheep on the hillside, I noticed how much they enjoyed the light of the sun. I was also struck by how little I would see any predators come out in the middle of the day into an open field. Coyotes and cougars would only creep through the cover of darkness and the shadows cast by the hilltop above. Their preferred time to attack was dusk and dawn when they could still see, yet hide and attack through the shadows of the night. These are the times as a shepherd I and my guard dogs were most alert for the danger.

David points out that not only has the Good Shepherd led him through a valley of darkness, but one filled with the shadows of death. He was fully aware of the enemy on every side as he walked his own flock through the dark valleys around Bethlehem, yet he led them with confidence, knowing he was watching over his sheep. He kept his eyes peeled on the shadows for the movement of any predator and he was prepared to defend his flock at all cost to himself.

Your life will take you through dark valleys and all around you the shadow of death will seek to encompass you. The snarls of the enemy will lurk from the darkness as they stalk and attempt to attack you from all sides. They howl and cackle in an attempt to cause you to run, but you must simply see the Good Shepherd to know you are safe. He is ever watchful with his all-seeing eye as he takes you through this valley of the shadow of death, and he is ready to leap to your defense should the enemy attack!

Go Enjoy The Shepherd.

June 14

I Will Fear No Evil
Psalm 23:4

I am completely amazed at how skittish and jumpy sheep are. Even under the care of a watchful shepherd they still at times are riddled with anxiety and fear. The slightest movement can set them in a panic and cause them to run. It could be something as small as a house cat or a rabbit running through the field, and they are off and running as if their life is in danger. Sheep by nature are afraid.

That is what makes this saying by David really stand out. He must have known the nature of his sheep and how easily they could be spooked. I am assuming there were times he had to go and gather the flock back in close after a small rabbit had spooked them into a run. His calming and reassuring voice reminding them that they were okay even though some small creature had put them into flight. I can see David giggling at his silly sheep, thinking, *If they only knew how safe they are with me!*

Today, you are faced with many small circumstances that are trying to unsettle you. They run in and out of your life in an attempt to unnerve you and turn your gaze away from the Good Shepherd's watchful eye. At times, you and I will fall for these attempts and will turn and run. However, we can rest assured that our Good Shepherd will gather us back in and calmly remind us that we are safe with him!

Go Enjoy The Shepherd.

For You Are with Me
Psalm 23:4

The sheep did not know what to think. The sounds of war had broken out all around us with "bombs bursting in the air." It was one of those nights that we as people celebrate by firing off fireworks for fun and games. However, the sheep were not quite as enthused as we were with the process. I was sitting on the porch watching the lights in the sky off in the distance, but the sounds of multiple fireworks going off that night was quite an earful. I could tell the sheep were disturbed, so I gathered them close to the house and simply spoke to them through the process. As long as I was close to them, calmly speaking to them, they rested. If I took a small break and went inside, they became nervous and unsettled again. Therefore, I decided to sit with them until the "war" was over.

David has built a beautiful portrait for us in this fourth verse of Psalm 23. He has painted a perfect picture of our life that is full of worries, concerns, and fears. He has related well the troubles we will face and the fact our life is a journey through both times of comfort and "shadows of death." However, he also has pointed out that through good times and trials we can rest in this simple fact, the Good Shepherd is with us!

Today, lift your hands in praise, no matter if you are in the fields of green pastures and still water, or if you are being led through the darkest valley, because your Good Shepherd is always with you!

Go Enjoy The Shepherd who is always with you!

Comfort of the Rod

Psalm 23:4

Shaped in the form of a baseball bat, the rod of biblical days was a perfectly crafted tool with a dual purpose. Its shepherd would spend hours perfecting his use of his rod, ensuring his ability to use it in both defense and protection of his flock. He would practice over and over throwing his rod with great speed, distance, and precise accuracy. Hoping he may never have to use it, he was prepared nonetheless.

As one of his sheep would begin to wander off, maybe approaching a poisonous weed patch or thick brush in which may be hiding a predator waiting to lunge out, the shepherd would throw his rod, striking his own sheep, forcing it to reverse course and return to the safety of the flock. Feeling the sting from the blow, the sheep would grimace and groan, maybe for a moment despising the shepherd. However, the shepherd would smile as he retrieved his rod, for only he would know the full reality of the danger that had been avoided.

Feeling the sting of a rod of correction is never something you long to feel, yet it is a necessary tool in the hands of the Good Shepherd. As you graze his pastures, like a sheep you will be tempted to press your boundaries and be drawn towards areas of danger, but you can take comfort in his perfectly perfected speed, distance, and accuracy with his rod. He sees the dangers you are headed toward, and with perfect timing, he will use his rod to return you to the safety of the body of Christ. You may turn and look at him with a grimace on your face, questioning what he has done, but he smiles knowing the great danger he has kept you from!

Go Enjoy The Shepherd.

Comfort of the Rod #2
Psalm 23:4

The sheep were in great distress. I watched in disbelief as this unwelcomed dog ran around my sheep field. I jumped out of my truck and ran into the field. Rocks in hand, I began to chase the dog away, pelting him with the stones I had brought with me. Unfortunately he returned each day, digging his way into my fields. I finally had to grab a modern day version of the rod of protection, my rifle, and I defended my sheep and slew their enemy.

When David wrote this psalm, he had most certainly used the rod of protection to defend his own sheep. He recounted to King Saul the stories of killing both a lion and bear with his hands, more than likely assisted by the rod in his hand. Surely a sheep who had been struck with the rod was not overly fond of it, until it saw that same rod used to defend it from the jaws of certain death.

The Enemy crouches at the edge of the field in which you live today. He watches and waits, looking for an opportunity to attack. He is patient in his craft of hunting, knowing he must only attack at the most opportune time. He lurches forward staring you down, jaws open, prepared to make you his next feast. He sprints forward, bearing down on you, death in his eyes. Until…his focus is broken by a bone-shattering blow to his head.

The Good Shepherd, the one who has perfected his skill with the rod with countless hours of practice, has run to your defense and has driven the enemy away. Day after day, this same enemy returns, staring you down, dreaming of devouring you in his starving jaws. As he tries again to swallow you up in death, The Good Shepherd casts his final blow, taking his rod and slaying the Enemy once and for all!

Go Enjoy The Shepherd.

June 18

Comfort of the Staff
Psalm 23:4

The year I purchased sheep, my wife and children decided to get me a very special gift, a shepherd's staff. In our area there was not many places you could find such an item; however, they hunted until they could bring it home. That staff is still with me today.

Sheep do not like to be caught in the hook of a shepherd's staff. It causes them to leap forward in an attempt to get away. However, for those sheep who are shy and timid, not trusting the shepherd, it is a necessary tool to draw them in close to his side when he needs to examine them intimately. I used mine on a number of occasions to get close to a sheep who appeared in need of medical attention out in the open field. Each time, the sheep would struggle, but the sturdy and strong staff held firm in order to draw them in to me. Although they did not like the feel of the staff, the purpose of it is to ensure their health and safety.

The Good Shepherd knows the hearts and tendencies of all his sheep. He knows those who are shy and timid, who struggle to trust his loving touch. So gently and tenderly, he uses his staff to pull you in close to his side so he can spend intimate time with you, checking you for any area that might need his attention. You will struggle against his staff, but it is strong and sturdy, drawing you in close to his side. As he gently searches you over for any areas needing his attention, you will suddenly find comfort in the care of his staff.

Go Enjoy The Shepherd.

Comfort of the Staff #2
Psalm 23:4

When sheep are going from one place to the other, they at times tend to get off course. If walking with them, the shepherd can take his long staff and gently reach up and put pressure in the side of the sheep to correct them back into the right path. I remember walking with my sheep, and a ewe attempted to steer off course. I was actually able to simply put my staff out in her direction and she quickly returned to the path leading to the place I was taking them.

As you walk through your life, there will be times you will drift away from the path in which he is leading you. He has carefully marked out your course, but something draws you away and you turn ever so slightly in the wrong direction. That is when the Good Shepherd gently touches you on the side with his staff; with slight pressure he prods you in the way of real and abundant life. When you begin to understand his tender proddings, you will eventually learn to return to the path with a simple sight of his staff pointing you in the way you should go.

Go Enjoy The Shepherd.

June 20

Comfort of the Staff #3
Psalm 23:4

One of the greatest mistakes sheep can make is straying off and getting themselves caught in a trap. Sheep, desperate to have the green grass they see at the bottom of a ledge, will find their way down to it. When they decide to return to the comforts of the flock, they realize their desire to taste the goodness of what their eyes desired has left them trapped. They will struggle to find their own way, but they soon realize they are without hope.

So, the shepherd takes his long and sturdy staff and will reach down to where the sheep is. He will hook them with its crook, pulling them up to safety. The staff in essence becomes an extension of the shepherd himself, carefully lifting up his sheep to solid ground.

How sweet of the Good Shepherd to always have his staff in his hand. He watches carefully over his flock, and when you become trapped because of your attempt to satisfy your own longings, he gently reaches down, his staff an extension of himself, and lifts you up to solid ground next to his side.

Go Enjoy The Shepherd.

A Prepared Table
Psalm 23:5

As I rode the tractor, running the disc over the field, I thought about the outcome of all my work. The sheep had been a little hard on the fields that year because of the lack of rain. The grass was low and it was evident the fields needed attention. I bought hundreds of pounds of mixed grass seed that I knew the sheep would enjoy and I started the process of sowing my fields.

Now the work was not easy or short. After breaking up the dry ground, I went over the land, casting the seeds out by hand. Since I had bought several different types of seeds, I decided to cast each one separately, thus going over the fields several times with the five-gallon bucket, casting the seeds. After doing this, I took a drag and ran over the ground several times, working the seeds in deep into the earth. About a month later, I began to see the fruit of my labor, and after two months, my sheep were able to enjoy a beautiful feast of winter wheat, rye, and fescue!

The Good Shepherd is preparing a place for you (John 14:1-3). He has diligently been at work, preparing the soil, casting out the seed, driving it deep into the ground, all in preparation for your arrival. The work is not easy, but he already sees the fruit which his toil will bear. With a smile, he gazes over the place he has prepared, and his joy is full when you enter the gate and partake of the feast he has prepared especially for you!

Go Enjoy The Shepherd.

June 22

In the Midst of the Enemy
Psalm 23:5

Here in the hills of Tennessee, you can guarantee that there are always hungry eyes on the sheep. Coyotes prowl the shadows and woods. Cougars and bears roam the hills. Packs of stray dogs look for a place to play and wreak havoc, and grey-headed vultures watch for arrival of newborns in order to take their life before it begins.

When David wrote this psalm, as a shepherd he dealt with the constant threat of lions, bears, jackals, and stray dogs. He knew a shepherd must be constantly on the lookout for attacks on his flock. With a limited supply of good grazing grounds, many times sheep would be forced to share their fields with their arch enemies. However, as long as the shepherd was on watch, the sheep could eat in peace knowing any threat would be handled with force by the shepherd.

As you feast upon the blessings that the Good Shepherd has provided for you, the enemy is watching every move you make. You live each day in a world which suffers under the strain of sin and suffering. Forced by the fall of man to share the blessings provided daily with the very ones who hate you and long to devour you can at times become a strain on your nerves. However, you can feast in peace knowing you are always under his watchful eye.

Go Enjoy The Shepherd.

June 23

In the Midst of the Enemy #2
Psalm 23:5

Because the grassy areas are spread out far and wide in the area where David wrote this psalm, shepherds would have to take their sheep on long journeys just to find a small patch of green, grazable grass. Scattered throughout the land, these small patches were considered extremely valuable to keeping the sheep alive. However, these areas of grass also tend to attract poisonous vipers as well. Looking for rest from the heat of the sun, vipers would burrow holes in these grassy areas and go hide just below the surface. Ever watchful, these vipers would lurch up at the first sign of dinner and strike with their poisonous grip.

This meant sheep with the soft tissue of their noses would appear to be a fine catch to these vipers. Many sheep suffered a bite from these snakes which left them with great sores and pain, or at times would lead to death. So, going before his sheep, the shepherd would enter this place of feasting first, searching diligently for the vipers' holes. Once spotted, he would pour olive oil down the hole, making it a slippery surface which the viper could not come up. Once every hole was found and filled with oil, the sheep could then feast in peace, not only in the presence of the enemies they could see, but also the ones who were buried right underneath their noses.

You may be able to look around and see the enemy lurking around while you walk in the fields he has provided for you. You can be on your guard, watching for their attack, trusting he will defend you. However, today you can also rest easy in the knowledge that he not only holds them at bay, but the Good Shepherd has also gone ahead of you into the place he is preparing and has eliminated the threat of the enemies you cannot see—the ones who lurk right beneath your nose!

Go Enjoy The Shepherd.

June 24

Anointed
Psalm 23:6

Flies, flies, and more flies. These pesky critters are extremely annoying, especially to sheep. They love to find any type of sore the sheep may have and then they dig in and make the matter worse. There is a disease among sheep actually called "fly strike." These parasitic flies will lay eggs on matted wool or open sores and the maggots will bury under the skin of the sheep and feast on the flesh until they reach the fly stage. Once a sheep is infected, the flies will continue the cycle until stopped by treatment. The cycle is endless and eventually can lead to death from the ammonia poisoning caused by this disease.

In order to avoid this, the shepherd would pour oil (olive, grapeseed, etc.) over the heads and down the backs of their sheep. If a sheep were to be infected by the buried maggots, the shepherd would shear the infected and surrounding areas and pour the oil over the wound. This would serve as a suffocating agent to the maggots, as well as a deterrent to any additional flies from attacking the sheep. The sheep would then be set aside for special care by the shepherd until it was fully healed.

Some of the greatest enemies you will face are the small and annoying things in life. After time, you may become resistant to the larger foes you have faced, but these pesky little details in life can be a constant annoyance, getting under your skin. Irritated by the nonstop movement of these little things, a deep and horrible sore can begin to evolve, threatening to take your life. So, the Good Shepherd anoints you with his healing oil, the Balm of Gilead, to both drive away the Enemy, but also to bring healing and restoration to the broken areas of your life. While going through this process, he sets you aside so that he may watch you closely until you have been healed.

Go Enjoy The Shepherd.

June 25

Continual Anointing
Psalm 23:5

Flies and parasites are not things that will go away with one treatment. I had some sheep who developed open sores and if they were not attended to daily, the flies would return to pester my sheep. If the wound was bad enough, I might even have to attend to it several times a day in order to keep the irritants away.

David knew that a shepherd had to anoint his sheep on a daily basis. He was aware this was not a one-time thing that would take care of the problem. It required daily attention and detail if the shepherd was going to keep his flock from being driven insane by the pesky little flies attempting to disturb his sheep.

You are under the care of the Good Shepherd who knows we face daily battles and struggles. He is well aware that the Enemy will be a continual irritant if he does not anoint you daily with the oil of his Spirit. Therefore, he comes to you daily with the oil of his love and care in his hand to drive away the pesky irritants trying to drive you to the brink of insanity.

Go Enjoy The Shepherd.

June 26

Anointing to Avoid Insanity
Psalm 23:5

Ever been pestered by a single fly? You know, the one who will not just go away, but decided to continue to land on your head, or face, or arm or leg. You swat at it, hoping it will just go away before you "lose it!"

Now imagine what it must be like for animals that are covered with hundreds of these critters. Sheep have no arms with which to shoo them away, so they constantly shake themselves and twitch a muscle here or there, hoping those little critters will just leave them alone.

In particular, nasal flies love to try and work themselves into the nose of sheep and lay their eggs in the nasal passageway. The maggots will then bury under the skin inside the nose and you and I can only imagine how irritating that would be. The sheep that is infected can be seen banging its head against a tree or the ground, desperately trying to rid himself of these pesky critters. Watching this behavior, the onlooker might assume that the sheep has lost its mind, as this banging, if done hard enough, can lead to insanity and death. With oil poured over the head and around the nose, these flies simply slide out and can no longer disturb the sheep.

Your life is surrounded by "flies" of the Enemy who is attempting to drive you insane. He comes to bury himself in a sensitive area hoping to cause you such irritation that you run around desperately attempting to rid yourself of the problem. However, in the hands of the Good Shepherd he holds the oil that will cause all these irritants to simply slide away in his truth.

Today, come to the Good Shepherd and let him pour over you the oil that will cause your "flies" to simply slide away from you!

Go Enjoy The Shepherd.

June 27

Must Come for the Anointing
Psalm 23:5

When my sheep are irritated by flies and mosquitoes, there is only one way to treat the situation. I must cover them with something that keeps the critters away. As we have seen, this is a daily thing and if not done, the sheep can suffer great irritation and in extreme cases, insanity or death.

However, there is something the sheep must allow me to do in order to defend them against these pesky little irritants, they must allow me to come close. I must be able to touch them and examine them, but if they are too shy or timid, the sheep will keep their distance. When I apply the protection and healing agent, it feels awkward to the sheep and if they do not trust me, they will attempt to run before I can finish the process. However, if they want to enjoy a day free from these insects, they must stand still while I apply the "oil."

If you are covered in a life of irritations and concerns that are causing you to be unable to focus on the joy the Good Shepherd has for you, then you must COME and allow him to anoint you with the healing oil of his Spirit and Word. You must place your head in his hands and trust him as he pours over you what may at first feel awkward or unnatural. However, if you desire to live a day enjoying the freedom of what he has provided you, you must come and submit to the anointing of his oil.

Go Enjoy The Shepherd.

Overflowing Cup
Psalm 23:5

When I have done all my work, when I have attended to all the needs of my sheep, something really cool happens. My sheep are able to focus on one thing, being sheep. They can eat freely of the green pastures and they can enjoy the waters given them. They go about their life in peace knowing all enemies, both big and small, have been taken care of. They can follow my lead, even through the dark shadows, because they have learned to trust in me. When this happens, the sheep respond by being healthy, happy, and simply enjoying life. They produce healthy lambs and raise them up to trust in the shepherd and become great sheep. As I watch them enjoy their life, it also brings me great joy.

Today, you can rejoice because you can simply be who he has made you to be, because he is the Good Shepherd, and he has taken all the steps necessary to ensure you have all you need. He has provided you the Bread of Life and a spring of Living Water. He has defeated the Enemy so you can walk through this valley of shadows without fear. He has provided the oil necessary to drive away the small enemies in your life. In turn, all you must do is simply enjoy the life he has given you and just BE! As you grasp today the realization that all your needs have been met, and that your cup is literally "overflowing," you can go out and share this great news, producing new "lambs" along your way. New lambs that he will allow you to train to trust in the Good Shepherd's care. As you do this, he is able to watch over you and smile with great joy as he enjoys you enjoying him!

Go Enjoy The Shepherd.

Follow After Me
Psalm 23:6

Let me be frank, I have not once seen a sheep who likes to be chased or followed. Sheep do not like to be driven, they prefer to to be led. Their instincts are to be afraid if there is something behind them. So what is David talking about when he says "goodness and mercy (love) follow after me?" He knew full well that his sheep did not like to be followed or "chased". So why would he use this picture at the end of this psalm?

There are many interpretations that one can gather from this passage, but I remember clearly the day it all sank in for me. I watched as my border collie moved with ease behind my sheep and I walked ahead. I realized in that moment that it was my love leading the sheep to something for their good, and Ben was an extension of my love, ensuring the sheep reached the blessings I had prepared. It was his pressure from the rear that kept them focused on me.

Today, as you follow the Good Shepherd, remember it is his love and mercy both leading you and following you. The things that press you, or chase you from behind are an extension of his love for you, pressing you on to the blessing of being close to him and enjoying him forever. Like sheep, you do not necessarily have to like those things behind you, pushing you forward, but whatever those things are, they are nothing less than his Goodness, Mercy, and his Love pressing you into the blessings he has prepared.

Go Enjoy The Shepherd.

June 30

Goodness and Mercy
Psalm 23:6

When on a long journey from one place to another, sheep have a tendency to become distracted. A simple clump of green grass can divert their eyes from the shepherd and before they know it, they have become separated from the flock.

Tired and weary from the long walk, some simply want to lie down and take a rest before they have reached their final destination. Unaware of the predators watching to pounce on those who fall behind, these tired sheep seek out a place to rest their weary legs.

Then the shepherd can be heard calling out commands to his herders in the rear to keep the sheep together and moving forward. The shepherd is fully aware of the tempting bite of grass, but he has a whole field prepared that his sheep can enjoy just ahead. He is also watchful, keeping his eyes on the predators who lurk in the high grass along the way. Fully aware of his sheep becoming weary, he calls back to his helpers to keep pushing because he intends to make it to the place he has prepared without losing even one of his sheep.

The Good Shepherd has such a beautiful role for those difficult things in your life that seem to press you and push you. He knows you are tired and weary, hungry and thirsty, but he also knows the dangers of allowing you to fall behind. He has seen the enemy who is waiting to snatch you away. So he calls out to those things he has placed behind you, each of them firmly under his command, pressing you forward to the place he has prepared for you. Why? Because he has determined to make it there without losing even one of his sheep!

Go Enjoy The Shepherd.

All the Days of My Life
Psalm 23:6

Years after reducing our flock to a small handful, I no longer needed a herding dog. However, I still needed my "goodness and mercy" when I was working with my sheep, so I replaced the dog with my wife and kids.

We were doing our best to get some new sheep to come into the shed we had set up so we could run our systematic check for worms and other issues they might have. However, I had not yet set up a great way to funnel them in, so we had to make a human funnel. Like I said, looking back, it was quite the comedic scene as over and over we attempted to gather in those final few sheep!

I share that story simply for this reason: whether it is a herding dog, or my family, it is necessary to have something to press the sheep forward every time we go to get them in or move them. Whether I am moving hundreds of sheep, or just a handful, I have realized to succeed I must have help from behind the flock. Why? Because in every flock there are a few who are not trusting enough to come in on their own. Every time I bring the sheep in, I always send out the extensions of myself to assist me in accomplishing the goal.

The Good Shepherd knows the tendencies to become complacent or lackadaisical that exist in the heart of his sheep. That is why EVERY DAY, he deploys the extensions of his goodness and his love to follow behind you in order to press you closer to him. He knows your heart is prone to wander and stray, so he lovingly commands his helpers to press you forward in your walk. Why? Because he is determined to keep his promise and lose none of his sheep!

Go Enjoy The Shepherd.

I Will Dwell
Psalm 23:6

Sheep find great comfort and assurance in being able to stay in a place for an extended period. They thrive if they are allowed to rest in contentment and peace. A sheep prefers to "dwell" somewhere instead of constantly being forced into a new place.

However, because of lack of grass, good water source, parasites, and predator danger, David had to constantly move his sheep from one place to the next. It was hard for David to find a place that provided his sheep everything they needed for an extended period of time. However, if he ever did run across such a place, both he and the sheep would treasure the ability to dwell in that abundant place for an extended stay.

The Good Shepherd knows your heart and the desire you have to dwell in one place forever. It is displayed in us through our dislike of moving around from town to town or house to house. We find comfort in having a place to dwell and call home.

However, in this fallen world, he knows that if we stay in one place too long, the dangers of lack of spiritual food, water, and protection will overcome us. Therefore, the Good Shepherd has gone ahead and prepared a place that one day you will call home because he longs to see you thrive in a place to call your forever home. But today, as he moves you through this sometimes chaotic life, remember he is preparing for you a place you will forever "dwell."

Go Enjoy The Shepherd.

In the House of the Lord
Psalm 23:6

David sums up this amazing picture of our life as the sheep under the care of the Good Shepherd by telling us where the journey ends. As a shepherd, David roamed the hillsides with his sheep. In order to keep them fed, he stayed with them, guarded them, and kept them safe. However, one of his favorite trips to make was the day he was able to return the sheep back to the family farm, and David and his sheep could enjoy the comforts of their home.

He had spent the nights out in the fields sleeping with the sheep. I can imagine him dreaming of the comfort of his own bed. He was constantly on the lookout for predators, daily fighting the lions and bears, as well as the worms and the flies. It was a long and tiresome job, one that took every ounce of energy and strength he could muster! It had literally been a battle day in and day out for their survival.

It was not only David who longed to be home, his sheep also looked forward to the day they no longer had to be daily moved and pressed just to find enough food and water to survive. In the open plains they were under the constant threat of attack; at home they would have safety and comfort. David knew in order to survive, they could not stay on the family farm all the time, and they would once again make the journey to find what the sheep needed. However, he would dream of a place where the sheep could live in abundance and safety and the shepherd could simply enjoy watching his sheep without the threat of attack any more. That would be a place both he and his sheep could call home!

This is a glorious picture of the final destination of each and every one of the Good Shepherd's sheep. He knows that you long for a place free from pain and suffering. He knows you long for a place where you will never again know need for food or water or the basics of life.

He knows you long for these things because he longs for you to have them. He knows you are tired from your journey and you desire to find a place in which you can dwell forever. He sees your heart that longs to be free from the constant attacks of Satan and his minions. He knows you desire all this because these are the same things his heart longs for you to enjoy.

That is why he came, why he has fought daily against the Enemy on your behalf, given you what you have needed to sustain through the journey, and has gone ahead of you to prepare a dwelling place you can enjoy forever. He is both with you as you walk through life and he is ahead of you longing for the day you will simply dwell with him in the comfort of his home for all eternity!

What a Good Shepherd we follow!

Go Enjoy The Shepherd.

July 4

Free To Be Dependent
Psalm 62:7-8

If you ever run across an "independent sheep," one who thinks it can survive on its own, you are looking at a sheep that will soon be dead. Yes, sheep who think they can live independently of the shepherd will soon meet their end.

Sheep are animals who are not self sufficient. They rely on the shepherd's care and attention for everything. Without the shepherd, the sheep would be without food, water, protection, and care when it is sick. Without the shepherd, the sheep would stay only in one place which would lead to its demise.

That is why David says his salvation and honor "depend" on God. David knew that without the Good Shepherd, his life would be in peril. He realized his safety came in being a dependent sheep.

On a day when the United States of America celebrates its Independence, you are free to celebrate your absolute dependence on the Good Shepherd. As long as you are dependent on him, you will find yourself independent from worry about what you will eat, drink, wear, or where you will live. In your dependence on him, you will find all these things are met through his bountiful supply. (Matthew 6:31-34)

Today, lift up your voice and celebrate your freedom to Depend on the Good Shepherd!

Go Enjoy The Shepherd.

July 5

Too Much Noise
1 Kings 19:11-13

There are some great benefits to having your farm close to town. You can run and grab things you need conveniently, and no one at our house is complaining about being close to their favorite place to eat out. However, there are a few times a year that this is not a convenient place to be for the sheep.

For the most part, the sheep live in peace and quiet. We are far enough away that the sounds of the town do not affect us too much. But on nights when the world is celebrating and the sky lights up, the tranquility of the field turns into a scene of nerves and frazzled dogs and sheep.

On nights like this, I have a choice as the shepherd. I can run out in the field and try and scream and yell above the noise so that the sheep can hear me, or I can walk out and simply be with my sheep and speak in a low and calm voice. If I did yell, trying to overcome the sounds around me, I would undoubtedly add to the stress of my sheep and guard dogs. However, when I speak calmly, they react to the stillness in my voice, and they too can remain calm in the middle of the noise.

The Good Shepherd knows the war you are in today. He knows the sounds of the battle can be terrifying and stressful. That is why, like a shepherd, he comes to you, not screaming above it all, but rather, whispering softly to you saying, "I AM here, everything is going to be okay!"

Go Enjoy The Shepherd.

Stand Firm
Exodus 14:13-14, 2 Chronicles 20:17

The greatest tactic a predator has on a flock of sheep is to get them running. If he can get the sheep spooked, they tend to separate and become easier to pick off. Each time I have found one of my sheep mangled and torn by a predator, it was when they had run and become separated from the other sheep.

Amazingly, the guard dogs I have seem to know this as well as I do. When the predators attack, I have watched my dogs time and again, circle the sheep and hold them in a tight formation, placing themselves between the frightened sheep and the enemy. As long as the sheep stood there with the dogs, they would be safe.

Oh, I love how the Good Shepherd has revealed his stories throughout the ages of how he handles the enemy. Moses told the people to "stand firm" and watch God fight for them. Hundreds of years later, Jahaziel, a prophet, delivered the same message to the people in Jerusalem. "Stand firm and watch the Lord fight for you!"

Today, you may be surrounded by the Enemy. He is pressing hard on you from every side. Like sheep, your heart tells you to panic and run, but that will only lead you right into the clutches of his teeth. Instead, today, the Good Shepherd has gathered you under his arm of protection. He has placed himself in a position to fight on your behalf, you need only to stand firm and watch the salvation of the Lord.

Go Enjoy The Shepherd.

July 7

Standing in the Storm
Ephesians 6:13, Matthew 8:23-27

If you drive by a sheep farm on the open plains during a storm, you will see an interesting sight. You will see sheep standing in the storm.

I remember the first time I looked out my window at my sheep in the middle of a great storm. I had provided a shed for them, but these sheep had all been born and raised on the plains of Texas, so they did what came natural to them. They went to a tree line and stood. Yep, they stood throughout the entire storm.

The reason they stand is because they know the water will shed off them because of the natural lanolin oil they produce. If they were to lie down, they would actually be more susceptible to becoming too moist on their skin. So they trust that their bodies will function as designed and shed the water.

You will certainly face storms in your life. It is a part of living in a fallen world. However, where once you would be overwhelmed by the storm, you now are able to stand in the strength of the Good Shepherd. He has redeemed you into his flock, and now you are covered in the oil of his righteousness which allows the "rains" from the storms life throws at you to simply roll off your back. Because you are his sheep, you no longer have to be afraid of the storm. All you need to do is simply stand!

Even more beautiful is knowing the Good Shepherd is in control of the storm (see passage in Matthew).

Go Enjoy The Shepherd.

July 8

The Shepherd's Patience
Psalm 86:15

I am not going to lie. Susie Q Knucklehead has a way of getting "under my skin." She is consistently causing me frustrations when she runs away from me because she always takes other sheep with her. If you remember, sheep follow sheep. If I were to be honest, there has been a time or two I have considered getting rid of her. However, each time I take a deep breath and press on to the next day ahead.

I am so grateful that God is patient and long suffering. Honestly, I am sure there are days I press hard against even his unending patience with me. However, I know, based on his Word, that as a Good Shepherd he will not stop his work in me until it is complete.

Today, you may feel as if you have pushed God beyond his breaking point. The thing about your Good Shepherd is, he knew what he was getting into before he started, yet he did it anyway because he loves you.

Go Enjoy The Shepherd.

July 9

Light in the Darkness
Matthew 5:14-16, John 1:4-5

I sat on my porch after the darkness had covered the landscape. Rain started to pelt the tin roof and I relaxed in my favorite spot outside. Winds started to blow and suddenly lightning lit up the sky. In-between the strikes of lightning, a complete darkness covered the earth. As I took this in, I began to notice that each time lightning struck, I could see my sheep like little bright balls of white in the field. They stood out in contrast to the darkness around them.

Jesus told his followers that they were like a city on the hill whose lights pierced through the darkness. He declared that we should let our light shine just as he had shone his. As I sat there that night, I was drawn into this Scripture as my sheep stood out so brilliantly against the blackness surrounding them in the middle of that great storm.

Today, as the Good Shepherd watches over you, let your light shine out for all those around you to see. Tell them about the amazing care you have received from his loving hands. As they watch, they will see your light stand out against the darkness of life's storms, and they will want to know if they too can be watched over by your Good Shepherd. Then lead them to his feet.

Go Enjoy The Shepherd.

July 10

Whatever It Takes
Jeremiah 29:10-14

As I drove up to the farm one day, I watched one of my rams looking up at some leaves on a small tree. They were much too high for him, but he seemed interested in having them for his own. So, he put his hooves on the bottom of the small tree and slowly pushed it over until he had gained the prize of eating those leaves. I sat there and chuckled at how he was willing to do whatever it took to get what he wanted.

Later that day I was pondering on the message in this passage of Jeremiah. God told his people—his flock, that he was going to bring them back to their homeland. He told them he had a plan for them and a future they would enjoy. However, he also said they had to be like that ram and be willing to do whatever it took to get to that place of hope in the future. He told them they had to Call on his name, Come and Pray to him. They had to Seek him with ALL their heart. He said if and when they did those things, that they would find him and that he would bring them back home.

Today, you may long to be back close to his side. You may be longing for a deeper and closer walk with him. Maybe you have strayed away and long to be back home. Like that ram, you are standing at the bottom of the tree, looking up at what you would love to have, but you must want it enough to do whatever it takes. You must call, come, pray, and seek earnestly with all your heart for the Good Shepherd. When you do, he has promised to be found by you and that he will bring you home.

Go Enjoy The Shepherd.

July 11

Reluctant to Come
John 5:39-40

As I walked through the fields with some friends who had come to see the sheep in the middle of the day, I called for them to come to me. I had brought some corn in my hand in order to give them a treat and allow my friend to see the sheep up close. However, the sheep stood up in their shady spot and only looked at me. They did not really want to leave their rest from the heat of the day.

Only one came that day, Caesar. He was the only one willing to leave behind the comforts of where he was and come to my side. When he got there, he not only received the corn I had brought, but he also was the recipient of lots of rubbing and petting (which he really likes). All the others stayed where they were and completely missed the blessing I had intended for them to have.

Are you like me and find yourself so comfortable that you really do not want to leave your place of peace and rest and go when the Good Shepherd calls? Is the warmth of the bed just too much to leave behind when he calls out your name? Is life going too good to run to his side when he calls your name?

Today, don't miss out on the immeasurable joy of simply spending time with the Good Shepherd. Each day he comes with a blessing for you in his hand, you only need to come and receive it from him. He longs to hold you and encourage you with his tender touch. Therefore…

Go Enjoy The Shepherd.

July 12

His Love Never Changes
Psalm 136

When some new dogs arrived, our long-time guardian, Vasella suddenly had a change in her countenance. She seemed dejected and worried. Her eyes reflected concern over whether or not she was being replaced, or if I was no longer going to love her as I had done before. Because these dogs were new to the farm, they required my attention and she would sit and watch me spend time with them. As soon as I entered her field, she was aggressive in her desire for attention, more so than ever before. It was as if she wondered if I still loved her.

The truth was, having the "new" dogs on the farm caused my appreciation for her to grow even more. Because these others were new, they really did not know what it took to please me. They would spend time trying to get to my house instead of staying in the field. We even lost a chicken to their playing too rough with them. On the other hand, Vasella knew her job and did it very well. Despite all her worrying, my love for her never changed.

Isn't this also true in our walk with the Good Shepherd. Are there not times we look up and see "new lambs" coming into the fold. We see all the rejoicing and attention they receive, and if we are honest, there are times we wonder, *Will He still love me like he always has*? The new lambs are more energetic and it appears they are receiving a lot of attention. So doubt creeps into our minds.

But the Good Shepherd simply smiles as he embraces every one of his sheep, young and old alike. He reassures you by telling you over and over, "My love for you will never change, it will always remain the same!"

Go Enjoy The Shepherd.

July 13

Always There
Matthew 28:20, Isaiah 41:10

Sometimes at night, or early before the sun comes up, I like to take a walk in the fields. On most of the occasions that I do this, I try and not draw attention to myself or disturb the sheep. I like to simply find a spot in the field and watch over them in peace and quiet. It is a refreshing time for my soul as I watch them enjoy themselves in the field. So, I just sit and I watch.

The Good Shepherd at times may appear to have left you alone where you are. In the "dark of the night" you may lift your head and not see him standing close by. You feel alone, and fear and anxiety start to creep in. Panic desires to overwhelm you, yet something inside reminds you of the truth. You look around and you may not see him, you may not feel him, but you can be certain he is watching over you!

Go Enjoy The Shepherd.

July 14

Not That Important
2 Timothy 2:23-24, John 17:21

One day while I was walking in the field with my sheep, I noticed two ewes having a head butting contest. The younger ewe had decided to challenge the older one, so she would walk back to prepare to butt heads with the older one. As I watched, I noticed a third ewe come and join in the fight. This is a very common scene on a sheep farm as the sheep set their "butting order," or as some may call it a "pecking order." Basically, they are trying to assert who will be the most dominant in the flock.

On this same day, as I walked by without saying a word, they looked up and seemed almost embarrassed to have been caught fighting. One might say they looked "sheepish" (pardon the pun). Upon noticing my presence in the field they instantly stopped fighting and went back to grazing right beside each other. Evidently, whatever they had been fighting over was not really all that important.

Often we are like those sheep, fighting among ourselves. We get into quarrels and fights in an attempt to claim a spot of higher respect. We long to be the first in line, hoping to be the first to whatever blessing we see in front of us. We fight among ourselves, and like the third sheep, when we see others quarreling we tend to take sides and join in the fight. That is, until the Good Shepherd walks by and we realize that what we are fighting about is not really all that important in the light of who he is and what he has done for us.

Today, if you are in a fight with another member of the flock, look up at the Good Shepherd and remember, whatever it is you are fighting about or over, it is not worth ruining his reputation as the Good Shepherd in the eyes of those who are watching you fight.

Go Enjoy The Shepherd.

July 15

They Are Everywhere
1 Kings 19:18, John 10:16

I was speaking to a sister in Christ one day and she mentioned how she sees sheep everywhere. She travels quite a bit, and everywhere she went, she started noticing the sheep.

That is such a true statement if you are looking for them. Basically, in every populated place on earth, you can find sheep in some form or fashion. They are literally everywhere!

The Good Shepherd wants his flock to know, that no matter where you go, you are never alone. He has his sheep literally everywhere on this planet. There are times you may feel as if you are all alone, as Elijah did, but the truth is you are constantly surrounded by members of his flock. His flock is massive and it covers every corner of this world.

Today, ask him to lift up your eyes to the hills and show you how big your family really is! Remember, you are never alone!

Go Enjoy The Shepherd.

July 16

Out of the Safety Zone
Leviticus 25:17-19

When I became a shepherd, countless hours were put in getting things ready for the sheep. I put up new fences and mended the old ones. I worked on buildings and stalls, bringing them up-to-date. I checked perimeters and learned all I could about sheep. What I was attempting to do was set up a safe zone for my sheep to live in.

Unfortunately, some of my sheep would find ways to leave the safety zone and go out on their own. I would come in and count the heads of sheep only to realize, 10, 20, sometimes 40, were not with the flock. So I would put on my boots, grab my staff, and start walking. It was only a matter of time before I would find the sheep and have to work to get them back inside the safe area, away from the predator's territory.

Just like sheep, we tend to go astray. The Good Shepherd has worked relentlessly to provide his sheep a safe place to live. He has set boundaries (rules) for our protection and inside those boundaries is guaranteed safety. But we are like sheep, and we stray outside the safety zone where we can easily fall into the hands of the Enemy. Thankfully, our Good Shepherd "puts on his boots" and he goes seeking those who have left his area of protection to bring us back.

Today, you may be living outside his area of protection. You may realize you are in the Enemy's sights as he prepares to pounce on you and drag you further away. Cry out today and ask the Good Shepherd to carry you back into the place he has provided for your safety.

Go Enjoy The Shepherd.

July 17

Among the Wolves
Matthew 10:16-25

I like to wrestle with Scripture, and this passage about being sent out as sheep among the wolves has always bothered me. Why would a shepherd send any of his sheep out among wolves?

Remember those sheep who tend to want to go outside the boundaries and find greener pastures? These sheep are often the ones who have yet to develop trust in the shepherd and his care. Therefore, once they are outside of his fences, they do not want to come back in. If they do not trust him, then they will not come to his call nor will they remain still enough to allow him to get close to them out on the "open plains."

However, a shepherd knows that sheep have a natural inclination to follow other sheep. So a wise shepherd may take some of his closest followers and lead them out into the "land of the predator" and let them mix in with the sheep who have gone astray. Then, he can call his trusting sheep to follow, and he knows by nature, the others will follow them wherever he is going.

What a beautiful picture of how the Good Shepherd knows how to bring all his sheep into the fold. He knows at times that it is important to allow the ones who are closest to him to enter the "den of wolves" in order to rescue those who are still not willing to trust his voice.

Today, as you look around at the lost around you, living in the land of the Enemy, offer yourself as the sheep who will be willing to go with the Good Shepherd into the enemy's camp and help him lead those lost sheep back home!

Go Enjoy The Shepherd.

July 18

Why the Closest Sheep
Acts 20:22-24

So yesterday we looked at the sheep who are sent out among the wolves. A very logical question comes up: Why send out the sheep the shepherd loves the most, the ones closest to him? Could he not use other sheep who usually come when he calls?

The answer is no! If I took some of my sheep out who are just okay with following me, but not ones who come every time I call, then I run the risk of not only losing the sheep who are already out, but also these others I have taken with me. They may do their job, but they could also possibly follow the wild sheep instead of coming when I call. If that happened, then I run the risk of losing all my flock and only having the one who is closest to me left.

Some have asked why God sent his own Son to save the lost of the world and not one of his angels. If you remember, it was a portion of his angels who went astray when Lucifer fell (Revelation 12:4). No, God had to send the one he knew would do everything he asked and never fail to obey his voice. That is why he sent Jesus!

Today, give thanks to your Good Shepherd for not sparing his closest sheep, but rather, he sent him out among the wolves to rescue you!

Go Enjoy The Shepherd.

So Others Can Enjoy
Roman 8:32

When the shepherd takes his closest sheep with him to gather in the ones who are lost and gone astray, he is taking a risk. He knows from the very beginning that something could happen to this sheep he loves so much.

If I were to go searching for my lost and stubborn sheep who had gone astray, and I took Caesar with me, I would be running a big risk. As we are outside the area I have set up to keep the coyotes and cougars out, we may very well come under attack and Caesar might possibly lose his life while attempting to rescue the ones who are wild and knuckleheaded.

As an outsider, one might say I was crazy for taking such a risk. Why not just let those sheep suffer their fate? If they are constantly going astray, why put Caesar's life at risk for ones who seem to not appreciate the shepherd's care? The answer is simple: Because all my sheep are valuable to me!

That is why the Good Shepherd did not spare his own Precious Lamb when he came searching for you. He knows your heart is turned against him and continually goes astray, but he considered you of such high value, that he risked his closest Son in order to rescue you!

Go Enjoy The Shepherd.

He Willingly Laid Down
John 10:17-18

A sheep who loves and knows his shepherd does not have to be coerced to go where the shepherd goes. If a sheep really trusts the shepherd, that sheep will willingly follow the shepherd anywhere, even into a dangerous situation.

Jesus, the ultimate Lamb of God, said he willingly walked out among the wolves with his Great Shepherd. When he was asked by his Father to go and lay down his life, he did so freely, by his own choice, because he loved his Father and wanted to bring home the lost and scattered sheep. He wanted to make the way back to God clear for them to see.

We too, as the sheep of God, are called to willingly lay down our lives, knowing in full confidence that no "wolf" can touch unless the Good Shepherd determines that our sacrifice will be used for the salvation of many more sheep. We can boldly tell others of the Good Shepherd and know that nothing can touch us unless the Shepherd says so. Then when that time comes, we can know in full confidence that our sacrifice here is merely a door leading to real life, life eternal for not only us, but also the ones he sent us out to lead back home.

Today, are you willing to "be the one" who will lay down your life so that others may know the joy of being with the Good Shepherd? I encourage you, do not count this life so valuable that you miss the high calling of being the sheep he will send out among the wolves to bring home those who are lost!

Go Enjoy The Shepherd.

July 21

Supreme Confidence
John 2:19, Titus 1:2

When I call for my sheep to come and follow me, there is one who will go with me no matter where I am leading. Caesar has come to a place in his life that he is supremely confident in his trust for the shepherd. He will go anywhere with me because he has learned to trust me in every situation.

Jesus was willing to follow his Father anywhere he was leading because he had supreme confidence that the Great Shepherd could be trusted. He could willingly lay down his life because he was confident his father would raise him up again.

The Good Shepherd you follow is, above all, worthy of your supreme confidence and trust. He cannot lie and he has never led any of his sheep astray. He has promised to walk you through the valley, guiding you through this difficult life, and into the place he has prepared for you. He promised the journey would be dangerous and difficult (John 16:33), but he has sworn to you that he will always be with you. You can follow him anywhere with supreme confidence because he is with you!

Go Enjoy The Shepherd.

July 22

Restored After the Trouble
Hosea 6:1

When I have taken a morning and worked through my sheep in the pen, the sheep tend to be a little stirred up after that. They do not like being closed up and handled like that. It is completely against their nature. Therefore, after I am finished and have turned them all loose, they tend to keep their distance for a bit. It is as if they look at me and remember that I was the one who had caught them, handled them, and caused them stress.

However, on the following day, when I call for them to come and receive the corn I have brought them, it is as if yesterday was but a distant memory. They forget the fact that I pulled down every eyelid to check for signs of worms. They forget that I laid them over to check for overgrown hooves. On this morning, they come to me knowing I am only there to bless them.

There are times in your life when the Good Shepherd has reached deep inside to help remove a "worm" from your soul. In his love, he cannot allow you to continue to live with the Enemy eating at you from within. This process is often painful, as he takes away yet another idol that is lodged deep inside. You may feel anxious toward him once it is over, as the pain is real and the area feels raw. Yet, he comes again fresh in the morning and invites you to eat from his hands once again. Although you feel anxious, you can come to him knowing the one who has "torn you" is the same one who will "heal you"!

Go Enjoy The Shepherd

July 23

Excited to See Him
Zephaniah 3:17

There are a few occasions where I will walk out into my fields and Caesar will see me before I say a word and he will come running to me. Typically I have to call my sheep to come to me, but every so often, this ram will simply come running at the mere sight of his shepherd in the field. On those days, I just smile because he has brought joy to my heart, coming even though I did not call.

The Good Shepherd loves his sheep. He enjoys watching them graze in the pastures he has provided and drink from the still waters. It gives him joy knowing he has placed them in a place under his protection. However, there is something that brings him even greater joy. It is when one of his own simply sees him and runs to be with him just because he is there.

Today, look up for he is near. Run to him and bring joy to his heart as you spend time at his feet! Your reward will be more than can be measured!

Go Enjoy The Shepherd.

Passing the Mantle
2 Kings 2:9-14

As a shepherd in the States, running a small flock, I have had to go through several ram changes over the years. One of the main purposes is to keep a fresh bloodline on the farm, but also, because as a ram ages, it is necessary to find a younger ram to continue producing lambs.

Each time this happens, it is inevitable that the younger ram and older ram will have "the fight." It is the struggle to determine who will be the leader of the flock. Typically the older, wiser ram, wins the first fight, but eventually, age gives way to youth. When this happens, the older ram always separates himself from the flock, sequestering himself away from the ewes. This is a time in which the older ram is acknowledging the passing of the mantle to the younger ram.

The Good Shepherd is very clear that we are never to give up, but he also was wise in knowing there always comes a time for the older and wiser to train the younger, then pass on the leadership to those who have been brought in by him to be the leaders for the future. It is nothing less than the passing of the mantle. Elijah passed his on to Elisha. David passed his kingdom on to Solomon. Jesus, the greatest of these examples, passed the mantle on to the disciples to carry the Good News into all nations. That mantle is still being passed on through our generations to the next to lead others back to the Good Shepherd.

Who are you training? Who are you discipling? To whom will your mantle pass?

Go Enjoy The Shepherd.

Wisdom and Guidance
Titus 2:1-10

When I notice the older ram has lost the battle and the leadership of the flock has been passed, I watch him to make sure he is still okay. Although he has sequestered himself away from the flock, he usually is still close enough to the flock to keep an eye on them. He no longer is considered the leader or head ram, but he still has much to offer.

One time during this "transfer of power," the mantle was passed to a young ram who had yet come to a place of trusting me. He preferred to keep his distance from me, not fully understanding my role in the flock. One day, when I came too close, he literally ran to the old ram and stood beside him. It was evident he was there because he felt comfortable around this other ram. It was like he had gone to him to receive guidance on whether or not this shepherd could be trusted. Although he had "replaced" the older ram as head of the flock, he still found comfort in being by his side when his own comfort zone had been breached.

The Good Shepherd smiles every time he sees the older sheep in his flock be there to impart wisdom and guidance to those younger leaders who are coming up. Although the time has come that the good news of Jesus Christ is to be carried on by the younger sheep in the flock, those who have gone before are to be there to give direction and comfort to these younger leaders. The elders have come to know the Good Shepherd and and have seen him work through troubling times, and it is their stories of the Good Shepherd's provision and Guidance that give courage to those who will soon lead the way!

Who are you training? Who are you discipling? Who are you telling your story to?

Go Enjoy The Shepherd.

July 26

Best for You
Proverbs 16:9

If you have not already figured it out, one of a shepherd's greatest joys are those times he can simply be with his sheep. His every move is in an attempt to do his best for his sheep. Sometimes, if there is something between the sheep and what is best for them, then the shepherd removes it.

Those poisonous weeds I pulled up, I burned them up. That over-abundance of grass, I cut it down. Coyotes and predators, I set up defenses to run them off. Whatever is trying to separate me from my sheep, whether it is good or bad, I remove it. Why? Because I enjoy being with my sheep. Sometimes, that process is painful, not only for the sheep, but also for the shepherd.

It may sound harsh that a shepherd would remove a blessing in order to draw his sheep closer, but without the shepherd, sheep would surely perish. From the outside it may appear selfish on the part of the shepherd; however, I know if the sheep stray too far away, or begin to ignore the shepherd's call, that could lead them to an untimely death. So everything I do, regardless of the appearance on the surface, I do because it is what is best for my sheep.

You may be in the middle of a great loss of what you considered a huge blessing. You may be struggling to understand why the Good Shepherd would ever do or allow such a thing. However, if you understand the heart of a shepherd, then you can know without a doubt, everything that is happening in your life is for your best because he knows what you need the most—to be close to him.

Go Enjoy The Shepherd.

Go Forward
Philippians 3:13-14

When my dad was just a boy, he had the privilege to raise a bottle lamb on my grandfather's farm. I heard the story over and over of how he loved this little lamb and cherished him as a pet. He spoke of the bond and affection they had for one another and what joy he had in feeding the lamb out in the barn. But his story had a sad ending.

He tells of the day he went out to the barn and he noticed an unusual quietness. There was not the typical jumping and excitement he heard when he approached. He called his lamb's name, but there was only silence. The room he had raised his lamb in had a wooden floor. In the floor there was a small wedge crack between two planks. His little lamb had gotten his hoof stuck in the wedge and had pulled backwards, only making his predicament worse. The lamb had thrashed around until it finally died. My dad said he looked down and said, "You silly lamb, all you had to do was go forward and you would have been free!"

This life is filled with "small cracks" in which we can find ourselves stuck and trapped. We love the feeling of life being steady, but in that trap we can become stuck. Before us is a great opportunity to experience the life he has provided, but we wrestle and struggle, holding on to what we know, afraid of the uncertainty ahead. If we are not careful, we can struggle so long, pulling backwards against the trap, until we find ourselves at the point of death. The Good Shepherd comes in, looks down on us and says, "Silly one, in order to live, you must go forward."

Today, let go of what is behind you, trust in his plan, and love forward into the abundant life of being with the Good Shepherd.

Go Enjoy The Shepherd.

The Shepherd Comes Close
Psalm 34:18

When sheep are sick or have become older, sometimes they separate themselves from the flock. When this happened with Mauro, our ram, he also stopped coming in when I called for the sheep. He maintained his place alone, refusing to leave his solitary spot. Therefore, I made a daily trip to where he was to see him. I could tell he was tired and had grown weak, so I took some corn and food to him. Not a day went by that I did not come sit by his side.

As I lived this out, I heard his small whisper again in my ear. "Ray, even when you fail to come see me when you are tired and weary, I never give up on you! I never stop coming to you to feed you, to strengthen you, to draw you back close to me."

When you fail to come when he calls, his love is so great that it pushes him to draw near to his wounded and hurting sheep to make sure you know he is always near. His heart never fails to pour itself out to go the extra mile to spend time alone with those who are hurt, tired, and burdened down. He calmly reminds you of his mercy and appreciation and reminds you that you are loved by him!

Go Enjoy The Shepherd.

The Only One
Luke 17:11-19

I walked among my sheep, as they were grazing early in the morning. I had chosen not to bring any corn that day; this was just a time to be with them. As they grazed by the pond, Caesar was standing right next to me, literally eating at my feet.

When it came time for me to go, I patted Caesar on the head and slipped off without a word. I did not want the sheep to leave their grazing area, so I simply walked off quietly. I got nearly halfway to the gate and I heard a thumping of hooves on the ground. I turned to see Caesar chasing after me. He was all alone, the other sheep were still down by the pond enjoying the morning dew on the green grass. But here was Caesar, following me all alone.

This is unusual for sheep, as by nature they have a tendency to want to stay with other sheep. It is called a "flocking mentality." But on this day, Caesar fought his nature and chose to be with the shepherd. He followed me all the way to the gate, and I rewarded him with a nice long rub on his back. All this time, not any of my other sheep followed me, only him. This was a huge display of trust and dying to himself simply to be with me.

The Good Shepherd has called you to follow him, even if you are the only one. It is so uncomfortable to stand out from the crowd, being different. Your natural instincts tell you to stay with the norm, not rock the boat, to simply blend in and be accepted. But he has called you to be set apart, to follow him even when no one else will. When you obey, there is the great reward of being with him!

Today, he is looking for those who are willing to follow him, even if they are the only one. I encourage you today, Be The One!

Go Enjoy The Shepherd.

July 30

Leading By Example
1 Peter 5:1-4

On the next day, I stood in the middle of the flock and Caesar again came to my side. I again had nothing to offer in the way of feed and I did not call my sheep to follow me. I simply stood there and spoke to them. As I spoke, more of the sheep started gathering around me. Having just had a storm, I went to go walk my fields and check for any damage. As I moved, Caesar again followed, but this time, so did all the other sheep. I literally walked a winding path in my search for downed trees or washed out places, and every step I took, all of the sheep followed. It was a line of me, then Caesar, then the rest of the flock. They literally all followed me back to the gate to my home even though I had no feed to offer and never once gave the call for feed.

This brought such joy to my heart that I went and got some of their corn and gave them a treat! I will have to admit, I was all smiles that day as I realized Caesar had led the other sheep to follow me.

The Good Shepherd loves when one of his sheep follows him even when others will not. He knows that through the obedience of one, others will see the good works God is doing and soon, they too will follow. His heart bursts with joy as he sees the obedience of the one who willingly followed him when no one else would, in turn lead others to do the same!

Today, be the one who will follow, because your obedience will not be in vain!

Go Enjoy The Shepherd.

Don't Lead Astray
Matthew 18:6, Luke 17:1-4

I read a story of a shepherd who had a gorgeous ewe whom he loved very much. She was a fine sheep and stayed healthy and raised good lambs. However, she had an issue with consistently wandering over onto the neighbor's farm. It was frustrating to go get her and bring her home each time, especially when the neighbor's farm was without anything for her to eat. It was as if she preferred to starve than enjoy what he had provided for her.

However, the shepherd indulged this sheep for a while because she was such a fine sheep and raised great lambs. He put up with her going off the farm, until she started to lead her lambs to do the same. Suddenly, the issue became worse, as other lambs would follow her as well, eventually leading them all away from his care. As much as it grieved him, he knew he could not tolerate these lambs being taught such bad behavior, so he slaughtered the ewe so that all the lambs would not be led astray.

This is a hard story to swallow, but it is necessary because it shows the love of the Good Shepherd. He loves his sheep so much, that he is willing to remove even one who others might call a "champion" sheep if that one starts leading the little ones away from him. He is a jealous God, and he will endure with much longsuffering the going astray of one of his own, unless that one starts leading the "little ones" into paths of destruction. He loves his sheep too much to let even one of his own lead them away.

Go Enjoy The Shepherd.

August 1

Different for a Reason
1 Corinthians 12:12-27

It does not take a shepherd very long to realize that each one of the sheep is unique. Each one plays a very different role in the flock and each role is vital to the health of the flock. Even the ones who may seem frustrating to the shepherd.

In my flock, I have a very special sheep, Caesar, who is like my closest friend. When I enter the field, he loves to walk by my side, he loves to be rubbed on, and he enjoys eating next to me. We are what some would call very close.

However, if all of my sheep were like Caesar, we would have a problem. You see, Caesar has no precautions about any person who might walk in the field. He sees all people as potential friends and he is not aware of potential danger from a person. However, Susie Q Knucklehead is extremely cautious by nature. She will flee even if she thinks her shepherd is moving too quickly around her. Her eyes are always peeled for danger, and if she runs, the other sheep will follow. This makes her a very vital member of the family if and when danger does come around. If each member of the flock were like Caesar, they could easily be led astray and into a place where their life would be taken from them.

The Good Shepherd, in his amazing wisdom, does not try to make each one of his sheep just like the other. He does not try to fit each one into the same sheep mold. He knows his flock needs to be made up of many different members in order for the whole body to be complete. His heart is to have a personal relationship with each sheep in their own unique way. He knows each member's unique personality is extremely vital to the life of the flock as a whole!

Go Enjoy The Shepherd.

August 2

Time and Patience
2 Peter 3:8-9, Isaiah 30:18, Psalm 86:15

Knowing that each member of the flock plays an important role really helps with my patience. Yes, I would love for each of them to trust me and be comfortable with my touch out in an open field, but for me to gain that trust takes patience and time.

Susie Q Knucklehead, whom I have mentioned several times, is one of my most difficult cases. However, I know her awareness and cautiousness is absolutely vital to my flock. Therefore, in my efforts to gain her trust, I am patient, knowing in time she will eventually be still in my presence. She has already come a long way, but we have much further to go.

The Good Shepherd knows his sheep very well. He knows your heart and how easily you tend to want to flee from his touch. Praise his name that he is patient and holds time in the palm of his hand. He never runs short of either patience or time when it comes to his sheep. He longs that each of his sheep would be still in his presence, trusting his touch is for your good, and he is willing to patiently work with you until that day becomes a reality!

Go Enjoy The Shepherd

Never a Waste of Time
Isaiah 43:13, Daniel 4:5

As you can imagine, there are days where frustration can set in when dealing with a sheep who simply will not trust you. Especially those times when I am needing to bring in the sheep and check them in the pen, and the knucklehead's head off in another direction, leading other sheep away. I will be honest, there are days I am ready to throw in the towel; however, I continue on and eventually I get them where I need them to do what I need to do.

You see, once my nerves are calmed, I remember that each sheep is valuable and therefore never a waste of my time. I know if I continue on, patiently moving forward, a time will come when those sheep will be still when I am with them. I also know they will produce more sheep that will increase my flock. Knowing the end of the story allows me to press on in my work and realize none of my time with any of my sheep is a waste.

The Good Shepherd, he not only knows the end of the story, he wrote it. He has given us clear words that absolutely nothing can stop his plans from coming to pass. Once he has set his heart on making something a reality, it simply will be. Praise his name, he has set his heart on all of his sheep, to make them his greatest prize and possession. He has determined to perfect his flock in accordance to the promise he made to his Son! Therefore, he never considers his work, his patience, and his time, to be a waste when he is working with his sheep!

That means he never considers any time he is working with you a waste because he loves you with all his heart! He sees the end of your story and he knows you will bring him great joy in the end!

Go Enjoy The Shepherd.

August 4

Determined Shepherd!

2 Chronicles 15:7, Philippians 3:12-17, Deuteronomy 9:13-14, Exodus 32:12-14

Let's be completely open and honest. Have I ever personally wanted to throw in the towel and give up on the sheep? Yes! Have I ever considered just catching and selling Susie Q Knucklehead so I would not have to put up with her jumpiness? Yes! Has she ever frustrated me enough that I was fed up with her and ready to quit? Yes!

In fact, one day, when bringing them into the pen, she literally turned on me, ran, and jumped in the air in an attempt to knock me down so she could escape. It was so frustrating because I simply wanted to check her for worms or other harmful issues. However, she did not want in the pen with the other sheep. On that day, I was ready to let her go and just quit trying to get her to trust me. However, I knew I could not just throw in the towel, so I made the choice to press on, knowing one day all my work would pay off.

The Good Shepherd also knows those moments where his knuckleheads press the limits of even his patience. Look at when he told Moses that he was ready to destroy the Israelites and just start over with Moses. The Israelites had pushed God to his limits, but for his own namesake, for his glory, he refused to throw in the towel. He continued on in his inexhaustible patience and love and he never threw in the towel, and he never will.

What an encouragement this should be to me and to you. Even when we do our best to frustrate him, or run from him, he is not a shepherd who will simply give up on his sheep. Rather, he presses on until his work is finished and he will look at us and call us "Perfect."

Go Enjoy The Shepherd.

August 5

When the Plan Falls Apart
Psalm 46:1-3

It was a foggy and damp morning when my son asked if he could join me in doing the chores and the devotional video for the day. Of course, when a six-year-old asks to hang out with his dad, you are certainly going to say, "Yes."

I had a great idea of doing a video of us calling the sheep together and discussing discipleship, when in the middle of the video a huge and nerve-racking fight took place. I was unaware that our two cats from the house had followed us into the field. Vasella, the guard dog, suddenly had one in the clutches of her jaws as I was shooting the video and quickly, everything changed. I rushed over and rescued the cat and my son and I took both of the cats back home. Needless to say, this really worked on my nerves because I knew how much the cats mean to both my daughters.

When my son and I went back to reshoot the video lesson for the day, it was clear we could no longer do the same one. After settling down and calming the sheep down (they had witnessed the whole scene and they were now on edge), we simply talked about "When the plan falls apart, the shepherd is still in control."

Today I praise his name that the Good Shepherd never loses control. He is never "surprised" by a fight and he never loses his nerves. He is our solid rock, our fortress, our defender, and the calm to our storm. When it appears our life is falling apart and our plans are all failing, remember, God is still in control!

You may be in the middle of a storm and your best laid plans may be crumbling beneath you. Take this moment and turn your eyes to Jesus and rest in his arms because he is still sitting on his throne!

Go Enjoy The Shepherd.

August 6

Remain Calm
Psalm 37:7-9, Romans 14:13-23

Sheep are jumpy, that is just a simple truth. Sudden movements, even around the calmest of sheep, will put them into a full flight-and-run mode. So, as the shepherd, I do my best to move in a slow and calm manner when I am around them.

As I walk among them, every now and then, one of my young boys (4 and 6) or Vasella (the guard dog), in their excitement to be with me will burst into a run, scaring the sheep and causing them to flee. Each time this happens, I simply turn and tell my boys or the dog, "Calm down! You are scaring the sheep!"

The same is true in our lives as sheep of the Good Shepherd. Our nature is to jump and run when the storms of life crash in around us. Or when others in their excitement to get close to him, are bursting with energy and those bursts of joy can cause panic in the other sheep. So the Good Shepherd reminds all of his sheep in a still, small voice, "Calm down, you're scaring the other sheep!"

Today, if you are excited to be next to him, do not fail to draw close and enjoy him. However, be careful in your excitement you are not causing other sheep to run away!

Go Enjoy The Shepherd.

August 7

The Trusting Heart
1 Samuel 13:14, Acts 13:22

I was offered the opportunity to travel up to Ohio to speak to a youth camp about the heart of a shepherd. I was truly blown away when I entered the camp and received such a huge welcome. I was amazed at the heart of these youngsters and it was evident they had learned so much about shepherds and sheep that week. I tested them by asking them several questions which they quickly responded to with the right answer. Questions like: "What is a shepherd? What are the names of some of my sheep? Which one of my sheep do I love the most? (all of them). However, this is the ultimate question that needed to be answered: "Which of my sheep do I use the most?" The answer of course is, "The one who trusts me with all his heart!"

When God chose David to lead his people as king, he did not pick the strongest. He did not choose the best looking or the smartest. He was not looking for a leader that the people would consider wise or attractive, God was looking at his heart. He wanted a heart that trusted him fully and would follow him no matter where he led. (1 Samuel 16:1-13)

Today, you may not be the strongest or the smartest. You may not look like a supermodel or have the appearance of a leader. You may not be able to speak well or feel like you can be used by the Good Shepherd at all. Remember, he is not interested in your strength, your looks, your wisdom, or your abilities. He is looking for a heart that completely trusts him and will go wherever he leads!

Go Be the One and Enjoy The Shepherd!

August 8

Not Perfect!
2 Corinthians 12:5-10

If you take one quick look at my sheep, the first thing you will notice is that they are not perfect. In the Old Testament, if you remember, any lamb brought as a sacrifice for sin had to be perfect and without blemish. My closest sheep, Caesar, is not one of these lambs. Caesar has a huge black spot on his side and would therefore have been disqualified from being a lamb who was worthy to be brought before God.

However, Caesar is the one sheep in my flock by which all other sheep learn how to follow me. He is used despite his flaw. I do not look at him and see imperfections. I see a sheep who loves me and trusts me with all his heart. Now, he is not perfect, at times even acting out around me. I have had to settle him down more than once so he would not accidentally hurt me or any of my children. However, in spite of all his issues, I still love him and use him to lead my other sheep.

The truth is, none of the sheep in the Good Shepherd's flock are perfect. We all have "black spots" which would disqualify us from service in his kingdom. However, through the sacrifice of the Perfect Lamb of God, all our blemishes have been covered and now he finds joy in using what the world calls "blemished" to lead his sheep back to him.

You may only see all your imperfections and faults, believing he would never use you, but all he sees is perfection, made in his image, and he is looking for a heart that trusts him fully! He is not looking for outward perfection, but rather, he is looking for the heart that is completely dedicated to him.

Go Be the One and Enjoy The Shepherd.

August 9

He Walks the Path
Psalm 32:8-11

There is a path on my farm which the sheep use to come to the gate near our house. This path runs right through the center of our field and is very easy to see. That is, until the spring and summer rains cause the fields to grow up tall with grass and suddenly the path can be harder to make out. During the mornings, as the dew is on the grass, it becomes even harder to discern.

This path is not just one the sheep use each day, it is also a path I use when going out to be with my sheep or feed them. Therefore, each day, I walk this path and something interesting happens when I do. With each step I take, the path becomes clearer and easier to see. So when my sheep come to visit the gate, the path has been made clear for them by their shepherd.

This is such a beautiful picture for me of how the Good Shepherd goes out before me daily to clear my path which leads to him. He knows that the cares and concerns of this world can often obscure the path of life which we are on, struggling to follow him. That is why he goes before us every day to make the path that leads to him a clear one for us to follow.

Today, lift up your eyes and see he is coming to you, clearing your path to follow him.

Go Enjoy The Shepherd.

August 10

Leaders Must Follow
1 Corinthians 1:11

When I call my sheep, the one who trusts me the most always leads the others back to me. If I am leading them from one field to the next, or taking them from one end of the field to the sheep shed, the one who trusts me, who is the leader, always is following me. As they follow me, the other sheep follow him / her.

When I am looking at my sheep, looking for the one who will lead the others, what I am really looking for is the one who will follow me. I know that sheep follow sheep, so in order for all the sheep to follow me, I need one who is committed to following me wherever I am taking them. When I find that sheep, I know I have truly found a great leader for my flock.

The Good Shepherd is not looking for great leaders to lead his sheep, he is searching for committed followers who will follow him wherever he leads. He is looking for ones like Paul who can say, "Follow me as I follow Christ." He is looking for a heart that is fully committed to going anywhere he leads, trusting he is in control and has a perfect plan!

Today, if he is calling you to lead, then what he is truly calling you to is to follow him. If you will follow in his steps, then and only then can you lead others to follow him.

Go Be the One and Enjoy The Shepherd.

August 11

Friends for the Journey
Hebrews 12:1

Sheep are not big fans of moving around. If they knew loading them on a trailer meant going somewhere new, I have a feeling they would never load up. They simply hate being moved. This is evidenced by the signs of discomfort and stress they display in their bodily actions. Stress can cause sheep to be sick and the nerves can give them the scours. The only thing that can somewhat soothe this move is if the sheep are moved as a flock. Being with other sheep they know can help calm their nerves.

This is another area in life that we are much like sheep. I helped a friend move across country once, and it is not so much the being in a new place, as it is leaving behind the comfort of the routine we have known. That causes great discomfort and stress to our internal systems and we tend to reflect signs of stress in our attitudes and our bodies.

The Good Shepherd knows that our journey through this life is a lot like sheep being moved. We are never really home here on this earth, even if we have found a place to settle in. Our journeys are full of change and constant motion, causing us to be like the sheep and display signs of stress. That is why he has given us his Spirit and other sheep to make this journey together with. That is why he has told us we are never alone. Surrounded by a great cloud of those to cheer us on, the Shepherd leads us into the Promised Land by his side!

Go Enjoy The Shepherd.

August 12

Quality over Quantity
Micah 6:6-8

On a visit back to Colorado, I was reminded that it is the number two state in our nation in the amount of sheep raised each year. Texas is the state in which most sheep are raised and Colorado follows it. As I thought that through, it reminded me of the difference in quality vs quantity.

Sheep are raised worldwide for mass production for wool and meat. Most "producers" as they are called, are raising the sheep for the ultimate purpose of increasing their personal wealth. Sheep are a vessel through which they can gain worldly wealth and provision. What matters most in these operations is numbers. How many head of sheep are there. How many lambs does one sheep produce. How can I expand my territory and raise more sheep? What can I do to make the most profit from this operation? That is the foundation on which a sound commercial sheep operation is run.

Sadly, this formula is used today in many of the flocks of the Good Shepherd. The entire organization is based on numbers which lead to "profit." How many salvations. How many baptisms. How many people come to each service. How can we increase the size of our operation. How do we expand the "sheep shed" to hold more sheep. How can I grow my flock?

Unfortunately, this in turn is projected on the Good Shepherd and how the lost sheep of the world might see him. If those who are supposedly representing him are most concerned with size and numbers, then it is easy to assume he is too. However, Jesus is not interested in numbers or profit. He already owns the earth and all that is in it. He does not need to expand his territory or increase his profits. What he desires is an intimate, personal relationship with his sheep.

I learned this principle when I went from 120 sheep to 20. With 120 I was not able to develop a relationship with each one. In fact, I could not even come up with or remember a name for that many. However, when we went to 20 sheep, I was able to focus in, learn their names, their habits, and attend to each of their needs individually. That is when I began to learn the true heart of my Good Shepherd and how he longs to have a Quality relationship with me instead of me simply being a part of a Quantity, or mass of sheep. He truly desires to know me deeply and in turn, to let me know him in every way!

He loves you and desires for you to not be simply a number in an "operation," but rather he longs to be known by you in a very personal and intimate way. **You** are the desire of his heart.

Go Enjoy The Shepherd.

The Undershepherd
1 Peter 5:1-4

On occasion, I have to take trips and be away from my flock of sheep. When this comes up, it is very important to me to have someone to attend to their needs. Sheep are extremely needy animals. Of all creatures on the farm, sheep are by far the ones who need the most attention.

If I have to be out of town, I typically ask my wife and kids to handle the sheep chores on the farm. If we are all going to be out of town, then I ask a family member or a trustworthy neighbor to see to my sheep. My point being, I never leave my sheep without care and supervision. To do so would be unwise and irresponsible.

How blessed are you today to be able to call yourself a member of the Good Shepherd's flock. How amazing of him that he has promised to never leave his sheep alone, but to always be with them and oversee them. How comforting to know he has placed undershepherds in your life to watch over you and care for you while he is preparing the next place for you to go. God is not unwise and he is never irresponsible. He always takes care of his own!

Go Enjoy The Shepherd.

August 14

You Are an Undershepherd
John 21:15-17, 1 Peter 5:1-4

When choosing an undershepherd for my sheep, I am looking for someone who is both willing and able to watch over them. My undershepherds must care as much for my sheep as I do. I am not just looking for someone who can deliver the food and water, but someone who cares about my sheep enough to do the chores regardless of the weather, the time, or the possible inconvenience to them. I am looking for someone who is willing to sacrifice their likes and desires to make sure the sheep are taken care of.

You may not realize this, but the Good Shepherd has called even you to be an undershepherd of his flock. Yes, no matter your age or place in life, you too have been given the charge to watch over his precious lambs and sheep. You may be a parent, an older sibling, a teacher, an administrator, a pastor, a secretary, or an owner of a small or large company. You may be an employee who works on an assembly line, or maybe you drive a truck or a delivery van. You might be a baker, a roommate, a landlord, or a tenant. It does not matter what your position in life, you have been specifically placed to help lead others to his feet. That is the role of an undershepherd, to lead the other sheep back to the Good Shepherd.

Today, ask God to reveal to you who he wants you to watch over, to protect, to guide, to care for, and **Feed His Lambs!**

Go Enjoy The Shepherd.

Woe to the Lazy Undershepherd
Ezekiel 34:1-10

I once came back home from a trip to find that my sheep and the dogs had not been looked after every day. I had left them in the hands of one I thought I could trust, but other concerns in life had distracted them from doing what they had promised to do. Needless to say, I was not happy! In fact, I was very upset. I never again asked this person to watch my sheep because I could no longer trust them.

In Ezekiel, we see this same reaction by the Good Shepherd himself. He cries out against those who had been given care over His flocks, but they had plundered them for their own gain and had mistreated them and left them scattered on the hillsides. They had ruled them harshly and had not sought after the ones who were lost. So the Good Shepherd cast aside all those evil undershepherds and went himself to redeem his flocks.

God has not changed in his heart and desire for his people through the ages. He looks out each day at those who have been given charge over his flocks and he is watching to see who is treating the sheep with care and who is abusing them for personal gain. He promises to all those who forget their role and responsibility, that he will treat them in the same manner in which they have treated his people.

Pastors, Parents, Teachers, Friends. You are an undershepherd, given charge over his sheep! Look to him today to be your example. Treat his sheep as he would, lest you hear him cry out against you!

Sheep of his flock, rejoice! He is watching over you and over those who have been given charge over you! He will never leave you long in the hands of a cruel undershepherd.

Go Enjoy The Shepherd.

August 16

A Job Well Done
Matthew 25:20-21

Once, after returning home from a five-day trip in which I had asked my children to watch over the sheep, I was extremely pleased to come home and see the sheep all in great health. Every detail had been attended to like I had asked and for that, I thanked my kids and rewarded them for a job well done.

Matthew recorded for us the words of the Good Shepherd as he spoke on this very topic. The parable used spoke of talents the servants had been given, but the lesson is manifold in how the servant took care of what he had been given charge over. He had been asked to be an undershepherd and because of doing a great job, he received a fabulous reward.

Watching sheep is not always easy. It takes determination, perseverance, patience, kindness, gentleness, and lots of self control. It is not as simple as sitting on a hill with your eyes open. It is a hands-on job which may require that you put your life on the line for the sheep. However, when the Good Shepherd returns and sees you have been faithful in your work, that you have grown his flock, that you have sought out the lost sheep and brought them home, great will be your reward! You will be called to enter in and share in his joy!

Go Enjoy The Shepherd.

For the Shepherd
Colossians 3:23-24

How awesome it would be to go out one day and hear my sheep say thanks! It would be such an uplifting experience to just have them reaffirm all the work I put in. However, it is a very rare thing that a sheep shows me his or her gratitude. I put out corn, they simply eat it. I walk out in the dead of winter and bust the ice on the water, they just drink it. In other words, they are just sheep and they simply take what I offer with little regard for all my hard work.

I once asked my teenage daughters if any of the animals ever thanked them for the times they did the chores. Both of them giggled and said, "Of course not!" However, when I asked them if **anyone** thanked them for their labor, they smiled and said, "Yes, Dad, you did!"

Many times we get caught up in trying to receive approval and thanks from those we are serving. We long for them to notice all our hard work and reward us, even if it is a simple thank you. Unfortunately, many times our labors go unnoticed by those we are serving; however, not a moment has escaped the eyes to whom it really does matter. The eyes of the Good Shepherd.

He is watching everything you are doing on behalf of his flock, and he has a great reward in his hands for you, an inheritance beyond your imagination. Today, do not labor for the applause of men, but rather, do your work as unto the only one who can truly reward you with an everlasting inheritance.

Go Enjoy The Shepherd.

Surrounded by the Enemy
Psalm 57:4

Coyotes are a smart hunting animal. They hunt in packs and often divide the forces in an attempt to lure away any guardians in one direction so they can attack from the other. In my time as a shepherd, I have watched this happen on multiple occasions. The coyotes would yelp from the west in an attempt to have my dogs chase after them, only to have a second squadron poised and ready on the east to come in.

Thankfully, each time I have watched my guardians act as they are supposed to, one would take off toward the enemy while the other maintained a close eye on the flock. If the second battalion of the enemy tried to attack from the rear, my guardians were prepared and there to defend my sheep.

We have a wise and cunning Enemy who is clever in his attacks. He sends in his foes from one side, all the while he has prepared a second wave to attack us from our blindside. But we are the sheep of the Good Shepherd, and he knows the ways of our enemy all too well. He has placed over his flock guardians who are trained and prepared for these tactics. When the enemy attacks, they will rise up and defend his flock.

Today, you may feel surrounded by the enemy, but know this, the Good Shepherd is defending you on every side! He will not fail you and the enemy cannot defeat him. Stay close to the Good Shepherd, for by his side you will find safety!

Go Enjoy The Shepherd.

Silencing the Enemy
Psalm 143:2

When coyotes attack, they have one plan in mind. They want to incite fear into the sheep in hopes that they can cause them to spread out, making it easier to pick them off. So coyotes fill the air with ear-piercing yelps that would drive any animal up the wall. Their goal is to make the sheep scatter, and they use their howls to start the process.

Every time this happens on our farm, the guard dogs respond by howling back at the coyotes. It is a signal to them that our dogs are aware they are there and that they will fight back to defend their territory. So many times I have heard this exchange take place, and within seconds of the coyotes beginning their yelps, they are quickly silenced and running away.

How sweet of the Good Shepherd to place around us defenders who have the sole purpose of silencing the enemy. The Enemy comes in, like the coyotes, and attempts to stir us up and draw us away from the Shepherd's care. Every time he attempts to scatter us with all his noise, the voice of the Good Shepherd and his guardians ring out and our Enemy is sent back home.

Go Enjoy The Shepherd.

August 20

Remain Calm
2 Corinthians 2:9-11

The predator has one goal when it attacks the sheep, to get them to run and leave the protection of the shepherd. No matter the tactic, whether using noise or straight-out onslaught attacks, if the sheep ever leave the shepherd and his protection, then that sheep is going to fall to the clutches of the enemy.

On the other hand, as long as the sheep is staying close to the shepherd, then it is completely safe. Near the shepherd, the enemy has no chance to ever harm the sheep without first going through the shepherd. Therefore, when the enemy attacks, the sheep needs only to remain calm and stand by their shepherd.

Today, you may be facing the most disruptive and severe attacks of your life. The Enemy may be coming at you from all sides and you feel life is falling down around you. You may think you have been left alone to fall to the Enemy's hands, however, if you stay close to the Good Shepherd you are safe. Remain calm and cling to his side, because under his shelter you will find complete peace during the attacks of the Enemy.

Go Enjoy The Shepherd.

Not a Number
Isaiah 43:1-2

When running a large sheep operation, the key to keeping up with your sheep is to have them tagged with a number in their ear. With that number you are able to track its results, its physical issues, and by that you determine if you want to continue to have that sheep as a member of your flock. This system is used in almost every commercial sheep operation in the world.

What this means is that each sheep is only known by its number. There is never any real connection to the shepherd of the operation. The sheep are to be good producers or they are simply discarded and thrown to the side. The life of the sheep is entirely weighed in the balance of the notes by its number.

The Good Shepherd does not run a highly sophisticated commercial sheep operation with his people. He is not interested in tagging his sheep with a number and judging them solely based on production performances. Does he keep a record of each sheep? Yes. However, he knows each of his sheep by name. He has formed a personal connection with each one and his judgement of that sheep is based on the righteousness of One, not the production of the number.

He knows Your name!!!!

Go Enjoy The Shepherd.

August 22

Engraved in His Hand
Isaiah 49:16

I visited a camp once to speak about the love of the Good Shepherd and as a gift, they handed me a shepherd's staff with names written on them in permanent marker. These were the names of some of the ones at the meeting, names I may only hear once in my life, but now that I have them written on a staff in my home, I can remember to pray over them by name.

I thought this staff was a beautiful reminder of the truth that my name is not just a name written on a staff, or even in permanent marker. Isaiah declared the Word of the Lord, and God himself said that the names of his children are written in the palm of his hand. The language used here refers to a tattoo that is permanent in nature and can never be wiped away.

That means your name is forever written in the palm of the Good Shepherd's hand. As a sheep of his flock, your name can never be forgotten amongst the masses of sheep he has as his, because each name is permanently tattooed in his hand.

Rejoice, the Good Shepherd knows Your name!

Go Enjoy The Shepherd.

August 23

Just as You Are
Matthew 11:28-30, Isaiah 1:18-20

There is something peculiar about my sheep. When I go out in
the field with them and call them to come to me, not once have I
watched them first run to clean themselves up. Not once have they
offered to take a bath before coming. Not even a quick dip in the pond.
They simply come to me just like they are, dirt and dust included.

I love how Jesus came to us right where we were. He did not
require the prostitute to clean herself before he embraced her. He did
require the leper be cleansed before he took him in. Rather, he told them
to come, just as they were, and then he lifted them up and set them on
solid ground.

Today, you may have been lying in some filth, some sin, and you
are afraid to come. You want to go take a "bath" before you run to him.
Do not wait, for in his healing hands is the cleansing you need. He
accepts you and embraces you exactly where you are. Today, the Good
Shepherd simply says to you, "Come as you are!"

Go Enjoy The Shepherd.

No "What Ifs"
Psalm 50:7-15

I was once asked, "What would you do to your sheep if you were no longer able to provide for them?" The answer to that is quick and simple, I would have to find them a place where they could be taken care of. Having sheep to me is not just something to do, it is a responsibility. If I am unable to care for them, then it would be irresponsible to keep them.

This made me so thankful as I thought about this in connection with the Good Shepherd. His supplies for his sheep are unlimited. His love and ability to care for his own knows neither measure nor end. There is nothing that he lacks, therefore there is nothing that those who are a part of his flock shall ever need. He gives generously to those who fear and follow him.

In other words, when it comes to his ability to care for his sheep, there are no "What ifs?" It is not a question he will ever have to answer. Even when his sheep face trials and tribulations, and troubles of all kinds, his supply of grace, hope, love, and mercy never ends!

Go Enjoy The Shepherd.

It Brings Me Joy
Psalm 149:4

I have been asked many times if my sheep could survive a day without my care. To answer honestly where I live, I would have to say yes. They have the fence and guard dog for protection. They have food to eat and water to drink. They have a place to lie down and rest. They have what they need to solely survive.

Therefore, the follow-up question is usually this, "So why do you go see them, or be with them, every day?" That answer is simple, because I enjoy it!

Being with my sheep is a place that I am able to simply be still and enjoy myself. I love watching them graze in the field or rest in the shade. It is calming and relaxing. I enjoy building my relationship with them, forming closer bonds with those who trust me, and working to improve my closeness with those who do not. When it all comes down to it, I just enjoy being with my sheep.

I love how this reflects the heart of the Good Shepherd and how he is with you and me. He has told us that it "delights" him to be with his people. Just as I enjoy being with my sheep, he enjoys time with you. He does not need to come see us and spend time with us daily, but he longs to because it brings him great joy!

Therefore, Go Enjoy The Shepherd.

August 26

Just Be His Sheep
Hosea 6:6

When I go out to be with my sheep, I am not necessarily interested in what they can do for me. Not every time do I want them to come to me, pawing at my legs for corn or feed. What I want to do is simply be with them and to know them and for them to know me. In other words, I just want them to be sheep and I to be their shepherd.

Many times, we get caught up in the running to our Good Shepherd for him to do something for us. We cry out for him to meet our needs and to supply our demands. When all along, he would like to simply just be with us, knowing us and us knowing him.

Today, go to him, but not asking for him to give you something you think you want or need. Just go be his "sheep" today. Enjoy him and allow him to enjoy you!

Go Enjoy The Shepherd.

Cease Striving
Psalm 46:10

I stood in awe and amazement, watching the wrestling match unfold in front of me. I had gone to learn from another shepherd on how to check a sheep for visible signs of worms and foot rot. He took me to his shed in which was a fairly calm sheep. We stood in the pen and the ewe did not seemed bothered by us at all. Until…

Until that shepherd grabbed hold of it and went to put it in the correct position to be checked. This seemingly docile ewe suddenly was giving him a run for his money. The sheep jumped and jerked, doing her best to escape his grasp. After what seemed like an eternity (probably 40 seconds), he finally had her on her back, head against his legs, and she was completely still. From there he was able to run his full check on her and teach me this great lesson, "Once I have them in this position, I can do whatever I need to do to help them."

That has stuck with me throughout my time with sheep. I have had a few wrestling matches of my own, you might say, and every time I get them in the position he taught me, I am able to help them as they need help. All they had to do was to cease striving against me.

The Good Shepherd loves to care for ALL the needs of his sheep, including the ones we are unaware of. Sometimes, that means getting us into uncomfortable situations where we wrestle and fight against his way and plans. Thankfully, he is not willing to give up on us, and he will continue to work with us until we cease our striving and allow him to tend to our deepest needs.

Today, cease striving! When you do, he will mend the broken inside of you.

Go Enjoy The Shepherd.

August 28

He Never Sleeps
Psalm 121:3-4

The fog hung over the fields as the sun hinted at rising that morning. I was on my way to a very early appointment, but before leaving, I stood and looked over my fields. My sheep were still resting peacefully in a small huddle, not yet daring to get up and graze at such an early hour. It was a scene of peace and serenity. My sheep were not aware of my presence; however, I was there watching over them.

As I stood there, I was reminded of how the Good Shepherd had told us through his servant that he never sleeps or slumbers. He is always watching over his sheep, whether we can see him or not. He is always there.

Rest in the comfort today, knowing your Good Shepherd never sleeps on the job. He never takes a break from watching over you.

Go Enjoy The Shepherd.

I've Fallen and Can't Get Up
Zechariah 9:16

I was out walking in the fields looking for my sheep to call them in that morning. As I walked, I began to hear the faint bleating of a sheep. It sounded like the sound of a newborn lamb, but I was certain none of my sheep were close to giving birth. Unfortunately, our farm tractor was broken down, and that meant some very high weeds had grown up. I searched by where I heard the sound, but found nothing.

As the sheep began to gather around me, I heard the sound again. That is when the sight of four legs, that appeared stiff, caught my eye. I rushed over to the tall weeds again and found one of my largest ewes on her side. She had become "cast," meaning a gas had built up in her belly and was prohibiting her from getting up. Thankfully for Kendra (the ewe), I found her in time and was able to stand her up and help her regain her footing. Within minutes of working with her, she was back with the other sheep grazing, even thriving once again. If she had gone unnoticed much longer, she certainly would have perished.

Our lives can become weighted down with the cares of this world and sin. It can build up into a "gas" inside of us that will literally hold us down and attempt to strangle the life out of us. We thrash and struggle, attempting to free ourselves from the clutches of death, only to find ourselves close to the end.

Then the Good Shepherd comes to your rescue, picking you up and setting you again on your feet. He works tenderly with you, removing the stiffness that has set in to your heart from the grip of the struggle. Coming to your rescue, saving you from the very clutches of death, he places you again in the middle of his green pasture, once again allowing you to thrive!

Go Enjoy The Shepherd.

Picking Out the Poison
Hosea 10:4

Here in Tennessee, we have an herbal plant that grows in the wild. It is known as perilla mint, or beefsteak weed to the locals. It is a plant with green leaves that have a purple underside. They smell like mint, thus the name. In many places in the world, it is used as a remedy for colds and allergies, transformed into an herbal tea. I have even personally used it and found it very helpful in tea form.

However, this plant has a negative effect on sheep. You can watch them out in the field, and they will avoid this plant. It is extremely poisonous to them, and a very small dose can actually kill them.

One summer, these weeds left the normal area of shades that they typically grew in and began to grow in the middle of the fields. These were the same fields that we had intended to use for a hay crop for the sheep. I knew that in order to use the hay, the weeds would need to be removed. So my family and I took several evenings and walked the fields and picked these poisonous plants by hand and removed them from the field. If I wanted to use the hay for the sheep in the winter, I had to first remove the deadly poison that would end their life.

What a beautiful picture of how the Good Shepherd goes before us and oversees the future ahead of us. He sees the things that could cause us to be "poisoned," and he is removing them before we reach that place.

Rejoice today, for he is going before you to remove the potential poisons that would most certainly bring you death.

Go Enjoy The Shepherd.

Disease and Death
Psalm 68:20

Whether we like it or not, as shepherds we have to deal with disease and death. Sheep are fragile animals and can be quickly overcome by diseases which lead to death. I can recount endless times coming upon a sheep who only hours before seemed perfectly healthy, and now it was dead.

I have also dealt with countless issues with perfectly healthy ewes being infected with deadly diseases. I have had to work countless hours in my attempts to save their life, sometimes being successful, others I have not. The point is, here in this world shepherds have to deal with the reality of disease and death.

The Good Shepherd was completely honest when he told us in this world we would have trouble (John 16:33). He did not hide the fact that we would wrestle with diseases and that everyone will face death. (Hebrews 9:27). However, he did tell us he would never leave us or forsake us. He told us he would watch over us, making sure we were cared for through the process. He promised victory over death (1 Corinthians 15:55-57).

So take heart today, for though you wrestle with the realities of death and disease in this world, Jesus is preparing a place for you where death and disease will no longer be allowed to affect his flock!

Go Enjoy The Shepherd.

September 1

The Thief
John 10:1

Sheep have always been the subjects of thieves and robbers. As shown here in the words of Jesus, thieves have always been attempting to steal sheep. It is not just wild animals a shepherd has to be concerned about, but greedy and hungry people as well.

When I first got into sheep, this was an epidemic plaguing some local shepherds. Most local farmers also worked full-time jobs, leaving their sheep vulnerable to these "two-legged" thieves. I was cautioned early on to be aware and take steps to prevent my sheep from being the victims of modern day thieves.

We have also been warned of one who is a thief who is coming to steal, kill, and destroy (John 10:10). His only goal is to wreak havoc on the life of the sheep and to plunge a dagger into the heart of the Good Shepherd by taking one of his flock. We have been given this warning so we can be on alert. The first tip we are given is how they attempt to enter the pen!

Today, be aware that your enemy, the devil, is seeking to steal you from the safety of the Good Shepherd's fold. Know he will never enter in through the gate, but will always attempt to enter another way. If you sense danger, run to the Good Shepherd, for you are safe by his side!

Go Enjoy The Shepherd.

September 2

Recognizing the Shepherd
John 10:2

After just a short time on my farm, I begin to realize how the sheep seemed to know which gate I was going to enter at. I would begin to call them as I walked up the farm road to the fields, and they started to meet me at the gate. I was quickly taken with their ability to recognize exactly where I was going to enter the field.

Here, Jesus gave us the very first sign of how to recognize the Good Shepherd. He told us he would always enter through the gate. The shepherd had no reason to climb in any other way in an attempt to get to his sheep. He always met them at a place of familiarity, the gate.

Are you wondering today if the one who has come to you is the Good Shepherd? You need only to look to where he entered in. If he did not come through the gate, a place you are familiar with, then be on guard and be alert, for a thief has come to steal you away. (1 John 4:1)

Go Enjoy The Shepherd.

September 3
The Watchman
John 10:3

I was warned early on in my shepherding career that sheep were subject to be stolen, not just by wild animals, but by people as well. Evidently, our area had become somewhat of a hotspot for some "sheep rustlers" who were looking for either fast cash or an easy meal. I was told to put a watchman over my flock, which I did in the form of the guard dogs.

On one occasion, I was able to watch my "watchman" work for me at the gate. A gentleman had come, not to steal my sheep, but to show them off to another prospective shepherd. He let me know they were coming, but instead of coming to my house, they decided to drive up to the sheep fields ahead of me. He intended to enter the gate and look around with this other gentleman. However, when I arrived the two men were standing behind the gate with a look of terror on their faces. Between them and the sheep stood Cheta (said cheetah), my guardian dog. When they had attempted to enter the field through the gate, he literally ran them out and would not allow them to pass. Only when I arrived and reassured Cheta everything was okay did he allow them to enter.

Yes, there is a thief who has come to steal, kill, and destroy, but our Good Shepherd has placed a watchman over his flock (Exodus 23:20). No one can enter the gate to steal any of the sheep unless he first makes it past the watchman, which he won't!

Rejoice today, for you are under the watchful eye of the Good Shepherd!

Go Enjoy The Shepherd.

September 4
Listen to the Shepherd
John 10:3

There have been many viral videos come across the internet showing sheep who listen to the voice of the shepherd. What made these videos viral was that others would try and call the sheep, mimicking the call of the shepherd, but none of them succeeded because they could not imitate the shepherd's voice.

I tried this on our own farm and found it to be true. One day, as we were coming up the drive, my youngest daughter began calling for the sheep. They did not even lift their heads. My oldest daughter tried, then my wife and two boys. I watched for a minute as they vainly tried calling the sheep. Then, from behind them, I called out. To my joy, each head lifted and they responded to my voice. With one more call, they came running my way. Not all of them could see me, but they knew the sound of my voice.

This world is full of voices calling out our names. Each one is trying to pull us in different directions. Success, popularity, and fame call from one way. The voice of greed and ill-gotten gain holler from another. Shame, anxiety, selfishness, and sin all ring out their voices. Yet, for the sheep of the Good Shepherd, there is but one voice that can lift up our heads—His. The world and the Enemy will attempt to mimic his call, but none can imitate the sound of his voice.

Today, simply listen. Listen to his voice, for he is calling you to come and follow him.

Go Enjoy The Shepherd.

September 5

He Calls Them by Name
John 10:3

Yes, it is true, sheep can learn their name. If a shepherd spends enough time with his sheep, he can single one out to come, and they will. On our farm, only a few who are willing to allow the shepherd to come close have ever learned their name. For these, I can go out into the field, call their name and they will lift up their head. When I call one out and they come, I always have something with which to reward them for responding.

In this passage, Jesus knew about how several shepherds would gather their individual sheep into a single pen for the evening. When the shepherd came out in the morning to take his sheep back out, all the sheep would have already mingled among one another and become one large flock. The only way to separate them back out was for the shepherd to call his own sheep by their names. When he would say their names, the sheep would lift their heads and come running to their shepherd. He would then lead them out into the fields and spend his day watching over his own sheep.

What a glorious picture of the Good Shepherd and how he knows his own sheep by name. We are all gathered into a single pen, this world, and we have become "mixed" in with all the other sheep. However, for those who know his voice, they listen, and when he calls their name, they run to him and are led out to enjoy time with him.

He knows your name today and he is calling you to himself so he can lead you out to simply spend time being loved by him.

Go Enjoy The Shepherd.

September 6

All of His Own
John 10:4

One of the most important tasks I undertook was making sure I had all of my sheep accounted for. In my early days as a shepherd, some might have called me a little too cautious, but I was wanting to make sure my sheep were okay. I would take count of them several times a day, and if any were missing, I would go find them.

When I would call them to come in, I would again take a head count to see if everyone had come. If there was even one missing, I would take to the hills to see what was going on. Many times I would find the lost sheep in a place where they could not hear my voice, or they had given birth to new lambs and would refuse to leave them in the field. Whatever the case, I was going to be sure I had all my sheep accounted for.

This is another glorious picture painted for us by Jesus himself about the Good Shepherd. He pointed out that the shepherd only went out once he had ALL his sheep. A Good Shepherd not only knows their names, he knows each of them so well he can easily spot when one is missing. A Good Shepherd would never head out unless he was certain all his sheep were accounted for.

Maybe today finds you in a place you cannot seem to hear his voice. Maybe you are engulfed in enjoying the pleasures around you and you have failed to hear him call your name. Be of good cheer my friend, for your Good Shepherd knows you are missing and he will not leave you behind. He will search for you until he has brought you back home to be under his care!

Go Enjoy The Shepherd.

He Goes Ahead
John 10:4

A story has been told of a man who visited Israel to see the area in which Jesus lived. While on the road to Bethlehem, he saw a man and sheep over in the field and he asked the driver to stop and allow him to snap a photo. "What a joy," he thought "to capture a picture of a flock with the shepherd in the Holy Land." As he was snapping the photo, the driver told him that he was not looking at a shepherd. Confused, the man asked him what he meant. Calmly the driver responded, "A shepherd leads his flock, that man is driving the sheep. The man in that field is not the shepherd, but rather, he is the butcher."

This story shows how a proper understanding of the sheep and his shepherd can make a huge impact in the lives of the sheep. You see, a good shepherd always goes ahead of his sheep, just as Jesus mentions in this passage. A shepherd is in front, not only leading the way, but also checking the path for potential hazards along the way. He is confident his sheep will follow, because he has spent plenty of time with them and they know and trust his voice. By taking the lead, the sheep can be certain that the shepherd will not lead them anywhere he is not willing to go himself.

Are you being led, or do you feel driven? Think about the simple truth in these words from our Good Shepherd. He will never lead you into a place where he has not first gone himself. He is in front, leading the way, all you must do is listen to his voice and follow.

Go Enjoy The Shepherd.

Reacting to the Stranger
John 10:5

I once took a pastor into my fields with my sheep. He wanted to do some video shoots for an upcoming event he had, and thought using the sheep would make for a good background. While we were there, I thought it would be fun to let him try and call the sheep. All I can say is that hilarity ensued.

He tried using his voice, but they did not listen. When he tried to get close to them, they walked the other way. He waved and gestured with his hands, but the sheep had nothing to do with him. He was a stranger in their field.

This reminded me of my first days with this same group of sheep. When they first arrived on our farm, they treated me just like this stranger. I would call for them, but they would not come. I would go out to them, but they would run away. Only through perseverance, patience, and spending lots of time with these sheep, did they come to know and trust me as their shepherd. Once I gained their trust, they were willing to come when I called.

Too often we expect a sheep who is new to the fold of Christ to instantly come whenever he calls. But the Good Shepherd knows he has a chore ahead of him, one he is willing to take on. He knows it will take time, but he works patiently, enduring all the initial rejections, teaching his sheep the sound of his voice. He longs for them to run when a stranger calls, but he also knows that will only happen if his sheep learn the sound of his voice.

Take time today to be still, to listen, and to learn the sound of the Good Shepherd's voice so that no stranger can ever lead you astray!

Go Enjoy The Shepherd.

September 9

The Bold Proclamation
John 10:11,14

If there has been one thing I have done my best to avoid, it has been to declare that I do a good job at attending my sheep. I have made so many mistakes in my time as a shepherd, I simply do not feel comfortable even being called a good shepherd. I strive to do my best on behalf of my sheep, but that has not kept me from making some foolish and costly mistakes.

Here, Jesus makes a bold, even an audacious, proclamation that he is the Good Shepherd. He has just finished talking about what a good shepherd does here on earth, then he compares himself with this portrait that he has painted. He has declared that a good shepherd knows his sheep and that they listen to his voice. He has talked about how the shepherd goes ahead of his flock, leading them in the correct paths. He has declared his sheep will find pasture when they go out, and that they would return to the pen of safety under his care. He has spoken of not only the good shepherd, but of the Perfect Shepherd, then he declares that he is this Good Shepherd.

This bold proclamation should bring you great joy today. Jesus has placed himself in the impossible position, then has declared that he would maintain his reputation by completing the task. He declared there was nothing that was going to keep him from being the Good Shepherd, not even death itself. He said, "I lay down my life for my sheep!" Only a Good Shepherd would sacrifice his own life in order that his sheep might live.

Not only did Jesus make this bold proclamation, he followed through so that he could be your Good Shepherd!

Go Enjoy The Shepherd.

September 10

More Sheep to Gather
John 10:16

There are two ways of growing a flock in size. First, you can simply keep some of the ewe lambs born and retain them for your own flock. The other way is to go out and find other sheep to purchase and bring back and mix them in with your current sheep.

I admit, I am always on the lookout for additional sheep to bring into my fold. I am not always buying, but I am looking. I enjoy the process of seeing the sheep others are raising, and on occasion, I purchase some and bring them home.

Each time I do this, it means I have to start the process again of teaching the new sheep that I am their shepherd. I have to earn their trust and teach them the sound of my voice. My sheep will automatically respond, but the new sheep take time and convincing in order for them to blend into the rest of the flock. When this process is complete, the goal is one flock following one shepherd.

The Good Shepherd declared in this passage that he had other sheep who were still outside of his fold. His heart is for all of his sheep, even the ones that are not "home" yet. His heart is set on having every one of his sheep in the safety of his care, and there are no lengths he will not go to in order to bring them all home!

Remember the time today that you were one of the missing sheep, and thank Jesus for seeking you out and bringing you home!

Go Enjoy The Shepherd.

September 11

A Firm Grip
John 10:28

I do not want to boast, but I consider myself a fairly stout guy. All my life I have enjoyed a strength given to me from the Lord through my parents. As part of this strength, I have always enjoyed a strong grip with my hands. Until the day it departs me, I will thank the Lord for it.

This grip has come in pretty handy around the sheep as well. When you grab ahold of a sheep's back hair or wool, you better have a firm grip if you hope to hold on to them. Sheep, if spooked, or if they feel "captured," are extremely strong animals. They lurch and jump, trying to get away. Without a firm grip on them, there is no way you can hold on.

Imagine trying to hold a sheep in your hand while fighting a predator. David mentioned twice fighting a lion and a bear, rescuing his sheep from their jaws (1 Samuel 17:34-35). What amazing strength and power to save a lamb from a lion of bear, then to grip it by the beard and slay the beast. David was determined to not lose any of his sheep, and he put his own life on the line to make sure that did not happen.

How awesome is the knowledge that your Good Shepherd refuses to lose you! He has made a promise, that of all his sheep, he is not going to lose any! You may be in the clutches of the jaws of the enemy, but he is going to rescue you because he is the Good Shepherd who refuses to lose even one of his flock!

Go Enjoy The Shepherd.

September 12

Attacking the Shepherd
Romans 4:25

So one thing is certain in a field with sheep, even the shepherd has to keep his eyes open. Sheep, especially rams, can become aggressive and attack people. You can watch countless videos of this happening on the internet, some are quite hilarious in nature. However, having been on the other end of an attack, it is not a pleasant experience.

Sheep have extremely hard skulls for the purpose of protecting their heads when they fight among themselves. This crusty shell at the top of their head serves as a great battering ram. However, my soft tissue and muscle do not offer a proper defense to these attacks, so I am always watchful in case one of the rams decides to turn on me at any time. No matter the case, ready or not, I know I am going to experience pain.

The Good Shepherd endures more of this than we could ever fathom. His sheep are consistently turning on him, and causing him great pain. The Good Shepherd of course loves his sheep through the pain, enough to allow himself to become tissue and muscle, only to be torn by those he came to save. Even after redeeming them, his sheep can still turn against him, battering him with the hardened skulls of our sin. Yet, he continues in his love toward us, even when we act as enemies of the one who died to save us.

Be humble today as you approach the Good Shepherd, knowing his love looks beyond even your worst attacks against him.

Go Enjoy The Shepherd.

September 13

Courageous Trust
Proverbs 3:5

As I sat in the field with my youngest son, I remember being amazed at how the sheep were so calm around us. Having had sheep for several years, I knew that sheep by nature are skittish and prefer their distance. But here stood Caesar and Mollie, letting us pet them without any worries or concerns. As long as we continued to pet them, they simply stood still.

What really made this special was knowing that it took every ounce of trust for them both to stand there. In reality, they were having to be bold and act courageously, as every instinct in them was telling them to move along. But they stayed, and because they did, we blessed them with enormous love.

The Good Shepherd knows it goes against your instincts and nature to remain calm in his presence. His holiness is literally unnerving to our souls, causing you to want to flee. However, he calmly asks you to stay close by, fighting every urge you have to run, so that he may bless you with the enormity of his love.

Go Enjoy The Shepherd.

September 14

It Does Not Make Any Sense
Romans 5:8

I finally gave in to my wonderings and said it out loud. "Why would any human being want to raise sheep?" The truth is, they are not the "sharpest knife in the drawer" or the "brightest light in the room." They are not really much to look at. They are constantly getting into places they should not and requiring attention and care. They can be a huge source of frustrations and concerns, completely taking over a full day for the shepherd who really needed to accomplish other things. It is just the honest truth, raising sheep can lead any outsider to say, "That does not make much sense."

How much more can the Good Shepherd declare, if he chose, that having his sheep did not make much sense. His sheep are constantly fighting against him, going astray, and getting into places they have to be rescued from. When he calls, they run the opposite direction, trying desperately to live without a shepherd. They run straight into the clutches of the enemy and need rescuing. From all perspectives, there is no benefit for him and none of it really makes much sense.

However, like any good shepherd, He does not care for his sheep because it makes sense. He does it simply because he loves us. Which means, he does not see you as a frustration, a renegade, or a problem, he sees you as the apple of his eye!

Go Enjoy The Shepherd.

September 15

Misplaced Confidence
Psalm 118:8

I was so distraught in the decision I had made. As I stared down at the ninth dead sheep in a two-week period, I grew completely frustrated. I stared at the miniature donkeys with complete disgust. How could I have been so foolish as to put my trust in animals who were not created to be defenders of sheep. My choice had led to severe consequences.

So many times we find ourselves putting our faith and hope in a person, place, or thing. We place our hope in a man to lead us, only to have them falter and fail. We put our hope in a place or a job, only to have it ripped away. Or we find our confidence in a padded bank account, only to see it all slip away. We stare in the mirror and wonder how could we have been so foolish.

When I placed livestock guardian dogs with my sheep, I never again lost a sheep to a predator. The ones who had been created to defend were now on the job, and I never had to worry again.

The same holds true when you place your hope and confidence in the Good Shepherd alone. He is the only one who has never, and will never fail at his job. He alone has the ability and power to hold you up and never let you go. Place all your confidence in him today and rest in the safety of his care!

Go Enjoy The Shepherd.

September 16

Blinded By Abundance
Mark 4:19

We had an abundance of rain that year in Tennessee and it had led to great growth in the fields. Sheep and cattle could not keep up, which meant the farmer did not have to worry about his livestock having plenty of food. The grass in my sheep fields had grown over waist deep, and we prepared to cut it for hay.

While awaiting the day for the hay cutting, I would go out and see the sheep. One day, I called for them to come to the shed for some corn, and I watched as they paced back and forth on the other side of the field. They were searching and hunting for the path back to the shed, but it had become overgrown by the abundant grass. It took several minutes for them to finally locate the overgrown path back to me. The abundance of grass had blinded them from being able to see the way back to the shepherd.

In our lives, we tend to live a life full of blessings and abundance. In America, we have what is called the "American Dream" which has filled more than we could truly ever need. Things begin to pile up around us, until one day we realize the abundance is keeping us from seeing the Good Shepherd.

Thankfully he carries with him a pruning rod with which to clear the path so we can see the one thing we desperately need, the Good Shepherd himself.

Go Enjoy The Shepherd.

September 17

Entangled
Psalm 116:3-4

Tessa was only four months old, still just a young lamb, and small in stature. As the older sheep made their way on the overgrown path through the hayfield, she struggled to make it. The grass was gripping her legs, causing her to stumble and fall. I noticed her stumbling along and went over to help her make it through the snares that were grasping her legs.

The things of this world are like that overgrown grass. They grow up around us and entangle us on our way back to the Good Shepherd. We are striving and struggling to get through, but we are held back by the weight of the world around us. Our only hope is for our Good Shepherd to lift us up and rescue us from the snares of our own overabundance.

Praise be to our Lord and Savior who has already made us a promise: that when we are entangled, he will hear our call for help, and he will rescue us from the snare of the Enemy. (Isaiah 55:6-7)

Go Enjoy The Shepherd

September 18

Not Listening
Zechariah 7:13

I found it quite interesting that the sheep suddenly began to ignore my calls to come in. I went out several mornings in a row and called them, but they refused to come to me at all. They would look up and then go back to eating. What was keeping them so occupied? The abundance of green grass.

In other words, they had more than enough to eat, so they did not seem to care to come to see what I had for them. They had become complacent in their abundance.

How many times have I found myself so engrossed in the bounty of my blessings, that I too ignored the call of the Good Shepherd to come be with him. How many times did he bring a blessing in his hand for me, yet I was too happy with what I had to let go and see what he was offering. I was so engrossed in my abundance that I simply refused to listen when he called.

Be careful not to allow the abundance of what is around you to keep you from the blessing in his hand. Yes, in order to receive it, you will have to leave behind what appears to be enough, but what he is offering is beyond your imagination.

Go Enjoy The Shepherd.

Every Single Inch
Psalm 37:23

I worked through the heat of that hot summer evening, carefully walking over every inch of the hayfield. I was pulling any poisonous weed or plant I could see in preparation of cutting the field for hay. Some of them were so small, hiding under the thick fescue grass. I was concerned I might miss one, and if I did, it could spell trouble or even death when the sheep feast on the hay during the winter. I lifted up my voice and simply asked, "Father, help me spot these weeds. I simply want to do my best for my sheep."

That was another one of those special moments in my walk with the Good Shepherd as he replied, "Me too, Ray."

So many times I fuss and argue in the moment I am in because it is not how I would like it to be. Then he reminds me that he has already gone before me in each step, preparing what is best for me. He has literally gone over every single inch of my life, removing the enemies who would cause me harm, and leaving only what is best and good for me. Because he is the Good Shepherd, I can be confident that he did not miss a single thing, even if it tried to hide from his sight.

Rejoice today, for your Good Shepherd has gone before you, going over every single inch of the path in front of you. He has carefully, and thoughtfully given himself to spot the poisons that are attempting to harm you, and he has removed them, leaving only what is best and good for you (even if it does not feel like it right now).

Go Enjoy The Shepherd.

September 20

Lift Them Up
1 Thessalonians 5:14

Once a ram has been replaced in the flock, and the leadership has passed on to a new ram, typically the old ram will simply go and be alone. This is especially true if the ram is older in age and does not have the strength or desire to try and regain his position in the flock. So, most of the day it will remain alone, sitting or grazing by himself.

However, it is not uncommon for the rest of the flock to come gather around the old ram and rest with him in the cool of the shade where he has gone. I have watched them as they have seemingly tried to encourage him to remember he is still a part of the family. What joy it brings my heart on the days I see him once again grazing the fields with the other sheep, having his head lifted up.

The Good Shepherd also smiles when he sees his sheep gather around and encourage those members of the flock who are discouraged, tired, weak, and feel alone. So often we try and separate from the flock and try and find comfort in our loneliness. But how great it is when the sheep of God gather around to lift up those who are broken and hurt, who are discouraged, and who feel alone. What joy must fill his heart when he sees those tired sheep once again grazing with the rest of the flock!

Today, look around you for those who are tired, weak, discouraged, downtrodden, broken, and confused. Go be with them, lift them up, encourage them, and remind them they are still one of his, a sheep of his pasture!

Go Enjoy The Shepherd.

September 21

Just To Be With You
Joshua 1:5

I am not a full-time shepherd as some might assume. I am a husband, father, minister of the good news of Jesus, a realtor, auctioneer, and a farmer. In other words, my days are full. So carving out time to just be with my sheep with no distractions can be difficult for me. However, it is one of my greatest joys, as it is a place of quiet for me, so I make it happen. At times, that means removing all distractions so I can focus on time with the sheep.

How grateful I am today that the Good Shepherd does not have to wrestle through a divided focus. His heart is on his people, and nothing can distract him from being with his flock. But it is not just that he is with them, it is that he enjoys simply being with his sheep.

That means today, the Good Shepherd is taking delight in simply being with you!

Go Enjoy The Shepherd.

September 22

Lost and Found
Luke 15:4

I walked up and down those hills searching and calling for my sheep. There was not a sound as darkness started to set in. All my other sheep were now safely in the new field, but I knew I could not leave this particular one out by herself. To do so would leave her and her new lambs as easy prey. I looked up the rocky hill covered in cedars and went searching.

I had no success on the way up and she still was not responding to my calls. I could understand her not wanting to give her position away to any predators, but I was there to help. I came down the hill and suddenly, in the corner of my eye, tucked away by a tree, was the ewe and her two babies. The biggest smile crossed my face as I went and lifted her twins into my arms and walked them all down the hill and over to the fresh green grass. As I passed by the house, my wife and kids all rejoiced with me on the finding of the one lost sheep!

Many today think it odd that so much effort would be put into finding just one. "Don't you have many more?" they might wonder? Yes I did, but to the shepherd, each one is highly valuable and worth seeking out.

Our Good Shepherd is seeking today all his lost lambs and sheep. Many think it odd that he would go to such lengths just to find one more, but that only reveals the fact that they do not understand the true heart of shepherd. A good shepherd is not willing that any should remain lost, but that each one will be found. So yes, today, the Good Shepherd is out looking for the One!

Go Enjoy The Shepherd.

September 23

Turn Around

1 Thessalonians 1:10

WLJ (initials for Wide Load Junior) was headed up the hill all by herself. She was nearing the time to have her lamb, and it was evident she wanted to be off to herself. Typically, this is not an issue, except, she was trying to burrow under the fence and get out of the field and into the wooded hillside. This could be extremely dangerous, especially with the coyotes who loved to roam those hills.

I quickly ran out the back door and jumped the gate. She was already half way under the fence when I reached her. When I got there, I reached through and hooked her with my staff and pulled her back into the field. With a loving tap on the rear, I urged her on back down the hill. If I had let her go, she certainly would have played right into the enemy's hands.

We are like sheep, and we love to go our own way. It may not seem like a big deal at the moment; however, like sheep, we are often unaware of the danger that lies ahead. Thankfully the Good Shepherd watches us and sees us heading into the enemy's hands. He runs to us and "hooks" us, which can feel painful, but it is a sign of his great love for us as he urges us back to where we are supposed to be.

Today, thank him for the paths He rescued you from which would have most certainly led you into a place of wrath.

Go Enjoy The Shepherd.

September 24

No Cutting Corners
Joshua 11:15

I never really like admitting my shortcomings in life, but that story yesterday about WLJ and the fence revealed a laziness on my part. You see, on that hill was a simple two-strand barbed wire fence that had been put up for cattle. It was never intended to keep sheep in; however, I had not done anything to change it because I figured sheep would not even want to go up on a rocky hillside.

WLJ showed me I was wrong and I could not cut corners if I wanted to be a good shepherd. A few weeks later, a new woven wire fence was in place to properly do the job.

This story reminded me of how our Good Shepherd did not cut any corners. When he came, he did not try and skirt the edges of the law, he kept it (John 8:29, 1 Peter 2:22). When securing his sheep, he left nothing undone. He made sure it was complete before he said "It Is Finished!" (John 19:30).

When he comes to you and extends his hand to invite you into his sheepfold, you can rest assured he has not left anything undone or overlooked. His work is complete and in his hands you are safe.

Go Enjoy The Shepherd.

September 25

Breath of Life
Genesis 2:7

That new fence got completed just in time. WLJ started her birthing process literally days after that fence was done. She had made her way up the hill against the fence, and it was clear we would soon see new birth.

Except, nearly the whole day passed without the appearance of a new lamb. WLJ had already had several lambs in her life, so one would assume it would not be a big issue for her to have another. That evening, I went with my daughters and we got close to WLJ. She was not happy to see us, as she would prefer to be left alone; however, this process had gone on too long. After a few minutes, we had her on her side and I realized what the issue was, her lamb was turned backwards.

I struggled to get the lamb pulled out, and once I did I assumed it was dead from its lifeless appearance. The strain of the birthing process seemed to have taken the life right out of it. WLJ came over and started to lick her newborn lamb, and a sadness swept over me, until—I saw the lamb take in a deep breath. The simple touch of its mother seemed to spark her to life, and a beautiful ewe lamb was born.

That reminded me of how I once was dead, seemingly with no hope at all. Then the Good Shepherd came to me, reached down to my lifeless soul, and just like he did with Adam, he breathed into me his breath of life.

Today, take a moment and reflect on the glory of our Good Shepherd and remember the time he breathed the breath of life into you. Then . . .

Go Enjoy The Shepherd.

Just Like He Is, Just As You Are
Luke 15:20

I drove up the drive after a day at work. I had on some of my nicer clothes, but I saw an opportunity to go hang out with my sheep for just a minute. I parked the truck, entered the gate, and was greeted by Caesar and the other sheep. I thought of a story my grandfather told me of how he used to drive his tractor while wearing his suit after work just so he could beat the darkness. How funny that must have seemed to onlookers, much like me walking in the field with my sheep in my nicer clothes.

It was a great opportunity for me though to hear another whisper from the Good Shepherd himself. He showed me how he too comes to me just like he is, in all his radiance and glory, not worried about his own apparel. He does not go dress up in a hazmat suit in order to be near me in the midst of all my filth. But rather, because of his sacrifice and payment for my sin, he now embraces me in all his glory while I stand in all my filth. Nothing can now separate him from his sheep because his sacrifice was accepted, and the price was fully paid!

Go to him today just as you are because he will embrace you just like he is!

Go Enjoy The Shepherd.

September 27

Momentary Afflictions
2 Corinthians 4:17

Susie Q was one very unhappy sheep. Not only was she in the pen, she had watched me work through all the other sheep and now it was just her, alone with me in the stall. Her nerves were on edge as she watched me come close. Seemingly calculating her escape plan, she made a dart for the door, only to be captured by the shepherd. She jumped and bucked for a moment until I had her on her backside and leaning against my legs. Suddenly she grew still while I checked her for worms and clipped her hooves.

I was hot and extremely tired after having worked through all the other sheep. Being a small operation, I have to physically handle each of the sheep and that can certainly wear you out. While working on Susie Q and some of the others, they tried to get away even when in the submission position, but what they did not understand was that these momentary afflictions they were enduring were going to lead to better health for the months to come. Though they did not like it, it was for their good to endure the momentary discomfort.

Are you suffering through some pain and afflictions? Have you gone through a trial of great pain or loss. Have you asked the question, "Why?" I know I have. It is hard to understand how pain can be a part of growth or how these heart aches can lead to something better; however, we must trust that the Good Shepherd knows what we need. We must be confident in our belief that he does everything for our good and even this momentary affliction will lead to greater glory.

Go Enjoy The Shepherd.

Just in Time
Romans 5:6

After the hay was cut, the field looked like a scene of death. Under all the thick and heavy abundance was what appeared to be a choked-out undergrowth. It was amazing seeing the difference between the grass I kept mowed and the hayfield side by side. The grass that I kept short looked full and green with life. Under the hay it was brown and yellow, on the verge of dying out.

Under all the brown though was a small hint of green. Short shoots of green grass were making their way up toward the sun above. We had literally cut the hay just in the nick of time which allowed the new growth a chance at life which would soon become the grass the sheep would need to live.

Many times in your life, you will feel the over-abundance of blessings around you. As we have talked about, they can choke the life right out of you. So the Good Shepherd comes along just in the nick of time and trims away all the overgrowth so the sprouts of life, growth in your walk with him, can spring up and bring you new life.

Go Enjoy The Shepherd.

September 29

Path of Life
Psalm 16:11

It stood out like a bright shining light in the middle of darkness. If you looked at our field, there was no way you could miss it. It was a skinny path of gorgeous green grass in the middle of all the brown left after cutting the hay. This was the path I walked every day when going to see the sheep, and the path they walked to come visit me at the gate. Now, with all the overgrowth cut back, its life of green grass stood out amongst the death all around it.

This was such a beautiful picture of the path of life that leads us back to our Good Shepherd. In his footsteps is life and life abundantly. It stands out like a light in the midst of the death and darkness of this world. It is easy to see as it springs up with life because it is the path that the Good Shepherd walks, leading all his sheep to follow him not only in life, but life more abundant.

Go Enjoy The Shepherd.

September 30

No Need to Worry
Matthew 6:28-30

Not once, in all my time as a shepherd, have I seen any of my sheep run around and wonder about what they are going to eat on the next day. As funny as that might sound, it is simply true. No sheep has ever laid down and concerned itself with what tomorrow holds. They don't fret or panic about food or water or the weather, they simply live and enjoy the moment.

There is a reason sheep can live like that, because they have come to trust the shepherd to make sure they have all they need. During the Spring, Summer, and Fall months they have all they need to eat and drink supplied by the fields and the streams. While that is going on I am preparing for the winter ahead and putting hay away in order to feed them through the Winter. They do not have to worry because the shepherd has already taken care of what they will need, not only today, but tomorrow as well.

Jesus told us that he is the Good Shepherd and that we can be like the sheep and just enjoy today. He has provided everything we need to live now, and he has already taken care of our needs of tomorrow.

Therefore, do not worry about what you will eat or what you will drink, or what you will wear, for these are the things the world concerns itself with. Do not worry about tomorrow because your Good Shepherd holds tomorrow in his hands.

Go Enjoy The Shepherd.

October 1

Hope with the Shepherd
Matthew 9:36

Sheep who live life without a shepherd are of all creatures to be most pitied. Sheep absolutely need direction and care. If there is no one there to watch over them, they will certainly perish and die. Without a shepherd, sheep are literally hopeless.

However, as long as the shepherd is with them, the sheep have absolutely nothing to worry about. Without him, they will go hungry, but with him they will always have food. Without the shepherd, sheep will be thirsty, but with him they will never lack for water to drink. Without the shepherd they are defenseless against the predators of this world, but with the shepherd they are safe under his watchful eye. In other words, as long as the sheep have a shepherd, they have hope!

You are the sheep in the pasture of the Good Shepherd. This means no matter what is going on around you or in your life, you always have hope. As long as you are under his watchful care, you will never lack what you need in the moment. He is watching over you and because he is good and his promises never fail, you will always have Hope!

Today, share the hope you have with the Good Shepherd with someone who is hopeless. Invite them to join you in drawing close to his side. Share the hope with those who are without it!

Go Enjoy The Shepherd.

October 2

God Chooses the Shepherd
Psalm 78:70-72

I have often wondered why God decided to put me in charge of some sheep. It just seemed to go against everything else in my life. Tending to sheep takes time, energy, and effort. I learned quickly that it was not a method of taking care of my family's needs as there was not enough money in a small operation to provide for our family of six. So why do this?

Over time God has revealed it is much bigger than just sheep in the field. He was pouring into me lessons which I could one day share in order to encourage the members of his flock. God consistently through Scripture shown how he will place men in a trade in order to teach them how to care for his people. In other words, what they were doing was much bigger than the small picture they saw at the moment.

The Good Shepherd was chosen by God to watch over us and to care for us as the sheep of his pasture. We could not have asked for a greater caretaker to be chosen for this position. His heart is to always please his Father, and he knows that properly caring for the sheep is what will bring his Father the greatest joy. Therefore, he was able to face the difficulties in his life with confidence because he trusted the plan of the Great Shepherd who was watching over him.

Whatever you are going through today may make little sense to you. You may not understand the point, the purpose of it all, but you can be like Jesus, and you can trust the heart of the Good Shepherd. You can believe he is preparing you and using this circumstance, not only for your benefit, but for the benefit of others in his flock as well. He has chosen you specifically for this moment and this time, so trust him through whatever you are facing! Something great is on the way.

Go Enjoy The Shepherd.

October 3

Before the Judge
Isaiah 61:3

What a grand site it is to watch these young 4-H competitors bring out their prized sheep they have raised and groomed for this moment. Hours of work have gone into making it to this very moment, to show off to the world their sheep they raised have raised. Children of all ages line up with their prized lambs and present them to the judges. Methodically the judge checks them over and inspects every last detail. The sheep stands still in the arms of its shepherd until the judge has completed his task, hoping to be accepted into the "hall of champions."

What a thought that one day our Good Shepherd will stand before the Judge and present us to be inspected in every detail. That thought can both be exciting and terrifying at the same time. To know that every inch will be checked, every detail will be gone over to see if you are worthy to be granted entrance into the eternal glory he has prepared for his own.

However, those who are members of the Good Shepherd's flock can stand there in peace because of this truth: it is the shepherd's responsibility to have you ready to be judged. No sheep is brought out to be judged in 4-H until the shepherd has completed their preparations. They are on a time limit and they must have their work finished before the time is out.

The Good Shepherd knows the task ahead of him when it comes to each of his sheep. Yet he has already promised he will finish what he has begun (Philippians 1:6). So you can stand confident today that he will have you ready to stand before the Judge!

Go Enjoy The Shepherd.

October 4

Going Back
Jeremiah 3:22

Nothing hurts quite as much as having a lamb you raised by hand turn away from you. I simply could not believe that this little lamb that I had spent so much time with had now decided to revert back to being a sheep who was shy and afraid.

I watched as she fell in with the sheep of my flock who were fearful of me. She began to mimic them and avoid me, ignore me, and refuse to accept my love. She had literally gone back to the old ways of a sheep and turned her back on the one who had given her life from the very beginning.

As much as that hurt me to watch, it pained me even more when I realized how I am so much like that little lamb. I have been rescued from the grips of eternal death by the bleeding hands of the Good Shepherd. I was given new life by the touch of his hands and lifted up from darkness into light. So often though, I turn my back on him, reverting back to the ways of those around me and ignoring him while I graze in the blessings he has provided.

But praise be to God, he will not give up on us. Just as I continued with hope and efforts of loving that little lamb, I know he will never give up on me. As often as I stray, he will never stop in his fierce determination to have me as his own. The Good Shepherd never stops drawing his sheep to himself, even when they have turned their backs on him.

If you are ignoring him today, choosing the way of death over the touch of his hand, he is calling out to you. Run back into his arms, Jesus longs to hold you once again.

Go Enjoy The Shepherd.

October 5

Be a Blessing
Zechariah 8:13

Sheep have an amazing talent. You can put them on an old, downtrodden farm, and if managed right, you can see a complete recovery of the land. A field full of weeds and thistles, after a time with sheep, can turn into a luscious pasture of green grass and return the farm to one of prosperity and usefulness.

When the Good Shepherd sends out his sheep into the harvest fields of the lands of this earth, his intention is for them to be a blessing to those around them. The world has been overrun with the weeds and thistles of sin and devastation, but the Good Shepherd has redeemed a flock and he intends on redeeming the land.

Today, ask God what he would like you to do in order to help him redeem what has been decimated by sin and return it to a beautiful display of his glory.

Go Enjoy The Shepherd.

October 6

Turning on the Sheep
Jeremiah 23:1-2

I simply could not believe my eyes. How could this beautiful puppy, whose job was to protect the sheep, become such a vessel of destruction. I was horrified at the sight of a young lamb who had become dinner for the one who had been given charge to defend it against all predators. Instead, the guardian became the destroyer.

The Good Shepherd has made it very clear what he will do to anyone who turns against his sheep in his pastures. He has warned all who would dare forget their role as guardian and decide to become an instrument of destruction. In other words, the Good Shepherd takes very seriously the role of watching over his sheep and he will defend it against all enemies, even those who are supposed to be their defenders and protectors. He is not willing that anyone should lead his sheep astray.

Pray for those today that God has given charge to watch over you. Pray they remain faithful in their watch. Then pray for those you have been given charge to protect and guard, and remain true to the high calling of being a shepherd to his sheep.

Go Enjoy The Shepherd.

October 7

Never Too Late
Luke 23:39-43

Mauro was probably one of the crankiest rams I had ever owned. He was not abusive like Bam-Bam, but he was extremely cranky.

He had been raised on a farm with wide open spaces and it was clear he had not been forced to have much human contact. He simply preferred not to be close to a person. He never threatened me or my kids, but he was in no way interested in being like Bob who was an extremely gentle ram we had owned prior.

As Mauro grew older, he began to be a little less contrary around me. He was a gorgeous red ram with a very thick mane, giving him the appearance of a lion from a distance. One day, much to my surprise, I found him nestled up next to me as I attended another sheep. I reached down and began to pet him and rub him, which he seemed to really enjoy. I could not help but think, "See, you're never too old to get to know the shepherd."

The Good Shepherd does not impose any restrictions on coming close to him. He never refuses anyone who will come, no matter the day, the time, or the year. His arms are opened wide and his love is never-ending. It is not too late to come today.

Go Enjoy The Shepherd.

October 8

Needless Death
Romans 6:23

I walked along the old trail on the hillside and found a disturbing sight. Just below the trail was the bones of what once was a sheep. She had been missing for a while, and after much searching it was determined she had been lost for good. On that day, I found the evidence of what I feared had happened—she had fallen prey to the coyotes who had attacked.

As I looked at her skeleton there, licked clean by the ravaging predators, I could not help but think, "Your death was so unnecessary!" Had she not run away from the safety of the field, she would have not had to endure such a horrible death. Had she not wanted what she was not supposed to have, if she would have been content with what had been provided for her, then she would still be enjoying the life of a well-cared-for sheep.

So many times, in our walk with the Good Shepherd, we act like this ewe. We see something just on the other side of his protective care, and we long to have it. We struggle against the fence and seek for a way to get where we think we want to be, only to fall into the hands of the Enemy. The wages of sin is death!

The Scriptures are full of stories of men and women who "kicked against the pricks" so much and so often that it led to an untimely death. Today, let us take heed to this warning and stay close to the Shepherd.

If you find yourself today outside of the fence of his protection, call him while he is near so you may be found! (Isaiah 55:6)

Go Enjoy The Shepherd.

October 9

A Sign of Wealth

1 Samuel 25:2

One may not think of sheep and wealth in the same sentence. I know I do not consider myself "rich" because I have sheep. I do however consider myself blessed to have them and learn from them about my Good Shepherd and his love for me.

However, in biblical times, when someone is mentioned to have been wealthy, many times you will see a number of sheep mentioned, like here in this passage. We also see them mentioned in Job as well and the story of Jacob and Laban. In other words, the wealthy owner was proud to have sheep!

What a glorious thought that our Good Shepherd considers himself "wealthy" because he has us as his sheep. He does not count his silver or gold or all the treasures that he owns as a sign of his riches; instead, when he wants to display his great wealth and glory, he shows people his sheep! That means he considers you the reason he is rich!

Go Enjoy The Shepherd.

A Sheep's Prayer
Psalm 119:176

It was the only sound in the field that morning. As I walked toward the gate, it was the cry of desperation I heard. There sat a little lamb by the gate, pacing back and forth. I wondered what in the world was going on? This was a freshly born, healthy lamb, but no mother in sight. If her bleating could have been words, she was saying, "Please save me, I am about to die!"

I felt fortunate to have found her before it was too late. She became a very special lamb in our lives and we spent many hours enjoying time with her. I am so glad I was able to hear her cry and rescue her from death.

The Psalmist has just completed the longest running song of his heart, and at the end he cries out just like that little lamb. He declares he has gone astray and he pleads with his shepherd to seek him and find him.

How amazing is it today that you have the opportunity to cry out to the Good Shepherd and plead with him to seek you out and find you. His ears are ever attentive to the cries of his people, and he longs to find all those who have gone astray. His heart is for his people, which means his heart is for you!

Go Enjoy The Shepherd.

October 11

Be Like Sheep
Philippians 4:5-7

As I scanned the field, everything seemed to be perfectly in order. The sheep were munching on the grass and the guard dog was basking in the sun. It was a quiet morning, a scene of peace and serenity. What struck me most was the contentment displayed by the sheep. They were doing what they were created to do, just be a sheep and enjoy what was put before them.

Life is full of distractions and frustrations which vie for your attention. Little hiccups to the "norm" of life come bouncing along in an effort to draw your eyes away from the reality that all your needs are taken care of. Life sometimes screams at you for attention, yet, the Good Shepherd gently whispers, "Be like sheep."

Today, be like those sheep. Remember the Good Shepherd already knows what you have need of. He has both supplied for today and he has taken care of tomorrow. So "Be like sheep" and simply enjoy him and the life he has for you today!

Go Enjoy The Shepherd.

October 12

The Son Always Shines
Proverbs 4:18

I walked with my daughters and we discussed the fact that the sun was hiding that day. Clouds filled the sky, causing a gloominess to the day. Sheep were grazing in the field as normal, nothing really seemed to distract them from the lack of the bright sun that day. We, however, were feeling the effects of the gloominess offered by such a "grey day."

I remember the day so well because I was able to share with my daughters that no matter what we saw from our side, the sun was still shining. We might not be able to see it for that moment, but its effects could still be realized. It was gloomy, but it was not dark. Though the clouds blocked part of the light, the power of the sun still brought us the light of day. So whether we could see it or not, the fact the sun was there had not changed and like the sheep, we could continue about our day as normal, trusting in the truth that the sun was still shining.

Your life may feel like one of those dark, cloudy days. You may look up and not be able to see the Good Shepherd watching over you, but it does not change the truth in his words that he will always be there. Circumstances may shroud the beauty of life in the moment, but you can rest assured, the Son is still shining.

Go Enjoy The Shepherd.

October 13

Who Am I?
Psalm 8

Every year, countless sheep are tossed aside in heaps of bodies, left to die because they are "not worth the effort to save." Large sheep operations bury sheep by the thousands each year, sheep who are dead or close to death. They are simply numbers in a mob of sheep and there are too many healthy ones to deal with the sick. It is easier to simply let them die.

My gallbladder is my least favorite organ. I know it has a very important function, but mine loves to give me fits during gallbladder attacks. These are long and painful hours of suffering, which I assure you have much prayer involved. Many times I think of all the others who are suffering at that moment, and I think "who am I" to be asking for help. However, I know my Good Shepherd is not interested in simply casting me aside to die in a heap of flesh. Rather, he is the shepherd who runs to me and holds me close and tends to my needs. His heart is to care for the sick and bring life to those on the brink of death.

Do you feel cast aside, left alone to die? Has the world or someone you love turned their back on you? Then be encouraged! You are being sought out by the Good Shepherd, so he can hold you close, lift you up, and rescue you from the brink of death. He desires to give you a life with him, which is the only real and true life!

Go Enjoy The Shepherd.

October 14

Sheep and Stars
Psalm 147:4, Isaiah 40:26

I enjoy the cool evenings of Fall as the skies are clearer than normal here in Tennessee. It is such a pleasure to go out in the field with the sheep and just look up into the vast expanse of space and stare at the beauty of the stars.

On one of these occasions I was pondering the words I had recently read about the marvel of these stars. How vast is the number of them. Some estimates have there being 300 million, billion, stars. That is a ton of stars. Their size and brilliance are unmatched in all the universe. Yet they rotate perfectly in an orderly fashion, all under the control of the Good Shepherd according to Isaiah 40:26.

What an amazing thought that the God of the universe would create such wonders, and know them all by name. How much more amazing is it that he then says, like a Good Shepherd, I know the name of each of my children, not one of them is missing!

What that means for you today is that, in his eyes, you shine brighter than the stars in the heavens above. His eyes are on you, and you are never missing from his sight!

Go Enjoy The Shepherd.

October 15

In His Image
Genesis 1:27

As I stare at the stars while hanging out with the sheep, I cannot help but think of all the shepherds in Scripture who did the same. They would be out for the entire evening with their sheep, and the stars would be their only companion. I imagine as I stare at them, they too were taken back by the glory of it all.

Stars are amazing, and though we have learned a lot, we know so little of them in reality. Some have been measured and estimated in size. One in particular has been said to be so large, that it would not fit between the earth and our sun. Now that is a big star! When I think on these things, I am simply astounded at how mighty our Good Shepherd is that he created these marvels for us to enjoy.

Then I hear the whisper in my ear, "Yes, they are marvelous, but I did not create them in my image! I made YOU in my image. You are the crowning moment of my creation. You are the apple of my eye. You stare at the stars in awe and wonder, but I stare at you and it takes My breath away. You behold the beauty of the stars, but I choose to behold the beauty of my greatest creation, You!"

Go Enjoy The Shepherd.

October 16

Thinking About You
Psalm 139:17

As I was preparing for bed, I was thinking about what I needed to get done for the sheep before going to sleep. As I was sleeping, I would wake up and remember something that had to be done for the sheep in the near future. I woke up and instantly thought of the sheep who needed special attention that day for sores and flies. All day long, I am thinking about my sheep and what they need for me to do for them.

I am constantly thinking about my sheep. Do they have enough grass or hay? Is there enough water for them? If it is going to storm, is the shelter properly prepared to house them? If they are sick, do I have the right things on hand to make them better? When the coyotes howl, do they feel safe and comfortable? Like I said, I am always thinking about my sheep!

How precious are his thoughts toward you, how VAST is the sum of them? I hope you understand today how much he is thinking about you. You are always on his mind. He is constantly making sure you are being cared for and have what you need. It may not feel like it, but it is true, the Good Shepherd is always thinking about you!

Go Enjoy The Shepherd.

Huddle Up
Romans 14:19

I listened with great enthusiasm as a fellow shepherd relayed the story of the guard dog he owned that had once lived on our farm as a foster pup. Red was a gorgeous Karakachan and from the sound of the story, she was great at her job.

As the coyotes bore down upon her flock one night, she hustled around her flock of sheep and acted like a herding dog more than a guardian. However, her herding was to push them all into the hallway of the barn. Once she had accomplished her goal, she turned and faced the enemy, sitting in the doorway. Her partner in defense, Junior (a large male dog who was born on our farm), raced off toward the coyotes, successfully defending the sheep from devastation.

Now, Red could have just reacted to the coyotes and went to join the fight, but her instinct was to huddle them up into a safe spot in order to better protect them. Her goal was not just to win a fight, but to make sure her sheep were safe.

The Good Shepherd knows that in order for us to be safe, his sheep must huddle up, especially when under attack. Our tendency sometimes is to race off just to win the battle, however, in our hurry to fight, we often leave the body exposed.

Today, the Enemy is on the move, attempting to scatter the flock of the Good Shepherd and pick them off. The Good Shepherd knows his plans, and he calls on his people to "huddle up," and from there we can watch him go and win the fight!

Go Enjoy The Shepherd.

October 18

It Is Not Okay
Deuteronomy 31:6

Today, things just do not feel right. Things are just "off" in the field and outside of it. The sheep do not settle in and something is amiss. No matter how many times I scan the field, there is no sign of agitation or anything out of place, but the sheep are not settled. It simply is a day where things are "out of whack."

On these days, there is only one thing that is steady, that is the shepherd. I cannot see what has them feeling troubled, but I can do the one thing I know to do, watch over them and make sure they know that I am there.

There are days in your life, maybe today, that things are just feeling "off." You may, or may not, know what the problem is. You may not be able to "fix" it. However, one thing remains constant, the Good Shepherd is watching over you. He sees your agitation, he knows what it is, and he is working to bring you calm in the middle of your storm.

Go Enjoy The Shepherd.

October 19

Redeemed
Ephesians 1:7

She was a lovely sight to see, bounding on the hillside behind her mom. Sparkling white, she stood out in the middle of the large green fields. She was one of the first lambs born in the new field near the beginning of our tenure as shepherds. We sat on our porch and stared at the marvel of seeing yet another lamb grown in our fields.

When I arrived home, the concern on my wife's face was real. "She has not moved much all day! I sent the girls to check on her and she is alive, but something isn't right!" Realizing the level of concern in my wife's voice, I immediately headed to the field and walked straight up the hill to the lamb. She was breathing, but she was not able to stand on her own legs. Her mom was close by with a look of concern as well, so I scooped her up and carried her to the shed.

Babe was diagnosed with White Muscles Disease, an almost certain killer at the stage of the disease she was in. She was not able to stand to drink, and it was clear she would soon die. I could have easily written her off and put her down, but I was determined to give it my best to make it work. Months later, I smiled as I watched her run and play in the fields. What was once close to death, had been redeemed back to life.

Like Babe, you may be close to the edge of spiritual death. Your very ability to drink the living water may have slipped away from you. All your spiritual muscles may be frozen and riddled with sin, but no one, yes, not a single soul, is too far gone to be redeemed in the hands of the Good Shepherd.

Go Enjoy The Shepherd.

October 20

Home of the Shepherd
Exodus 26:14

It is no secret that sheep's wool and leathers have been used for years for clothing and protection from weather. In war, many wool outfits and blankets have been used to shelter the soldiers from the cold weather. Leathers have been used to make sandals and coverings for the feet.

Even God himself used the skin of rams as the covering of his first tent here on earth. He made his home inside the skins of rams dedicated to the Tabernacle. He commanded each family to dedicate a certain number of skins to be used for the purpose of creating the covering for his tent in the middle of them.

Now he has chosen to make his home inside of you and me (1 Corinthians 6:19), the sheep of his pasture (Ezekiel 34:31). He still has chosen the "skins of sheep" to be his preferred home. That means he has chosen you as his preferred dwelling place.

Go Enjoy The Shepherd.

October 21

Used as Payment
Genesis 12:16

Often in the Old Testament, sheep have been used to buy land, pay dowries, and to secure peace. Kings would attack lands and part of the payment to secure peace would be flocks of sheep. Abraham received many sheep from Pharaoh when he lied about his wife and allowed her to be taken by the king of Egypt. Sheep were traded for many things in order to gain something of greater value.

That is why it took a lamb to secure the price of the slaves to sin. When God required a payment to be made, he said only a lamb without spot would satisfy his demands. Eventually the time came for the final price to be paid, and only the perfect Lamb would suffice.

The Good Shepherd became the Lamb so he could gain something he considered to be of far greater value. You!

Go Enjoy The Shepherd.

October 22

About to Explode
Matthew 24:8

Wideload has by far been the largest pregnant ewe I have ever owned. She came in with the initial load of sheep from Texas, and months later she appeared ready to literally burst. I watched her intently for weeks, eventually thinking something was wrong. Were these lambs ever going to make their entrance into the world?

Giving birth to a new lamb takes time. In order to fully develop and be prepared for birth, the lamb must be allowed its fully allotted time inside the womb in order to be ready to take on life ahead. It must not be rushed or the lamb will more than likely not make it when it arrives.

The Good Shepherd knows this as well, and although, like me, he looks with longing anticipation for the birth of the new believers, he knows it must come at the proper time. Otherwise, the newborn may not be prepared to face the reality of the life ahead and will quickly die. So he watches and he waits for when that perfect moment arrives, then he leaps with joy as he embraces his new little lamb!

Go Enjoy The Shepherd.

October 23

The Day of Birth Is Here
Romans 8:18-22

As I walked up to the field, I noticed my guard dog, Cheta, pestering Wideload. Immediately upon arriving in the field it was clear why—she was in labor. I quickly gathered her up and put her in a small lambing stall in the shed. The day of birth had arrived.

My excitement level went through the roof as my two young daughters were with me that day. How much fun was it going to be for them to witness a birth of a lamb for the first time. True anticipation filled the air as we waited for these lambs to arrive.

The whole earth groans in anticipation as the good Shepherd watches with joy the beginning stages of the new birth of one of his own. What joy floods his heart as you share the good news of the Gospel with those around you, then life starts to form. As the time draws near, he is present, watching with all the host of angels, for life to burst forth and a Birthday of a new child of God to be created!

Join him today in great anticipation over the birth of new disciples around you! Be ever watchful, mindful, and in prayer as the birthing process begins.

Go Enjoy The Shepherd.

October 24

A Little Help
Ephesians 2:8, Luke 15:17

We watched as the little lamb's head poked out. My daughters were giddy with glee as they watched the lamb being born. However, something was not right as the process came to a standstill. I watched for a moment, then I made a phone call. Little did the girls know, this was my first time watching a lamb be born as well.

I called Bill, a much more experienced shepherd, and explained what was going on. He quickly gave me my marching orders, which included preparing to pull the lamb(s). I knew with Wideload, it was going to be more than one lamb, because she was so big.

Nervously I washed my hands in the warm water my wife brought up, then I slowly reached in and grabbed the body of the lamb. What a moment to be a part of, helping give birth to a new life on the farm. My girls were ecstatic when the lamb made his arrival. A healthy ram lamb appeared. Moments later, I assisted in the birth of the second lamb, another healthy ram lamb. What a beautiful moment to share with my family.

You may be in the middle of long "birth pains" as you have been sharing the love of the Good Shepherd with a family member or a friend. You may have been watching with anticipation, longing for the moment of birth to arrive, yet it seems to not come. Let me encourage you with this. He is watching, and he is helping. His hands are ready to reach down and bring forth the life ready to be born. What you must do is simply ask him to bring it to pass.

When the moment arrives, Jesus will rejoice with you as the new life is born!

Go Enjoy The Shepherd.

October 25

More Than Expected
2 Corinthians 9:6

I walked to the house, slightly exhausted from the whole ordeal of helping Wideload give birth to her two new ram lambs. That had been my first experience of "pulling lambs," and once the joy and excitement wore off, I admittedly felt the adrenaline rush subside. I sat for about 20 minutes, listening to my girls bubble in excitement of what we had just done together.

Catching my breath, I decided to walk back up to the shed and make sure the lambs were doing okay. When I arrived, I was not prepared for what I was about to see. There stood Wideload with her twins, but protruding from the birth canal was yet another head. A triplet was ready to make his arrival. I had to assist again in the birth, but when it was over, our farm was the proud owners of its first-ever set of triplets. Overjoyed, I ran home to share the news and we all came back to bask in the joy of this beautiful sight.

Sometimes, when you are sharing the love of the Good Shepherd with another, you may think you are only sowing seeds in one individual's life. However, the Shepherd has a greater plan, and you may reap much more than you ever imagined. So keep sowing and trust him for the harvest—it may be more than you ever expected!

Go Enjoy The Shepherd.

October 26

Beware of the Fence
Exodus 19:12

The original fence on the old farm place was a five-strand electric fence. For the purpose of the sheep, I added two more strands to the bottom. When this fence is on, it is extremely hot and will turn any animal around once touched. The point is to keep the animals where they are supposed to be.

One day, I was out working on another issue on the farm and let's just say, I got lit up. The fence was working at full strength and it lifted up my body off the ground and I made a thud as I landed on my belly. Just a little pop reminded me of the power of electricity and why I so often saw one of my sheep leap when it got too close to this fence.

As I lay there recovering from the thud of my body hitting the ground, I thought of how much he must love me when he allows the sting of my creeping too close to temptation to shock my soul. When I walk too close to the boundaries he has placed for my protection, the Good Shepherd allows me to receive a huge warning before I go too far. He may even lay me flat out in order to keep me from death and destruction. It does not "feel" good, but how gracious of him to care enough for his sheep to set boundaries for our protection and even allow us every so often to be reminded of the shocking death of sin.

Go Enjoy The Shepherd.

October 27

Foolish Trade
Philippians 4:11-13

I was completely fed up with how things were going. Sheep were dropping on me left and right. I was trying my best to keep them alive, but these sheep were determined to die. I decided I had endured enough of this with hair sheep, and I sold them all and told my wife I was going to buy me some more "hardy" wool sheep for our farm.

I arrived late in the evening with my new flock of wool sheep. I had purchased four to start, and figured I would grow my flock from there. As I opened the trailer, these four sheep went berserk and tore through the panel fence and ran into the darkness.

That was just the beginning of my issues. They were completely different than my hair sheep. They did not know me like the others had come to, and my guard dog seemed to strike terror in their hearts. After 30 days, I completely regretted my decision to sell my other sheep. I simply did not realize how good I really had it and that the issues I was having were something I could learn from for my future in raising of sheep. Needless to say, it was not long before I abandoned this new project and became the owner of hair sheep once again.

The lesson in this is simple, contentment. So often we look at what we have and we get tired, or bored and decide we need a change. Without consulting the Good Shepherd, we head off in a new direction which only leads to greater frustrations. Today, be still and be content, thanking him for everything you have and trusting him to lead you down the next path. Otherwise, you might be like me, sitting in the middle of the field and shaking your head wondering what you have done.

Go Enjoy The Shepherd.

October 28
The Common Denominator
Hebrews 12:14-17

I stood in awe of what I was watching. My ram was standing there, nose to nose with my guard dog and both seemed to be enjoying themselves. Although by nature they should be enemies, because of their unique relationship with me as the shepherd, they had now become friends. In other words, they had something in common which brought them together.

Each member of the Good Shepherd's flock is unique in their own way. Some are laid back, some are aggressive. Some tend to be tender, others coarse and rough around the edges. Some are timid like prey, others are fierce like the predators of the wild. So what can hold all these unique pieces together in unity? The one thing they have in common—the Good Shepherd.

Today, as you live with those who may by nature cause you to want to be enemies, remember you serve the same Lord and allow him to bring unity in the midst of your diversity!

Go Enjoy The Shepherd.

October 29

Helping One Another
1 Corinthians 12:27

At certain times of the year, you can find gathered together in one field my sheep, cows, chickens, a horse, and every so often one of the cats. That is a lot of different types of animals in one place at one time. However, each of them provides a benefit for the other.

The chickens peck around and eat ticks and bugs in the grass that could be a pest to the sheep. The sheep stir up more insects for the chickens to eat as they walk around. My guardian dog provides protection against the wily coyotes for all the animals in the field. The sheep and other animals provide a family for the guard dog. The cows and sheep do not share the same parasites, therefore as they graze, they help to eliminate potential worm problems for one another. The horse provides a sense of dignity and stability to all the creatures, having eyes peeled in all directions. In other words, they each are different, but they each play a significant role as a family.

How true is that of the flock of the Good Shepherd. His fields are full of members who are all different, yet each plays an important role for the function of the whole. If one part is missing, the rest will suffer from it. However, when each member is functioning properly, the body can accomplish much good together.

Today, be sure to do your part as an unique member of his flock.

Go Enjoy The Shepherd.

October 30

Red, Yellow, Black, and White
John 17:23

In my short tenure as a shepherd, I have had the joy of owning many different kinds of sheep. This is true mainly because the first loads that came from Texas had such a wide variety. I was once asked, "How many kinds of sheep are there?" If you do a quick search, you will find there are over one thousand different breeds of sheep.

To name just a few, I have owned, White Dorper, Black Face Dorper, White Katahdin, Red Katahdin, St Croix, Hawaiian Black, Painted Desert, Southdown, Hampshire, and Speckled Sheep—just to name a few. There are hair sheep, wool sheep, and sheep with fiber coats. I have had sheep with horns and sheep without. I have had red sheep, white sheep, black sheep, brown sheep, yellow sheep, red with white spots, black with white spots, white with black or red spots, yellow with spots, and the list goes on.

However, one fact was always true. When I put those sheep in a field together, they all acted like sheep. They would all flock up and eventually live as a single family. They did not see differences, they saw other sheep.

The Good Shepherd longs for the sheep in his flock to act like these sheep I have owned. He longs for us to lay aside our differences and focus on the one thing that is true, he is the Shepherd of us all. We do not need to see color, or race, or things that will separate us. His heart is that we would be one with him and each other, just like he and his Father are one.

Today, let us lay aside the things that seem to separate us, and let us live as one body, with one Head, the Good Shepherd.

Go Enjoy The Shepherd.

October 31

No Fear
2 Timothy 1:7

"Come on Dad, let me try!" cried my oldest daughter. She was all of eight years old at the time, but she wanted so bad to catch a larger lamb by herself. She had determination written all over her face, despite the fact the lambs already outweighed her at only five months old.

Reluctantly, I agreed to let her try and catch one of the jumpy lambs that we were preparing to load up and haul to another farm. Best of all, she wanted to do it "all by herself." My little redhead was fearless in the face of such a great challenge. She threw herself into the fray, and let me just say, once she got ahold of the lamb, she refused to let go.

My daughter was not able to win the fight, but she gave it all she had. She refused to back down from the challenge because she knew when the lamb was about to overtake her, the shepherd was going to step in and help. She had confidence in the fight and went into it with no fear because she knew her dad was going to be right there with her.

You can go into this day with boldness and confidence because there is one truth that will always remain the same: your Good Shepherd is with you. When he allows you to face a "giant" in your life, you can grab ahold of it with confidence knowing that he will be right there beside you. He will not let it overcome you because when you cry out for help, he is right there. What a blessed assurance we have that we never will face a battle without the Good Shepherd at our side.

Go Enjoy The Shepherd.

November 1

Finish the Fight
Joshua 1:9

In her tug of war with the lamb, my daughter suddenly lost her footing. In her tenacity to not let go, she was being dragged along the ground. As I rushed to assist her, she was suddenly caught between the lamb and the fence. As he struggled to free himself from her ferocious grip, my daughter's head was being scraped along the woven wire. I yelled out, "Let go, honey!"

Because of her fierce determination, my baby girl received some scrapes and a small cut to her head. When I arrived at her side, she was nothing but all smiles. She had held that lamb until I came over and grabbed him. Though battered and bruised, she had conquered her task and helped me catch the lamb. I tended her wounds and smiled down at her and simply said, "Good job, Sugaboog!" (her nickname)

In your life, you will face many trials and struggles. It is a promise the Good Shepherd gave us (John 16:33). At times, he will lead you into a task knowing you will not be able to stand on your own. You will have to rely on him to overcome. However, he wants you to face this fight with the determination of a soldier who will never give up, never give in. If you stand strong and finish the task, imagine the smile you will share with him as you stand battered and bruised and hear him say, "Well done my child!"

Go Enjoy The Shepherd.

Enough
2 Kings 2:23-25

After my struggle in the barn with Bam-Bam in which I employed the rod of correction, we seemed to be on good terms. I kept a close eye on him in order to avoid another tussle in case he decided to try me again. Thankfully we had no more problems, until . . .

My family stood at the gate staring at the sheep. My daughters were picking some fresh strands of grass to feed through the gate to several of the ewes. Bam-Bam stood close by watching and then, without warning, he took his head and rammed my daughter's foot that was propped up in the gate.

In a moment of adrenaline and rage, I jumped the fence and faced him head on. He lunged at me and I snagged him by the horns and lifted him in the air, only to slam him to the ground again. My daughter's cries were in my ears as I dared him to come again. I supposed he remembered our last tussle and he turned and walked away. But my mind was made up, he was leaving my farm immediately. Within a few days, he was sold to another farmer with a good understanding of his temperament. Because he attacked my daughter, he was no longer welcomed on our farm.

The Good Shepherd is kind and gentle, loving and caring. He tenderly loves his sheep and cares for his lambs. He moves slowly among them, being careful not to stir them up. His voice is soothing to their ears and his tenderness is a calm to their soul. However, when his flock is attacked, even by another sheep, he is swift to act, swift to protect, and he knows when it is time to say it is enough. He is not timid or shy, nor is he weak! He will quickly remove anyone who is attempting to hurt his sheep!

Go Enjoy The Shepherd.

November 3

Do the Right Thing
Micah 6:8

Holstein (yes, my daughters named one of our lambs after a breed of cattle) was a very good-looking ewe lamb. She stood out among all the other sheep due to her appearance. Because of her uniqueness, we asked a higher price for her. I took her to the barn the evening before her new owner was to arrive and put her in a stall. In the morning she would be on her way to a new home.

When I arrived for early morning chores, it was clearly evident something was wrong. Holstein was having trouble standing up. I checked her over and saw nothing that stood out as being the issue. When I came back in an hour, she had only gotten worse.

I called the buyer and informed her of what was going on so that she would not make the long drive for nothing. I told her if things changed we would let her know first. She thanked me for our honesty and agreed to seeing how things went. Later that day, Holstein died. I still today am not certain of what happened to her, but I knew despite our need, we had to do the right thing.

Today you may be facing personal struggles and there may seem to be an answer to your current situation. However, that answer may require you to sacrifice your integrity in order to make things better for you personally. The Good Shepherd is watching and all he asks is that you remember what he did for you and treat others just the same. He could have bent the rules several times to benefit himself, but to do so would have meant losing you! (Mark 4:1-11)

If you are facing a broken situation, then do as Jesus did and turn your eyes to the Good Shepherd. Trust him to fulfill his promises as you walk humbly before him.

Go Enjoy The Shepherd.

Chasing Cheta
Psalm 139:7-8

Cheta (said cheetah) was the fastest dog I had ever owned. He was extremely brave in battle, and lightning quick to wherever he had to go. I used to take pleasure in watching him run along the fence, barking at our neighbor's dog who was walking on the outside of the field. It was truly a beautiful thing to behold as he seemed to take joy in his speed.

That is, except for those times Cheta decided to venture outside his field to explore instead of doing his job. The first few weeks of owning him, he and I had some real "catch me if you can" moments. On one of these occasions I was in no mood for his games. He knew I could not run and catch him, so he would run for a bit, then wait for me. When I got close, he would run some more. Frustrations mounted in my spirit, but I determined I was not going to lose, so I pressed on.

Finally, he made the mistake of letting me get close, then he jumped in the pond. He must have assumed this sweaty old farmer was not going to follow him in the water, but he was wrong. I dove right in and snatched him up like a mother carries her puppies. I refused to let go until I had him where he was supposed to be, in the field guarding my sheep.

The Good Shepherd is relentless in his pursuit of his sheep. Like Cheta, we tend to run away from him, hoping to enjoy freedom outside of his prepared places. We attempt to taunt him as he draws close, then we sprint away, not understanding we are running from his love and care. However, he will never give up on his pursuit and there is nowhere he will not go, no lengths he will not reach, in order to rescue his flock from the hand of his enemy.

Go Enjoy The Shepherd.and his relentless pursuit of you!

November 5

Standing Shepherd
Micah 5:4

I remember doing a search for pictures of shepherds on the internet and being amazed at the percentage of them which showed the shepherd standing by his flock. In the heat of the day, or in the blistering cold of winter, these ones watching over their flocks were standing. Some looked tired from the evident long hours, yet they stood. I know first hand, that being on your feet for extended periods of time can set in a fatigue in the legs, making it difficult to not want to take a rest. However, a true shepherd knows that in order to keep an eye on all his sheep, he must stand.

I love this portrait of the shepherd presented by Micah in this passage. Here we see the Good Shepherd standing and watching over his flock. His job is never ending, yet he stands. Through countless days and nights, through stifling heat, heavy rain, or bone-chilling cold, he stands and he watches.

In a garden, he shook off fatigue and the desire to sleep, and he stood so he could watch over his flock. Beaten and torn, ripped to shreds, he stood as he carried his cross. Suffering death, rejection, and certain defeat, he stood as the Good Shepherd for his flock. Risen and standing at the right hand of God, he continues to watch over his sheep!

Go Enjoy The Shepherd.

November 6

No Waste
1 Corinthians 15:58

As I stood outside the huge facility in Colorado watching the sheep line up to enter the slaughterhouse, and as I listened to the gentleman talk about what all took place inside and how the sheep were processed, I was amazed at how nothing seemed to go to waste. They had a purpose and use for every part of the sheep as it was going through the processing line.

This caused me to think of how it was in biblical times. Shepherds in those days also did not waste any part of the sheep when it was slaughtered. They used the wool for clothing and coverings. The leathers were used for shoes, tents, and other things. Horns were used to blow the trumpet sounds and to carry oil in. To waste anything of the sheep, in life or death, was considered a misuse of God's provision.

How great is it to know today that the Good Shepherd will not waste anything in your life at all. There is no situation or circumstance that he will not use for your good and his glory. His ways may seem hard or difficult to understand (Isaiah 55:9), but he has promised to cause all things to work together for your good (Romans 8:38) in order to perfect you for that day you stand before him. How comforting to have a Good Shepherd who will waste not a moment of our lives. There is no sickness, no sorrow, no joy, no suffering, not even our death, that is not for our good and for his ultimate glory!

Go Enjoy The Shepherd.

November 7

Unique Reflection
Ephesians 4:11-13

In the time I have had sheep, I have had a few that looked similar. Some were almost perfect copies of one another. However, there was always something, even if it was minute, that made each one unique. Even when identical twins are born, their personalities allow them to stand out as individuals. They are each unique.

Did you realize that you are unique and special in the eyes of the Good Shepherd? You may feel like you are just another cog in the wheel that turns, but in his eyes, you are unique, and the only one like you. He created each person to be a unique reflection of his glory and character. Only you can reflect God to the world in the way you do! Just like sheep are all unique individuals in the eyes of the shepherd, you are the only one he has made to be you! In his eyes, you are extremely special.

Go Enjoy The Shepherd.

November 8

Unity Shines Bright
Matthew 5:16

There is nothing better than walking out in the field and seeing all my sheep getting along. Each one either grazing in the fields or resting in the shade, enjoying what I have prepared for them. They do not see color differences or size differences. They do not separate into miniature flocks based on their differences. They look like the leaves of Fall, all different colors creating a portrait of beauty and peace. As I look upon this scene, my heart is warmed and my smile shines bright.

As the sheep of the Good Shepherd, we are all unique and different. Composed of many different races, colors, sizes, and backgrounds. We all have different customs, thoughts, and beliefs about things like doctrine and association. Many things exist to divide us, yet our Good Shepherd calls us to stand in unity, as one flock, one body, with one head, Jesus Christ.

When we lay aside our differences, and lift up the name of Jesus, our Good Shepherd, standing in unity, the world will look on and just like different color sheep grazing in the fields, they will see a portrait of beauty and will long to know more. That is when our unity and good works bring him the most glory, and a smile to his face.

Today, let your light shine brightly by standing in unity with those he has placed around you as members of his flock.

Go Enjoy The Shepherd.

November 9

Awe and Wonder
Zephaniah 3:17

I stared out over the fields after a long day of work. It was a brisk Fall evening and the sheep were enjoying their final taste of grass before huddling up for an evening of rest. I looked out over the scene with awe and wonder as I enjoyed what I was looking at. These sheep were precious to me, each and every one, and I simply enjoyed the opportunity to take in such a gorgeous sight.

Today, the Good Shepherd is looking out over his flock and his heart is flooded with awe and wonder. He is taken back by the beauty he is beholding. He sees all the flaws and imperfections in each sheep, however, he is not focused on those. What he sees is beauty beyond compare and his heart is full as he enjoys looking over the sheep that are grazing his pasture.

Remember this, he sees you, all of you, and today he is singing with joy and thanksgiving that you belong to him.

Go Enjoy The Shepherd.

November 10

Nameless No More
John 10:27

Every sheep I have ever bought and brought to my farm came as a numbered sheep. I have only bought three total in my time that had a name and they were all established rams from other flocks. Every ewe or lamb I have bought simply had a tag in its ear and were known by their owner as number such and such.

Until they came to my farm. One of the first things we do with any new sheep that comes on our farm is that we give them a name. This process was actually started by my two daughters when we first got sheep. My girls are the ones who God used to teach me the importance of naming the sheep. Once the tradition took hold, we have named every one of our sheep. As soon as they join our flock, they receive a name.

Before you were a member of the Good Shepherd's flock, you were nothing more than a number to your previous owner. He had you tagged and numbered and he cared nothing about who you really were. You were nothing more than a member of his mob.

On the day you were purchased by the Good Shepherd, he instantly gave you a name, your name. It was a name he had for you from before you were born (Jeremiah 1:5). Your first moments in his care, you became nameless no more.

The Good Shepherd knows Your name!!!!

Go Enjoy The Shepherd.

November 11

Under Constant Attack
Isaiah 14:12-15

I do not have to worry too much about a band of raiders coming through and stealing my sheep away, at least not in the place we live right now. Our focus is more on predators and disease. However, in the days of Scripture, and in some places of the world today, this was/is still a reality. Bands of thieves would come in and attempt to steal the entire flock away. There is only one way they could accomplish this, they first had to get rid of the shepherd.

For a thief to be successful, it was of extreme importance that the shepherd be eliminated as a threat. The protection of the sheep fell into the shepherd's hands, and there was no way he was going to allow his sheep to be taken without a fight. Throughout the ages, many shepherds have given their lives in their attempts to fight off the thieves who came to take away their sheep.

The point is, the shepherd himself was a constant focal point of attack. Not only was he dealing with lions, bears, wolves, and coyotes, he dealt with these men who wanted to take away his prized sheep. The Good Shepherd, from the very beginning, has been under constant attack. The Enemy, the great thief, Satan himself, has one thing on his mind—he wants to steal all of the Good Shepherd's sheep. The only way to do that is to eliminate the Shepherd, therefore he is constantly attacking the integrity, validity, and reality of the existence of such a Good Shepherd.

Praise be to God, we already know this is one fight the Enemy can never win because the Good Shepherd willingly laid down his life so that his sheep would be eternally free from the danger of being carried away by the great thief!

Go Enjoy The Shepherd.

November 12
Undershepherd Excitement
Proverbs 22:6, John 13:15

As I was leaving the farm, a beautiful sight caught my eyes. My daughter Raygan, 12 at the time, was walking out in the field to go tend to her horse. I stopped and stared for a moment as I watched all my sheep get in a line behind her and follow her around. Raygan was a constant visitor to the field because of her love for her horse, and all animals for that matter, so the sheep were very accustomed to her. As I watched, a swell of pride and joy arose inside of me as I saw a beautiful picture of discipleship in front of my eyes.

Raygan had made many trips to the field with me, walking beside me and helping me with my chores. She knew how to act around the sheep because she had seen me do it many times. She knew to walk instead of run. She knew to lead instead of push from behind. In other words, she had watched me closely enough to go and do things exactly how I did them, and that meant the sheep trusted her just like they trusted me.

The Good Shepherd calls to us to watch him closely, and then to do as he is doing. Remember, sheep follow sheep. Jesus became the Lamb of God so he could lead all the other sheep back to the Great Shepherd, God the Father. He came and taught his disciples how to lead by following, and he has left that example for us to live by as well. I can only imagine the smile that crosses his face and the huge wave of joy that floods his soul as he watches his disciples do as he has done and lead the sheep to where they should be—at his side!

Go Enjoy The Shepherd.

November 13

Bring Him Joy
John 15:9-11

There are days I am not able to get up and go see the sheep. I have some obligations in life that require at times that I leave before the sun arises and therefore I have to leave the daily chores in the hands of my great family. It truly makes me happy to know I have a wife and kids whom I can trust to handle things at home when I am not there.

But if I were honest, I actually miss being able to go out and see my sheep on those days. Even when it is cold or extremely hot, I enjoy those moments watching my sheep simply enjoy themselves, and enjoy each other, and enjoy me. Those moments fill my heart with joy!

Today, the Good Shepherd longs to spend time with you. Not only is this time vital for the survival of his sheep, but it literally is a time that fills his heart with joy. He loves to see his sheep enjoying themselves, enjoying each other, and enjoying him. Take time today to make his joy full by allowing him to simply enjoy time with you!

Go Enjoy The Shepherd.

November 14

The Only Safe Place
Psalm 18:2, Psalm 91:2

In a flash, they were standing at my side. These poor sheep were terrified by the new addition to the field, a puppy who would one day be their guardian. This pup was full of energy, way too much for the sheep. Bertha was just too excited, and it was unsettling for the sheep. Therefore, they drew in close in order to enjoy the safety that could only be found next to their shepherd.

Today, you might be dealing with something very unsettling. You may be having something that is stirring your life into a tizzy and you are not sure how to handle it. Run to the Good Shepherd, stay at his side, for only there will you find a safe place!

Go Enjoy The Shepherd.

November 15

Choosing the Ram
Daniel 2:21

In all the time that I have been raising sheep, not once has a ram been allowed to be over my flock unless I put him there. I always went out and picked the best ram I could and I placed him in the flock so he could bring about growth and multiplication of my flock. He was put there for a very specific purpose, and he was put there by me.

Many kings and kingdoms have come and gone throughout history. Many nations have risen and many have fallen. These leaders at times have been good and kind, others have been evil. Yet one truth has remained throughout all ages, no leader has risen to power or his position over the people of the Good Shepherd without him being hand chosen by the Shepherd himself.

At times this knowledge can be unsettling and disturbing. It can draw out questions from us as we wonder why certain leaders are put in place. However, we can know this for a fact, the Good Shepherd always chooses his "ram" so that his flock may grow and draw closer to him and will multiply throughout the earth.

Take time today to pray for those who are over you as leaders of your church, your community, your county, your state, and the nation. Thank the Good Shepherd for his chosen leaders and draw ask him to draw you closer to his side.

Go Enjoy The Shepherd.

November 16

What Does He Profit
Deuteronomy 7:6

Sheep producers worldwide typically have one goal, profit. Sheep are used for their own benefit to increase their position and place in life. They raise sheep for the purpose of selling them or their wool so that they can "get ahead" in life. Sheep are simply a tool for them to get what they want out of this life.

For the Good Shepherd though, his purposes are completely different. He is not after a profit or to "get ahead." He has one thing as his purpose and goal, the sheep. His treasure is his sheep, not what he can gain from them. His desire is for his sheep, not for the wealth he could obtain if he sold them. In other words, simply having the sheep is his profit. To him, they are his gain.

You are a member of his flock, a chosen people, and you are his treasured possession. When he looks at you, he has all that he wants. You bring satisfaction to his soul! (Isaiah 53:11)

Go Enjoy The Shepherd.

November 17

Wounded Hands
John 20:20

I reached in where the lamb was stuck in the middle of the briars. She had gone in to find a place of safety and rest, only to get herself snagged in the heavy thicket. I probably would have walked right past her had she not been crying out for help. I had not come into the field properly prepared for such an extraction, but I knew she needed to be free in order to be back with her mother. As I pulled her out, the thorns tore the flesh on my hands, but in a few minutes, she was back to running and playing with the other lambs. Watching the lamb enjoy its freedom, I considered the pain I had endured and the blood that was now flowing from my hands a small price to pay.

As I looked at the blood on my hands, I could not help but think of my Good Shepherd and the wounds in his hands. He heard my cries as I was trapped in the thicket of my sin. He did not hesitate to reach in with his nail-scarred hands and rescue me from my snares so that I could be free to run and enjoy the bounty of his love. His flesh was torn and his blood was spilt, all so that I could be free!

Today, as he looks at the scars in his hands, on his back, in his feet, and in his side, he smiles as he watches you run and enjoy freedom bought with his blood and he says, "You were worth it all!"

Go Enjoy The Shepherd.

November 18

Still the Shepherd
Jeremiah 10:6-7

There have been good times and there have been tough times on our farm. We have laughed at the frolicking lambs, we have cried at the death of others. Some lambing seasons have gone amazing, others we have suffered great loss. Most days the sheep are fine, but some days we have had trouble with them. For the most part the sheep have rested in safety on our farm, but we have also lost some of our sheep to coyotes and other predators. Through it all, one fact has remained, I am still the shepherd. As long as we have sheep, nothing will ever change that.

Our lives are filled with ups and downs. It is a simple truth if you live long enough. It will take you on quite the roller coaster ride with its twists and turns. At times it can feel like it is actually out of control. But one thing remains the same and will never change, Jesus will always be our Good Shepherd. No one is going to replace him and he will never give up his position to another.

Is your life seemingly spinning out of control today? Then find confidence in this fact alone, Jesus is, and will always be, your Good Shepherd.

Go Enjoy The Shepherd.

November 19

The Drought
Psalm 63:1

We had just finished the hay cutting for the Fall and put all the square bales in the barn. It was a bountiful year in hay as the rains had made the hay grow thick and heavy. Underneath the freshly cut hay were new sprouts waiting to shoot forth, only the rains that we had enjoyed all year suddenly ceased. We actually went through nearly eight weeks of no rain in October and November, and the grass in the field quickly dried up in the heat. We suddenly found ourselves having to feed hay and put out more water on a daily basis much earlier in the year than expected.

Droughts are a part of life. All over the world, shepherds deal with these times when the rain seems to simply avoid their area for the sheep. During these times, the sheep have to remain closer to the shepherd, leaning more heavily on his provision than ever before. Only he is able to provide for them, especially in times of drought.

Have you ever experienced a season of "drought" in your personal life. A time when the everything seems barren? Have you been so thirsty in your spiritual walk that your physical tongue felt as parched as your soul. It seems that all around you is a wasteland and you are on the verge of death.

This is when the Good Shepherd invites you to rely all the more on him to meet your every need. Only he has the nourishment to revive your soul and give you life. So instead of dreading these times in life, embrace them. They are the times that allow you to be closer to him than you've ever been before.

Go Enjoy The Shepherd.

November 20

Lift Your Eyes
Psalm 121:1

That was one of the worst weeks I could remember in quite some time. Our family was struggling to just get by. My income was at an all-time low and our ability to simply put food on the table was a huge struggle. While this was going on, the sheep decided to start lambing in the middle of a snowstorm and over fifty percent of the newborn lambs did not survive. Our sheep were on our new farm and we lived twenty minutes away, and every morning I arrived to seemingly more trouble. "What are you doing, God?" I cried out as I looked to the sky!

When my sheep are in need, they look to the one who is standing watch over them. When these lambs were dying, the mothers looked up at me as if to say, "Why did this happen?" It was as if they felt the same pain I was feeling, and the only one they had to look to was me, their shepherd.

How glorious the thought, that when life is at its worst, we have a Good Shepherd who stands watch over us and he calls out, "Lift your eyes up and look to me!" He is our Shelter in our storm. He is the Healer when we are hurting. He is the Mender when we are broken. He is the Savior when we are lost in our sin! We need only to lift our eyes and cry out to him for mercy!

Today, are you broken? Are you hurting? Does it seem your life has been shattered? Are you entangled in sin and cannot wrestle yourself free? Then lift your eyes to the One who stands watch over you. He stands ready to heal the hurting, mend the broken, renew the shattered, and save the sinner. Lift up your eyes to the Good Shepherd, his arms are open wide and ready to embrace you!

Go Enjoy The Shepherd.

November 21

You Must Trust
Jeremiah 17:7

I poured out the organic corn for the sheep to come enjoy. I stood by the trough and smiled as I watched them gobble up the delicious treat I had put in front of them. Standing about 50 feet away was Tony, our ram. He had been with us for about 5 months, but he still did not trust me enough to come eat with the other sheep. Sadly, he stood there and just watched as the others enjoyed themselves.

As I took this in, I could hear that still whisper again in the field. The Good Shepherd reminded me that in order for me to enjoy the blessings he has for me, I must trust him and draw near to him. If I continue to stand back, uncertain of his true love for me, I would be like Tony and completely miss out on the blessing he has placed out for me.

Let me encourage you today, as the sheep of his pasture, learn to trust his loving hands. Allow him to have his way with you and draw close when he calls. Don't be like Tony and miss out on the great blessing Jesus has prepared for you!

Go Enjoy The Shepherd.

November 22

Giving Thanks: The Basics
Isaiah 55:1-3

It is the season of Thanksgiving, and I simply love this holiday. It is my favorite one of the year, and I am blessed to spend it with my family and friends.

So what do sheep have to be thankful for? For starters, the basics of food and water. They need grass, hay, grain, salt, mineral, and water to survive. Who do they look to for the provision of these things? Their shepherd. He/she is responsible to make sure these basics are met, and when they are, the sheep respond by being full and content which is their way of saying, "Thanks."

In our walk with the Good Shepherd, we need the basics as well. We need the Bread of Life and the Fount of Living Water if we are going to survive. There is only one place we can find these things, in the hands of the Good Shepherd. He alone can provide our needs.

The Good Shepherd invites you today to come and eat, take a bite of the Word of God himself. He implores you to come and drink until your thirst is satisfied. He loves for you to come and be satisfied. To be filled with the things only he can provide. As we respond with contentment, he can hear us say, "Thanks!"

Go Enjoy The Shepherd.

November 23

Giving Thanks: Protection
Proverbs 18:10

Sheep have absolutely no way to defend themselves. Without protection from the shepherd, a good fence, and some guardian dogs, sheep can and will be decimated quickly by all types of predators. Wolves, cougars, bears, lions, and coyotes are just a few that can be named that enjoy a good sheep feast if they are left unprotected.

That is why so much time is spent on making sure the sheep have a safe place to eat, drink, and rest. On our farm, fences have been raised, guard dogs have been brought in, and I feel many times I sleep with one eye open, especially during lambing season. All this is an effort to make sure the sheep are safe. The sheep thank their shepherd by resting in the fields under his protection. Their peaceful rest is thanks enough for him.

The Good Shepherd has gone to amazing lengths to make sure his sheep are under the protective care of his hands. He has set boundaries for their safety to keep the enemy out. He has placed guardians over them to watch them day and night. He keeps his eyes peeled, watching over his flock both day and night. How he loves to see his sheep give him thanks by simply resting under the hand of his protection.

Today, simply say thanks by resting at his feet!

Go Enjoy The Shepherd.

November 24

Giving Thanks: Healing Care
Psalm 147:3

Sweetheart was really struggling to move around. As I walked out into the fifty-acre field, I moved past all my other sheep and went directly to her. When I reached her I was shocked at what I saw. Her neck was "bottle jawed," a clear sign she was suffering heavily from barber pole worms. I ran back to the house and immediately grabbed all the necessary treatments for these deadly parasites. I gave Sweetheart a healthy dose of several medications then watched her closely for the next few days, giving her additional treatments. In a short while, she gave me her thanks by being strong and healthy again, and soon after, raising a set of twin lambs.

The Good Shepherd knows the condition of his sheep at all times. He sees when we have become infected with the parasites of hidden sins which quickly drain our life from within. He knows the only cure is to immediately fill us with a dose of confession and humility. I can see his smile beam across his face as those he has brought back from the verge of death say thanks with a healthy life. Once healthy again, we are able to share the good news of what he has done for us, therefore discipling others to follow Jesus as well.

Go give thanks, and Enjoy The Shepherd.

November 25

Giving Thanks: Guidance
Psalm 139:24

Sheep have no true sense of where they should go. If left to themselves they would wander aimlessly out in the open, driven only by their desire to satisfy their hunger and quench their thirst. Without a guide though, they would become lost and simply die wandering around in search of what they needed.

That is where the leadership and guidance of the shepherd comes into play. The shepherd knows where the good food and the water is. He has mapped out the proper course which will allow the sheep to receive their needs in full. The way they can say thanks is to simply follow!

Like sheep, we are desperate for direction. The greatest desire of humans is to have purpose and the direction to get them where they need to go. Like sheep, without guidance we are doomed to a life of endless wandering through desert lands. But the Good Shepherd knows exactly where our needs can be satisfied. He knows where we need to go, all we need to do is to say thanks by following him.

Go Enjoy The Shepherd and give him thanks by following where he leads.

November 26

Giving Thanks: Drops of Grain
Psalm 33:12

My sheep love little more than the mornings I ring out my voice and call, "Hey, Sheep!" They instantly come running because they know that means I have brought them their favorite treat, organic corn and grains. Little excites them more than seeing that bucket in my hand and their anticipation grows with each step I make toward the feeding area. Heads are held high as they watch for me to pour out the blessing they long to enjoy. My thanks comes when the sheep simply enjoy the treat I have given them.

How the Good Shepherd loves to pour out his blessings on his sheep. Nothing brings him greater joy than to give abundant life and gifts to his children. His heart is thrilled as we come running to him as he calls our name. He holds tremendous gifts in his hands and he walks us to exactly the best place where we can receive them and enjoy them to the fullest. He receives his joy simply by watching us enjoy the gifts he has blessed us with!

Go Enjoy The Shepherd.

Giving Thanks: Patience
Joel 2:13

Sheep love to test the patience of their shepherd. I have mentioned before that I have often considered just getting rid of my flock for good. They can be such a hassle. No other animal on a farm needs more attention than a sheep. They require an enormous amount of attention and care. Without it they would die. That is why being patient with sheep is so important. A shepherd with little patience is a shepherd who will not have sheep for very long. However, a patient shepherd knows the joy of seeing a flock prosper and grow in trust of him and in size as the sheep produce more lambs. This trust and growth are the thanks a shepherd receives.

The Good Shepherd has had ample opportunity to just throw in the towel with his flock. How often do we test our boundaries, push our limits, get caught in traps and need to be rescued? That is why it is said he is "LONG suffering" (2 Peter 3:9), because we press hard against his patient care so often.

Thankfully he is the Good Shepherd and he is able to see beyond our thoughts. He has a bigger picture in mind than the moment we are living in. He knows, with patient and loving care, his flock will respond and prosper under his care and multiply, bringing more sheep into his care. As we learn to trust and then help others grow in their confidence in him, he smiles knowing a life lived for him is a life of thanksgiving!

Go Enjoy The Shepherd.

November 28

Giving Thanks: For the Shepherd
Psalm 86:12-13

Each expression of thanks given by sheep is not just a thanks for what they have received, but rather a means of saying thanks for the shepherd himself. Without the shepherd, sheep would have nothing to be thankful for. However, when the sheep are content and satisfied, when they rest in the comfort of his protection or recover from their illness, when they follow and enjoy the blessings from his hands and learn to trust him, each of these are ultimately saying to the shepherd, "Thank you for being so good to me. Thanks for being my shepherd."

When we choose to be content and satisfied with what he has provided, we are saying, "Thanks for being my Good Shepherd." When we rest in the comfort of his protection and recover from the sin he has saved us from, we are lifting our voices in praise to him. As we enjoy the over-abundant blessings he gives us in this life and learn to trust him, even through the valley of the shadow of death, our voices are ringing loud in his ears as we sing praises to his holy name!

Today, lift up your voice by being content and satisfied in Jesus alone. Rest in the safety of his protection and care. Let your life sing to him as you enjoy everything he has given you and give yourself to trust him no matter what life throws your way. In this way, your life will be one of giving thanks to the One who loves you more than any other, The Good Shepherd!

Go Enjoy The Shepherd.

November 29

Trophy Sheep
2 Corinthians 2:14-16

Contests are held every year around the country to determine which sheep is the "Grand Champion." These shows are held in the highest esteem by all the the sheep world, and prized ewes and rams are drooled over by those who want the best for their flock. These winners are paraded before a host of potential producers and prices can only be considered as near "ridiculous." For the one who put in all the hard work to raise the champion, this opportunity to "show the sheep off" is a treasured moment in which all their hard work is shown the appreciation and praise it deserves.

I love the picture shown here in 2 Corinthians of the parade of the "captives" as it relates to the Good Shepherd. In the days of Rome, a conquered city was taken captive and a huge parade was held. The conquering general would parade through the city and the "trophies" were displayed for all to see. It was an opportunity for the general to have all his hard work appreciated and praised.

The Good Shepherd is working daily to prepare his "Grand Champion" to show off to all the universe. He will display with pride the handiwork of his long and hard hours put into making the most desired, the most beautiful, the most treasured one in all the universe, You! He literally is longing for the day that he gets to march you out in front of all the beings of the universe and say, "Look at my Beloved!" The major difference is he is not interested in the highest bid, because he is the one who paid the ultimate price so he could have you! The Good Shepherd has no desire to sell his prized possession, but rather he is looking forward to treasuring you forever.

Go Enjoy The Shepherd.

November 30

The Glory Ahead
Hebrews 10:36

Every glorious ram or majestic ewe, once had a beginning as a little lamb. Lambs can easily get sick. They are the most susceptible to worms and parasites. Predators single out the young and even the weakest of the young. They are looking for easy prey. In order to survive and develop into a full-grown sheep, lambs must make it through this very delicate phase of life.

As they grow, sheep must go through the natural process of having bones stretch to length and muscles to develop in strength in order to carry them about. This process is not free from pain as the sinews and fibers of every inch of their being are pressed to make it to its full potential. More struggles come as sheep go through the "right of passage" being beaten and hammered by the elders in the flock fighting to maintain their place of dominance. Many lessons of humility and recovery come along the way, all leading to that day when they can stand as fully mature sheep, ready to be productive members of the flock.

Our walk with the Good Shepherd is not an easy one. He warned all who chose to follow him to count the cost (Luke 14:25-35). The process of growing from a lamb in the arms of the Good Shepherd to a productive member of the flock is filled with setbacks, struggles, and sufferings. The path is not one to be taken lightly; however, he knows what is coming, and if you follow, the day is coming when he will declare you a perfect and productive member of his flock.

Lean into him as you endure hardships and trials, for the day of glory is coming.

Go Enjoy The Shepherd.

December 1

Don't Run Ahead
2 John 1:9

"Silly Sheep," is what I say every time they make an assumption about where I am going instead of following me. They leap ahead, thinking they know where I am going, only to get there and turn around and look sheepish (pardon the pun). It never fails for them to have the expression on their face of "Where is he going? I thought for sure he was coming here." I simply smile, continue walking as they file back in line behind me to make it to where I intended for them to be in the first place.

Do you ever act like that? Do you ever run ahead, assuming you know the Good Shepherd's plan? I know I do. I look out in front of me and instantly assume that I know where he is taking me only to end up looking sheepish myself as I realize I have jumped ahead and made a fool of myself.

Thankfully he is a patient Shepherd who simply calls us to get back behind him so he can lead his people to where he intended for us to be all along. He turns and says, "Silly sheep, do not run ahead, just follow me. I know where you need to be!"

Go Enjoy The Shepherd.

December 2

At the Sheep Gate
John 5:1-15

If you have gathered much at all about sheep, you probably understand they are not very hardy animals. They easily become sick and weak, have no effective defense mechanisms, for lack of a better word, they are puny. When they get sick, they literally lie down and wait to die. They require a lot of oversight and help to survive.

That is why this story in the Gospel of John is so intriguing to me. You see all the "blind, lame, and sick" gathered at a pool by the "Sheep Gate." These puny and dying people acted just like sheep in the sense they went to a place where they could just go "live till they die." The one focused on in this passage had been there for 38 years awaiting his final breath to come.

Then along comes the Good Shepherd. It should be no surprise to us that he would come to the Sheep Gate to find his lost, hurting, blind, lame, and dying sheep. What a glorious picture of how he knows exactly where to find us when we are hurting, suffering, and at times dying.

Are you hurting today? Do you feel sick, lame, or blind? Does your heart feel faint, leaving you with the overwhelming reality you can do nothing to heal or defend yourself? Then be of good cheer, for the Good Shepherd knows exactly where you are and he knows how to find you!

Go Enjoy The Shepherd.

December 3

Honored by the Shepherd
Zephaniah 3:19-20

Despised, rejected, left alone to die, the little lamb was the most pitiful sight. None of the sheep cared for the little lamb, not even its mother. In its current condition it would die in a matter of hours. This lamb was the epitome of what it is like to be unwanted and hated. It already carried the bruises given it by the beating its mother had given it each time it attempted to get some milk. Its pitiful cries reached my ears and I gathered it up and took it home to raise.

Though unwanted by its own, it was most treasured by me. When I came to see the sheep, all the sheep received my greeting and gifts of grain, but that lamb got a double portion. I spent a great deal of time tending to and caring for that lamb, making sure it had all it wanted. As the other sheep looked on, I gave that lamb a great deal of love and I lifted it up for them all to see.

In this world, the sheep of the Good Shepherd are much like that little lamb. Scattered, despised, beaten, broken, and unwanted. The world looks on and hates the poor, sickly little lambs of God, seeing them as not having much to contribute to the common good. All they can seem to do is speak of the kindness and love of their Shepherd, which causes them to be hated all the more. Though it is painful to endure this rejection and hate, the sheep of his pasture can hold their heads high, looking forward to the day which has been promised. The day the Good Shepherd will gather in all his sheep and give them "praise and honor among all the peoples of the earth."

Though today you feel despised and rejected, a day is coming where he will lift you up and honor you before all the ones who have put you to shame!

Go Enjoy The Shepherd.

December 4

Heart of the Shepherd
John 11:35

My time as a shepherd has led me to experience the whole range of emotions. I have been elated and thrilled. I have been torn and broken. I have experienced joy and also great agony. I have lots of easy decisions I have made, but I have also been faced with heart and gut-wrenching ones.

I once prayed God would allow me to feel what his heart feels, to beat as his heart beats. I believe he gave me sheep in order to answer that prayer. There are days he experiences the joy of seeing his sheep simply resting and trusting in him. There are other days his heart is in agony over those who have gone astray and become lost in their own way. His heart burst with the elation of bringing another one back home, and yet his heart yearns for those who are still wandering around, lost in a dying world.

Today, the Good Shepherd both sings over the ones who are experiencing the safety of being in his fold, and he longs for the return of those who have been scattered by the attacks of the enemy. His heart is set, as he wipes his tears away, and he goes forth to rescue All his sheep.

If you are feeling lost today, if you are broken, tired, and drenched in the filth this life pours over you, know for certain, his heart is longing for the day you are with him once again!

Go Enjoy The Shepherd.

December 5

Personal Sacrifice
Titus 2:14

If I only had a full record of the countless hours I have put in both day and night raising these sheep. I think I could fill a log book up to the brim, as could anyone who has ever cared for sheep. In fact, many shepherds keep very detailed records of their sheep and can go back years later and recall favorite memories with individual sheep. What such record books show is the great deal of time and personal sacrifice it takes to raise sheep.

Just a few of the things given up for this endeavor has been time, energy, sleep, comfort, and finances. There have been days when I was ready to hang out with my wife and kids, but the sheep required attention. I have had days I had no energy, was sick, not feeling well at all, but my sheep needed me, so I went. Countless hours of sleep have been sacrificed in order to raise bottle lambs, check on birthing mothers, or running off the predators. Hours spent in blazing heat or bone chilling cold in order to make sure the sheep were okay. Time and again, money was needed to buy feed, hay, or medicine to tend to the flock when I would have preferred something for me or the family. In other words, in order to raise sheep, you must consider the cost.

The Good Shepherd did not accept his role as our shepherd lightly. He knew before he began what all he would have to give up in order to have us as his sheep. He would have to leave behind everything he knew, become a mortal with flesh, spill his own blood, and give up everything that was precious to him, in order to become our caretaker and guide. He weighed the cost, considered his options fully, then accepted the position at great personal sacrifice because he considered you worth more than all he would leave behind!

Go Enjoy The Shepherd.

December 6

Going Deep
Psalm 139:23-24

I was sitting out with my sheep one day, and Caesar decided to come see me for a little rub. How he enjoys it when I dig deep into his thick hair and rub down his spine. His tail will shoot straight into the air as he wags it back and forth. At times I wonder if he is more of a puppy than a sheep.

On this particular day, Caesar's coat was looking shinier than normal. His white hairs glistened in the sun as he stood there beside me. I dug my fingers in deep, knowing he enjoyed the extra attention. When I was finished, I looked at my hands and saw they were black with the dirt hidden under his shiny coat. Under the surface there was a filth hidden that only a deep search would ever be able to find.

On that day I again heard that still, small whisper in the field. The Good Shepherd told me how at times I too looked nice and shiny to all those around me. My self-righteousness was on display for all the world to see, but he was looking deeper, beyond my surface cover, into my heart. He wanted to dig deeper than just the outside in order to free me from all the filth hidden underneath. The process to remove this mess of course would not be easy, and would require the shepherd to put his hands deep into the grime I had hidden, but he was willing to do it in order to bring me to a place of true righteousness, not just something that looked good on the surface.

If you feel the hands of the Good Shepherd reaching down deep into your soul, grinding away at the blackness of hidden and deep sins (pride, selfishness, worry, anger), then know his love for you is truly beyond measure as he works to free you to live a life of true abundance with him.

Go Enjoy The Shepherd

December 7

Wiping It Away
Psalm 51:7

When I had finished rubbing Caesar and my hands were covered in black, grimy filth, I simply wiped my hands together and all the dirt quickly came off. In other words, the filth he had on him was not able to fully attach itself to me. All I had to do to permanently remove the dirt was wipe it away.

My heart leapt with joy as I realized the deeper impact that little moment had in my life. I realized because of what Jesus had done on the cross, he was now able to embrace me in all my filth, allowing himself to remove my sins from me, and simply wipe them away. His sacrifice allowed him to become my Good Shepherd and allowed him to go deep into all my wretchedness and simply wipe it all away. His spilt blood allowed him to take my sins, place them on his hands, stand before his Father's throne, and in that place simply wipe his hands together, eternally erasing my filth from existence.

Praise Him today, for he washes away your sins as easily as I wiped that dirt off of me! What a Mighty, Good Shepherd we serve!

Go Enjoy The Shepherd.

December 8

Carding the Wool

Luke 22:31

Over the years, as a son of an auctioneer and becoming one myself, we have sold numerous sets of Wool Cards in middle Tennessee. These older cards are outfitted with thick steel bristles which were used for brushing through the wool once removed from the sheep. The purpose is to separate the fibers of wool and remove any imperfections of dirt from them. Doing one sack of wool would take hours of intense work in order to make the wool useful for banding, spinning, and ultimately weaving.

I can picture the Good Shepherd now as he sifts through our outer layers and works through the "wool" (actions) of our lives. He is not one to waste anything, not even our mistakes. So he brushes through every inch of our lives, combing it out, removing the imperfections and dirt, in order to band it, spin it, and weave it into something beautiful that he can use in the lives of those around us.

As he works through your "wool," be still and allow him to do what only he can do, taking even your mistakes, even your sins, and transforming your life into a spectacular display of his glory that he will use in the lives of those around you and those who are to come.

Go Enjoy The Shepherd.

December 9

Anointed to Avoid the Fight
Galatians 5:15

Rams often fight in a flock to see who will be the mating ram for the year. Sometimes this fight can lead some of the rams to suffer significant injuries, and in some cases, even cost them their life. In order to avoid these losses and injuries, sometimes a shepherd would put a slick and greasy oil on the rams' heads so when they butted one another, their heads would simply glance off one another, leaving them looking at each other with an embarrassing and confused glare.

I love how this speaks to how our Good Shepherd anoints his own flock with the oil of the Spirit to stop us from our bickering and fighting. When we turn on each other, the world looks at the spectacle of our fighting and laughs at our declaration of love for one another. The only outcome our fighting can produce is injury or even death to the members of our own body. In other words, when we hurt one another, we are only hurting ourselves because we need each other in order for our entire body to function properly.

Today, ask the Good Shepherd to anoint your head with the special oil so when you do rise up to fight against your brother or sister, you will be left standing there, looking foolish, as your blows simply glance off one another.

Go Enjoy The Shepherd.

December 10

Brute Force
Psalm 147:5-6, Psalm 130:7-8

I am not sure the following is one of my proudest moments as a shepherd, but it did happen and it was a lesson to me. Sometimes you have to listen hard to hear the most important.

My sheep were filing into the shed so I could check them for worms, when suddenly, "Nutzy" (yes, we had one named that) decided to turn and charge me. There was nothing she hated more than being confined in a stall with other sheep and the shepherd. Once she realized what was happening, she determined she was going to get out. She lowered her head, darted toward me at full speed, and then jumped in an attempt to leap over me. I stepped slightly to the side, raised my left arm and caught her in a clothesline sweep. Her body fell backward and she once again was in the stall she was attempting to escape. We looked at each other, both in a little shock at what just happened, and then she nestled in with the other sheep and awaited her time to be seen.

Many times in my own life I have sensed that the Good Shepherd was bringing me in for an up-close-and-personal look. These moments frightened me because I knew all the "worms" I had hidden inside would be exposed. In desperation I made my effort to run through or over Jesus to get away only to have him use brute force to keep me where I really needed to be, under his close and careful watch.

You may not like the reality that sometimes Jesus will use force to do what is best for his people, especially if the force is used on one of his own. But had I not forced that sheep to stay in the stall, because she was sick, she would have died soon afterwards. Therefore, instead of bucking against him, today, I choose to praise him, even for those times he has had to "clothesline" me.

Go Enjoy The Shepherd.

December 11

Only the Best
Psalm 113

My wife loves to do all things healthy. She came to a place in life where eating unhealthy and living unhealthy was no longer acceptable to her. When that happened, that meant everything in our household had to change, including what our sheep ate.

When we first got sheep, I was going to the local farmer's Co-op to get pellet feed for them. That is what I knew and it was what was the cheapest. After a while, we began to get grain from the local Amish community, thinking it was better for the sheep. When Katie found out even the Amish were offering corn with GMOs, she immediately went and found a place that offered certified organic grains. Only the best for our sheep would do, even if it cost much more.

I am so grateful for my wife leading our family in this area of life and for the lesson I learned from this change. I was not very happy about the extra expense and travel to pick up this "best feed for the sheep," but I begin to realize that what we were now doing was simply a picture of the Good Shepherd's care for us.

He is not willing to simply give us what will do, he wants and provides nothing less than the best care for us. No cheap substitute is acceptable for his own. That is why he does not allow any other shepherd to watch over his sheep, because his sheep deserve the best, which only he can provide.

Give thanks today that he is not willing that you should have anything other than the best, and the best he is giving you is nothing less than himself.

Go Enjoy The Shepherd.

December 12

Turning on the Sheep
Ezekiel 34:7-10, Luke 17:2

Fifteen years before I raised sheep, my brother and I had some goats. As part of our operation we had a couple of Great Pyrenees guard dogs. Unbeknownst to us, our female had gotten pregnant with the neighbors big Chow dog. When she had her puppies, she did something very unusual, she started killing the goats she was there to protect in order to feed her pups. In order to satisfy her own natural instincts, her own desires, she turned on the very ones she was meant to protect.

Unfortunately, the body of Christ is not immune to this same occurrence taking place. Sometimes those who have been put in charge of guarding and defending his sheep turn on them in order to satisfy their own personal desires. It can be absolutely devastating to watch this take place, but it does not go unnoticed by the Good Shepherd.

Because that dog refused to stop killing goats, and her pups now had the taste for blood, my brother did the only thing we could do, we put them all down. We could not allow our herd to be threatened by them any more.

The Good Shepherd, he has already promised any of those who would dare hurt his own, that he will one day remove them as he protects his flock. He loves his people too much to allow anyone, even those meant to guard and defend them, to hurt them.

Go Enjoy The Shepherd.

December 13

Birthday Gift

Romans 6:23, Luke 18:29-30

I have a confession to make, today is my birthday. On my maternal grandfather's 45th birthday, I was born into this world. I wish I could tell you a story of a lamb who was born on this day, but I personally do not have such a story to tell. However, I could think of no better day to share about the best gift I have ever received.

I spent a good amount of my life building up a great wealth, a wealth that no one wanted. I sought to satisfy my every longing and filled my account with all my wages I had earned. However, as the account grew larger, the heavier the burden of it felt. My savings was composed of the many sins I had committed in my pursuit of self gratification. As my wealth increased, I felt crushed under its weight. As I was suffocating under the weight of it all, I gasped out a breath of desperation, which landed on the ears of Jesus, the Good Shepherd.

What an amazing gift I received as he emptied my entire account and left it at a zero. He picked me up out of the miry clay, carefully washed away every deep-soaked stain I had received, and then set me free to enjoy a life by his side. This life of following him has had its share of troubles and trials, but I have never again felt the weight and oppression I was under when my sin account was full.

Not only did he replace my wages of sin with a full account of his righteousness, he also offered me a HUGE bonus as well: Eternal life living in the green pastures of his paradise with him constantly at my side! I can think of no greater gift!

Go Enjoy The Shepherd.

During this season where we think about giving back and being a blessing to others, I think it would be great to take several days and focus on the many ways in which sheep give back to the world. I hope you enjoy how each of these relate to how we have been redeemed so that we can give back to those who are around us.

December 14

Giving Back: Covering of Wool
Matthew 5:14-16

One of the top products sheep are known for is their wool. Sheep were created with an amazing ability to supply a continual flow of this much needed and much used product. Wool has been incorporated from the very early days as a use for clothing and means of warmth. One of my favorite coats I had growing up was a denim coat that was lined with wool. Even on the coldest days, this particular coat would keep me warm.

What a beautiful picture of how we, as the sheep of the Good Shepherd, can be used in our world today. For those who are members of his body and are going through the cold and dark experiences of life, we are a people who can provide the warmth of Jesus to get others through those difficult and tough times. To those who are not part of the body, our "wool" is an outreach tool through which we can share the warmth of the love of Christ into the chilling reality of a life frozen by sin.

Sheep would prefer to keep their wool, but if they did, it would not be able to serve the desperate need of warming so many in this world. If we do not share the "wool" of his love in our lives, many who are desperate to know the warmth of his love will perish in the bitter cold of their sin.

Go share your wool as you Enjoy The Shepherd.

December 15

Giving Back: Delight
Proverbs 11:25

One of my favorite things to do is shooting a game of pool. I fell in love with it as a boy watching my father and grandfather play their friends. As soon as I could hold the stick, I began a lifelong joy of playing this fantastic game. In college, I might have been known to skip a class or two in order to play a few extra rounds. (That is a confession, not a recommendation.)

Little did I realize that the baize, or the covering over the slate was often made of wool. Only through recent research did I come to find out that sheep have been a part of my life much longer than I realized. Because of their sacrifice of wool, I have been able to enjoy a lifetime of delight shooting games of pool.

This is only one example of recreation we enjoy that sheep wool is used in. Many others exist, each one to bring delight to the one using it.

As his sheep in this world, we should seek to bring joy and be a delight to all those around us. They should know us by our love for each other, and our acts of kindness should bring smiles to their face. Sometimes, in order to fulfill this chore, it will require pain and sacrifice on our parts, but the smiles we will see and the delight in their eyes is worth far more than any price we can pay.

Go be a beacon of hope and joy today in the midst of a dark and dying world! Be a blessing as you . . .

Go Enjoy The Shepherd.

December 16

Giving Back: Holding Up Others
2 Corinthians 9:8

Another common use for wool in the world is for covering of furniture and for use inside of a mattress. Wool has been used for centuries as one of the finest upholstery covers and to provide comfort in the process of rest. In both cases, the wool is underneath whoever is on it, holding it up and keeping it from falling.

We are to be a people who continually hold up each other in prayer and petitions before the Father. As the Good Shepherd uses our "wool," we are a means of keeping others lifted up when they are struggling to make it through. As we come together in a tightly woven knit, we can be a source of encouragement to hold up those who are weak and tired.

Give back of yourself today and allow your life to encourage and hold up someone you know who needs a shoulder to rest on.

Go Enjoy The Shepherd.

December 17

Giving Back: Comfort
Hebrews 13:16, Psalm 34:18

The wool from sheep is extremely soft and it provides so much more than warmth when spun into a sweater. It can be one of the most comfortable things you can wear. Blankets made from wool can be found worldwide wrapped around someone simply looking to get cozy and be comfortable. I know my children like to snuggle up and let all their worries slip away in the comfort of their blankets.

As members of the Good Shepherd's flock, we should be a place the people around us can come to seek the comfort only found in Jesus. The way we live should draw those who are hurting into a place they can find peace, comfort, and care. Like the coziness of a wool sweater, Jesus wants his flock to be a place the world can find comfort in his love.

Go Enjoy The Shepherd.

December 18

Giving Back: Soak It Up
Matthew 5:39

One of the most intriguing uses of wool in recent history has been the discovery that wool is extremely absorbent for oils. It has the ability to repel water while at the same time soaking up the oil. This has been a great discovery especially when it comes to oil spills in open waters. The fleece from many sheep has been found to be one of the best products out there to both remove the contaminant from the water while also protecting some of the wildlife. In one case wool was used to put on penguins affected by an oil spill in order to spare them from being covered in the nasty oil.

This is yet another beautiful picture of how the flock of the Good Shepherd can give back in the world we live in. We are constantly barraged with the darkness of sin all around us. People lash out against us, even members of the body "spill oil" on us through their words and actions. Yet, like the wool from sheep, we can literally "soak up" these sins and forgive one another. As we forgive, we reflect the covering of protection given us by our Good Shepherd which prevents our sins from contaminating us permanently, and we as his sheep begin to remove the stains of sin from the world around us.

Has someone "spilled oil" on you? Allow the wool of righteousness he has covered you in to "soak it up" and forgive them today, just as the Good Shepherd has forgiven you.

Go Enjoy The Shepherd.

December 19

Giving Back: Strength in the Bond
Ecclesiastes 4:12

If you take a minute and do a little research, like I did, I bet you too would be amazed at all the uses there are for wool. In fact, I bet a whole book could be written on the subject. Another "unusual" use I found for the product is a manufacturer who puts wool in their bricks. Yes, they put wool strands in the clay to form their bricks, and they have been found to be much stronger. This also makes them able to withstand and endure whatever is thrown at them over a longer period of time.

The Good Shepherd told us of a "building" he was putting together with him as the cornerstone. The wool from his sheep are infused in the building of the body, so that when it is formed together, it will provide strength for all who are members of it. When woven together, these strands are not easily separated, forming a strength which can withstand the strongest of foes over a long period of time. That means each individual strand is of great importance to the strength of the whole building/body.

You are a member of his body, a strand needed to complete the whole. The Good Shepherd is using you to build up his body, his church, so that it can withstand the test of time and hold strong under any attack. As each strand joins together, allowing its strength to combine with the strength of the others, Jesus is building a glorious thing which will last for all eternity!

Today he wants you to know you are a vital part of what he is building! He loves you and longs for the day when you will finally see what he has been working on all along.

Go Enjoy The Shepherd.

December 20

Giving Back: Suppress the Weeds
1 Peter 4:8

Wool is also used in the manufacture of mulch bed products, specifically for weed suppression. It has been found that the density of wool when placed in mulch beds or around plants is able to keep weeds from sprouting up and choking out the plants. Most amazingly, these products are found to not only be better at the job of weed suppression, but also more environmentally friendly than plastic-based mulch bed products.

This is just another example of how the Good Shepherd is using his sheep in this world. By allowing the "wool of the Spirit" of love to be used, much sin can be covered over, but not only that, many sins will be completely suppressed from even starting. As we allow Him to use us like sheep, we will be able kill off many sins before they ever have a chance to grow, allowing the fruits of the Spirit to thrive and grow as the sins are suppressed.

Today, if you sense a sin beginning to sprout up, allow the Good Shepherd to use your "wool of love" to snuff it out before it ever has a chance to grow.

Go Enjoy The Shepherd.

December 21

Giving Back: Mend the Broken
Luke 4:18, Psalm 147:3

For centuries wool has been used in the world of medicines for many purposes. It has been used in clothes for the purpose of dressing open wounds. Its ability to absorb and also help bind up wounds and bring healing with the lanolin oil was essential in the medical field. In more recent days, proteins extracted from the wool have been used in bone grafting procedures. Sheep have played a very intrical part in helping mend broken and bleeding bodies around the world.

The Good Shepherd declared that he was sent to heal the broken, bring freedom to the oppressed, and to bind up the wounds of the hurting. He in turn told his followers, his sheep, to go and live as he lived. Which means we are called to help heal the broken, bring freedom to the oppressed, and bind up the wounds of the hurting. He has equipped us, like sheep, with all we need to do these things through his Spirit.

Look around your world today, in your community, in your neighborhood, in your city, even in your church, and identify the broken, the bleeding, the hurting, and allow yourself to be the instrument through which the Good Shepherd can bring the healing they need.

Go Enjoy The Shepherd.

December 22

Giving Back: Hold It Together
Colossians 3:14

Sheep have glands that secrete a very unique oil into their wool. This oil is used as a means for them to shed water so they do not suffer from skin rot from having overly soaked wool. It truly is an amazing oil found mainly in sheep.

There are huge commercial usages for this oil in the tape industry. It is used in the production of highly useful tapes and items which induce bonding and holding together. It can also be found in adhesive plasters which bond together to hold up walls and seal up cracks.

How beautiful it is to know that the Good Shepherd allows his sheep to be a useful agent in the bonding and holding of things together. The oil of our love can permeate so deep that it acts like a glue which forms a permanent bond. As the world looks at the flock of his sheep, they should see a unity, formed through the "oil" of love that is secreted through us by the Spirit that lives within. As they see a steadfast unity, praising his name, they too will be drawn together into this bond formed in the family of God.

Allow yourself to be used today as an instrument of love, an adhesive which holds together the body through the Spirit who lives in you.

Go Enjoy The Shepherd.

December 23

Giving Back: Preventing Rust
Psalm 133:1-2

Many car care products, including motor oils and cleaning products, contain this very unique and fine lanolin oil supplied by sheep. Their purpose is to prevent rust buildup and corrosion from setting in, thus locking up the engine or eating away at the metal of the car. The oil allows things to continue to run smoothly and prevents deterioration.

The Good Shepherd, he smiles as he sees our "oil of unity" being used to prevent buildup of grudges, bickering, quarrels, and the "rust" of selfishness and pride. As we allow the oil of the Spirit to rush over us and run through us, we can continue to run like a well-oiled machine, firing on all cylinders, and not succumb to the corrosion and deterioration of sins which are the destroyers of souls. Just like the oils from sheep used to keep a car running smoothly and looking great throughout the years, the oil of our unity will allow the world to see our lights shine brightly, bringing him glory and honor, and drawing them close to the Shepherd's feet.

Today, if you have allowed the rust of selfishness, gossip, or pride to cause build-up between you and other members of his flock, ask him to pour the oil of unity over you so that the corrosion of sin can be removed and he can be seen through your unity together. If you know a brother or sister who is deteriorating because they have allowed a buildup of these thing in their life, allow yourself to be poured out, as the Good Shepherd was, so your life will act as the lubricant which will bring them to once again enjoy a smooth relationship with the Good Shepherd and all the members of his flock.

Go Enjoy The Shepherd.

December 24

Giving Back: Removal of the Old
Ezekiel 36:26

One of the most common usages of lanolin oil is in cosmetic products. You will find it in hand lotions, creams, balms, skin care products, and shaving creams. Some of these are designed to soften up what is hardened in order to remove the older, outer layer, so the new layer can come through. The body oils and creams are intended to keep the skin soft so no cracks are formed, allowing in harmful bacterias. Lipsticks are made with this oil so that they will not break and crack under the extreme heat or chilling cold of the weather. It is all used in order to keep the body safe and functioning properly, removing the old layers so the new can shine through.

As the Good Shepherd produces this oil in us through the Holy Spirit, its entire design is to soften up the hardened, outer layers of the old man so they can be removed and the new man can start to shine through. His Spirit defends us against the hardening caused by sin, keeping our hearts tender with His love. Each day, as it is applied, the glory of who we are becoming shines more brightly.

The Good Shepherd loves to use each of us to help sharpen each other in our walk through life. As we help each other grow more into the likeness of the Good Shepherd.

Go Enjoy The Shepherd.

December 25

The Good Shepherd Is Born
Luke 2:7

Have you ever really considered this night, the night Jesus was born? Looking past all the seasonal stories and the manger scenes, into the depth of this event? Though the exact day is unknown to us, this is the day we have chosen to celebrate his birth.

Mary's water breaks and Joseph is desperate for a place for her to be comfortable to have the child. He rushes around looking for anywhere they can find a room. Mary doubles over in the pains of birth and the innkeeper points to the only thing he has left, a stable with a manger full of hay.

Into this scene, the one who was the Great Shepherd of the Israelite people through the wilderness, the one who oversaw all of creation and guided it as only a shepherd could, lowers himself to become a "lamb." He is fragile and cold. For the first time he experiences the lack of clear sight, the brush of the cool air in the night, the warmth of his mother's embrace, the need to have his hunger satisfied with her warm milk. The one who had it all, left it all behind so he could become the perfect "Lamb of God."

So many have asked the question, "Why would he do such a thing?" Many have tried to answer. If you truly want to know his motivation for the "Greatest Gift" ever given, simply take a minute and go look in the mirror. His answer to "why" will be staring back at you!

Go Enjoy The Shepherd.

December 26

Shepherds in the Field
Luke 2:8-18

If we are not careful, we might miss the significance of this particular announcement that was made on the night of Jesus' birth. Did you notice who first received the word that a Savior had been born? Shepherds! Ever considered the significance of that?

To understand a little more, look at the setting. The shepherds were all out tending their flocks in the dark of night. They were standing watch over them while no one else wanted to. The night shift was the most dangerous and the most difficult.

These men stood watching over their flocks when suddenly they receive word of the birth of the one who came to stand watch over them. They were keeping watch through the dark of night when all others were asleep. The angels announced to them that the one who would watch over them during their darkest hour, through their greatest needs had now come to earth. Who better to understand and spread the word of Christ's birth than shepherds who knew what it meant to tend to sheep.

We are told David was called from the sheep fields to shepherd the people of God. The prophet Amos declared he had been called from his shepherding job to deliver a message to God's people. Here God chose shepherds to be the ones to first spread the news that the Good Shepherd had arrived. No wonder all who heard the news were in awe and wonder at the news they had heard from these poor men!

Go tell someone today the Good News that the Good Shepherd was born and lives today, watching over all his sheep!

Go Enjoy The Shepherd.

December 27

The Lamb Grows Up
Luke 2:41-52

Every lamb goes through the process of growing up. The Lamb of God was no different. Just like a lamb who is curious and wanders off, Jesus is found in this passage to have wandered away from those who were given the responsibility to watch over him. Joseph and Mary searched like shepherds hunting a lost sheep, frantically looking for their lost lamb, the Lamb of God. I can hear even now, as down through the ages, their massive sigh of relief exhaled as they laid eyes on their lost lamb for the first time in several days.

As Jesus grew up and learned about sheep and how to be the Good Shepherd, he remembered the time his earthly father and mother left their other kids to come in search for the one who was missing. He remembered the scolding he received for causing them this great anxiety. He also remembered how determined they were in their search, never giving up, and how they celebrated once they again had him safely in their arms.

From this experience, he learned a valuable lesson that molded him into the Good Shepherd he needed to be over his flock. He learned to be focused and determined in his pursuit of his lost sheep, never giving up, even when all hope seemed lost. He also learned how to throw a huge celebration each time one of his sheep is brought back home!

Aren't you glad he relentlessly pursues you? He promises he will never give up on you! He will never quit until the day he gets to throw a huge party in celebration of your coming home!

Go Enjoy The Shepherd.

December 28

The Lamb Leads
John 13:15

My whole motivation in raising Precious, Caesar, Babe, and other bottle-fed lambs was knowing that one day they would help me lead the other sheep where I needed them to go. The long hours, the lost sleep, all the cleaning, the smell in my house, the frustrations, the playing in the backyard, it all had a purpose. I looked forward to the day all the hard work would pay off and others would follow.

Jesus, as the Lamb of God, learned and grew in knowledge and favor with God and man. As he listened to stories of God's work through the Old Testament and works of David, he began to understand what he came here to do: lead others back to his Heavenly Father. As he grew, he endured trials, tribulations, sufferings, insults, and being rejected. Through all this he learned how to train others to live the life God intended for man to live, then he began to impart that knowledge to those the Father had given him. In other words, in order to lead, Jesus first had to learn to follow his Shepherd, God the Father.

In some of his final days, he knelt down and washed the feet of his followers. He then told them, "As you have seen me do, go do the same." In other words, as I have followed the Father, follow me as I point you back to him. Before he was the Good Shepherd, he first was the Rejected Lamb!

Today, go and follow him as the Spirit leads you, and you too will lead others back to his feet. It is a simple plan, but one only the Good Shepherd knows how to teach you!

Go Enjoy The Shepherd.

December 29

The Lamb Is Slain
Matthew 27:32-56

As the Lamb of God got closer to the end of his earthly life, it was becoming very clear where his path would lead. He knew the law of the Old Testament, having memorized it as a child. He knew that a perfect lamb had to be slain in order to cover the sins of the guilty. He realized he was the One Isaiah spoke of in his 53rd chapter, the man of sorrows, acquainted with grief, whom it would please the Lord to crush so the price could be paid.

Did you know I could easily take a butcher's knife to the throat of my closest sheep and kill them without them even flinching. Yes, if I wanted to I could. These sheep have absolute trust in their shepherd, even if it means death. Jesus had come to a place where he learned an absolute trust of his Great Shepherd, so he too was willing to lay down his own life so that other lost lambs could be saved. The decision was not easy, as he sweat great drops of blood, agonizing over the suffering he knew was coming. However, he counted the cost, saw what he was going to gain, and therefore willingly laid down for you and me.

Today, take a moment and allow the wonder of this all to sink in. The Lamb of God willingly laid down his life for you, because he trusted that his Father would consider him worthy and raise him to life again. Because he, as the Lamb of God, willingly laid down his life for you, he was given the honor of being raised up to become your Good Shepherd.

Oh, what a Savior!

Go Enjoy The Shepherd.

December 30

The Lamb Shall Be Lifted Up
Revelation 5, Revelation 19:6-10

He only was gone three days, then to the amazement of all those who were in despair over his death, Jesus rose again. He had told them he would be back, but they had very little faith and no real understanding. Then before their very eyes, Jesus stood, risen again.

He then went on to show John a glorious vision of a mighty Lion, the Lion of Judah, who appeared as a Lamb who had been slain, standing next to the throne of God. He had been lifted up from his low place and received power, and wealth, and honor, just as the prophets had foretold (Revelation 5:12, Zephaniah 3:19-20).

But not only that, he saw all those who had believed on the Lamb, who had chosen to follow him as their Good Shepherd, whom he had purchased with his blood, reigning on earth. He had given them real life, abundant life, and the ability to live free from the cares and concerns of this world. They no longer had their eyes set on earthly wealth and gain, but on the eternal gain of being with the One they longed for, the Holy Lamb of God.

I simply cannot wait to see him face to face. Can you?

Go Enjoy The Shepherd.

December 31

The Lamb Will Be the Good Shepherd
Revelation 7:14-17

The year has come and gone, and a new one is about to begin. Another year of joys, thrills, heartache, and sorrow has passed you by. Through it all, one truth has remained, Jesus is still your Good Shepherd.

As each additional year passes you by, and each day comes and goes, no matter what they hold, this one truth will always remain. Death cannot stop him. Sorrows cannot overcome him. No barrier can block him. Nothing will keep him from his sheep.

As you enter this new year ahead, I would like to encourage you to embrace the words of the Apostle Paul in Philippians 3:13. Forget those things which are behind you, set your eyes on what is in front of you. And what do you have in front of you?

The Lamb who will forever shepherd his people. (Revelation 7:17) There is nothing that can separate you from his love. There is nothing that will snatch you from his hand. There is no distance he will not travel to find you when you are lost. There is nothing that will keep you apart from him!

With this knowledge, with this truth, go out today and live your life with all the joy a lamb displays as it jumps and frolics in my fields. Live your life with the ease and comfort my sheep display as they rest in the shade. When the enemy attacks, be still in the knowledge Jesus is watching over you! When death comes to bring you to his side, embrace it with the joy of one who is gaining more than they are leaving behind. Simply be like sheep and revel in the joy of his great love!

As I have said each and every day, I say with all the same joy and energy and desire for you today: I pray you will Go Enjoy The Shepherd.

Made in the USA
Middletown, DE
13 December 2016